Augsburg Commentary on the New Testament
I CORINTHIANS
Roy A. Harrisville

Augsburg Publishing House
Minneapolis, Minnesota

AUGSBURG COMMENTARY ON THE NEW TESTAMENT
1 Corinthians

Copyright © 1987 Augsburg Publishing House

All rights reserved. Except for brief quotations in critical articles or reviews, no part of this book may be reproduced in any manner without prior written permission from the publisher. Write to: Permissions, Augsburg Publishing House, 426 S. Fifth St., Box 1209, Minneapolis MN 55440.

Scripture quotations, unless made directly from the original languages by the author, are from the Revised Standard Version of the Bible, copyright 1946, 1952, and 1971 by the Division of Christian Education of the National Council of Churches.

Library of Congress Cataloging-in-Publication Data

Harrisville, Roy A.
   1 Corinthians.

  (Augsburg commentary on the New Testament)
  Bibliography: p.
  1. Bible. N.T. Corinthians, 1st—Commentaries.
I. Title. II. Title: First Corinthians. III. Series.
BS2675.3.H34 1987   227'.207   87-17561
ISBN 0-8066-8866-1

Manufactured in the U.S.A.   APH 10-9024

1 2 3 4 5 6 7 8 9 0 1 2 3 4 5 6 7 8 9

TO MY MOTHER

CONTENTS

Foreword 7

Abbreviations 9

Introduction 11

Outline 23

Commentary 27

Notes 295

About the Author 301

FOREWORD

The AUGSBURG COMMENTARY ON THE NEW TESTAMENT is written for laypeople, students, and pastors. Laypeople will use it as a resource for Bible study at home and at church. Students and instructors will read it to probe the basic message of the books of the New Testament. And pastors will find it to be a valuable aid for sermon and lesson preparation.

The plan for each commentary is designed to enhance its usefulness. The Introduction presents a topical overview of the biblical book to be discussed and provides information on the historical circumstances in which that book was written. It also contains a summary of the biblical writer's thought. In the body of the commentary, the interpreter sets forth in brief compass the meaning of the biblical text. The procedure is to explain the text section by section. Attempts have been made to avoid scholarly jargon and the heavy use of technical terms. Because the readers of the commentary will have their Bibles at hand, the biblical text itself has not been printed out. In general, the editors recommend the use of the Revised Standard Version of the Bible.

The authors of this commentary series are professors at seminaries and universities and are themselves ordained. They have been selected both because of their expertise and because they worship in the same congregations as the people for whom they are writing. In elucidating the text of Scripture, therefore, they attest to their belief that central to the faith and life of the church of God is the Word of God.

The Editorial Committee

>Roy A. Harrisville
>Luther Northwestern Theological Seminary
>St. Paul, Minnesota
>
>Jack Dean Kingsbury
>Union Theological Seminary
>Richmond, Virginia
>
>Gerhard A. Krodel
>Lutheran Theological Seminary
>Gettysburg, Pennsylvania

ABBREVIATIONS

ACNT	Augsburg Commentary on the New Testament
ANF	*The Ante-Nicene Fathers*, ed. Roberts and Donaldson (New York: Scribner, 1903ff.)
APOT	*The Apocrypha and Pseudepigrapha of the Old Testament*, ed. R. H. Charles (Oxford: Clarendon, 1913)
KJV	The King James Version of the Bible
LCL	The Loeb Classical Library (Cambridge, Mass.: Harvard University Press)
LW	The American edition of *Luther's Works* (Philadelphia: Fortress, and St. Louis: Concordia, 1955–1986)
LXX	The Septuagint (Greek translation of the OT)
NEB	The New English Bible
OTP	*The Old Testament Pseudepigrapha*, ed. James Charlesworth (Garden City, N.Y.: Doubleday, 1983, 1985)
RSV	The Revised Standard Version of the Bible and the Apocrypha
Str-B	(H. Strack and) P. Billerbeck, *Kommentar zum Neuen Testament aus Talmud und Midrasch* (Munich: Beck, 1922ff.)
WA	(Weimarer Ausgabe) Critical edition of Luther's works (Weimar, 1883 to the present)

INTRODUCTION

1. Principal Events in the History of Corinth

Like many a great city of antiquity, the origins of the city of Corinth, situated on the isthmus between the Peloponnese and the Greek mainland, are shrouded in myth. In the earliest identifiable period of Greek history, tyrants ruled Corinth and were extending its influence toward the west, and as far east as the Black Sea. But with Corinth, colonization was less a military than a commercial affair. The city's artisans were the envy of their neighbors—building ships, working in bronze, and producing on their pottery a naturalistic style which most Greeks had never seen and came more and more to desire. As a result, when Athens later challenged Corinth's commercial hegemony, and the entire upper coast of the Corinthian Gulf passed into Athens' hands, there was little decline in Corinthian prosperity. From the beginning, Corinth's colonies had been independent, and amicable relations with the mother-city were retained in midst of all the political filling and tacking.

Following the Greeks' victory over the Persians at Salamis in 480 B.C., trade rivalry between Athens and Corinth precipitated a 10-year war (431–421 B.C.). Corinth attacked her unfilial daughter city on the Adriatic, Corcyra (Corfu). Athens sent ships to relieve the island. Corinth called off the attack, and a year later spurred Potidea, a restive ally of Athens, to revolt against her mother-city. In retaliation, the Athenian Pericles issued a decree that all produce from the Sicilian city of Megara, Corinth's ally against Corcyra, should be banned from ports of the empire. Corinth, undaunted, called a Congress of the Peloponnesian Confederacy, and, together with the initially reluctant Sparta, broke up the Athenian empire.

When, following the battle of Chaeronea (338 B.C.), Philip of Macedon, father of Alexander, became effective master of Greece, he summoned all the Greek city-states to a congress at Corinth. There, the League of the Hellenes was founded, with Philip as king and commander-in-chief. The Macedonian had two principal objectives: to invade Persia, and to employ the combined strength of the league to insure that there should be no execution or banishment contrary to established law; no confiscation of property or redistribution of land; no cancellation of debts or freeing of slaves for purposes of revolution.

Following Alexander's death (323 B.C.) and the division of his rule, and after Macedonia had gone to war three times against her neighbors to the south, Rome dissolved the Macedonian empire, reduced Macedonia to a Roman province, and annexed to it all the Greek city-states. The independence of Greece came to an end till 1834. In the struggles, Corinth had been laid waste. Its paintings, bronzes and sculptures, the works of its great artists were stolen and used to decorate the homes of the upper class in and about Rome.

In approximately 44 B.C., Corinth was rebuilt as a Roman colony (by decree of Julius Caesar; in honor of his sister, Colonia Laus Julia Corinthus?), and annexed to the Roman province of Macedonia. Augustus later detached the city from Macedonia, and made it the capital of the senatorial province of Achaia, ruled by a separate proconsular governor. At the time of Paul, L. Junius Gallio, younger brother of the philosopher Seneca, held the proconsular post (cf. Acts 18:12).

All the cults of the Mediterranean were represented at Corinth. Near the city stood a statue of Poseidon, a temple of Aphrodite and the sanctuaries of Asclepius and Isis. In the city itself stood a sanctuary of the Ephesian Artemis, a brass statue of Athena, a

Introduction

temple to Octavia, sister of Augustus Caesar, and a sanctuary of Jupiter Capitolinus. On the way to Acrocorinth, high to the west, stood the sanctuaries of Isis and Serapis, the altars of Helios, temples to "Fate" and "Necessity," and, above them all, a temple to the mother of the gods. On the rocks of that towering mountain stood the famous temple of Aphrodite. Strabo, geographer in the time of Christ, wrote that this temple contained 1000 hierodules (cult prostitutes). He was no doubt in error. Other ancient writers make no mention of cult prostitution, merely of the Corinthian courtesans' participation in their patron's worship. Whether or not Corinth was the site of sacral prostitution, it was Corinth's name which came to be a Greek term for living immorally, for the prostitute and whoremonger. It was at Corinth that Paul wrote that famed description of the ruin of culture in the pagan world (Rom. 1:18-32), and of Corinth that the Latin poet Horace wrote, "The voyage to Corinth is not for every man." As one scholar has noted, readers who have seen Edinburgh Castle in Scotland will have a view in their minds of a fortress high in the air, safe from an enemy with no long-range guns, and round the rock at its foot growing something of a town. Such a town was Corinth, on that neck of land between the two seas (*bimaris Corinthus*, as Horace called it), with its mountain that gave the widest view over all of Greece.

2. Corinth and Paul

According to Acts, Paul arrived at Corinth on his so-called second missionary journey. He began his activity in the Jewish synagogue, and subsequently in the house of Titius Justus. Acts 18:8 reports the one sensational fact that the ruler of the synagogue, Crispus, together with his whole house, was baptized (cf. 1:14). In addition, "many of the Corinthians" who heard Paul believed and were baptized (were the "household of Stephanas," and also Fortunatus and Achaicus among them? cf. 16:15,17). At first, the Jewish community left Paul unmolested. The troubles began during the proconsulship of Gallio.

1 Corinthians

At the turn of the last century, a letter in stone was found at Delphi which proved to be of significance for the chronology of Paul's life. In it, the Emperor Claudius refers to himself as "acclaimed for the 26th time as emperor," and to Gallio as "my friend and proconsul." The 26th acclamation of Claudius fell between the end of January and the beginning of August in A.D. 52, at the time Gallio was in office. If Gallio entered upon his responsibilities according to the date fixed by Tiberius Caesar for accession to office in senatorial provinces, then he did so on July 1st in A.D. 52. If (!) the apostle was hailed before Gallio only after several months' activity in Corinth (18?), then his sojourn in that city fell between the years A.D. 50 and 52.

At the time of writing, Paul was in Ephesus, to which he had come—though perhaps not directly—following his activity at Corinth, and where he spent more than two years preaching and teaching. Since the apostle indicates his intention to leave Ephesus for Macedonia, but to remain in Ephesus till Pentecost (the month of May, cf. 16:8), our "1 Corinthians" was perhaps penned toward the conclusion of Paul's activity in Ephesus, thus in the spring of A.D. 55.

The congregation at Corinth consisted primarily of Gentile Christians, most from the lower classes (cf. 1:26-29), though the presence of Jewish Christians in the congregation is highly probable. At least, the presence of Jews in Corinth cannot be denied. Among the artifacts gleaned from the city is an inscription from a door which reads, "Synagogue of the Hebrews" (the inscription to the door of the synagogue in which Paul first preached?). Moreover, in his *Embassy to Gaius*, Philo of Alexandria, Paul's older Jewish contemporary, refers to Corinth in his list of the cities of the Jewish dispersion.

Prior to our "1 Corinthians," Paul had written a letter to the congregation (cf. 5:9ff.). He may even had paid it a brief visit. After composing 1 Corinthians, Paul traveled from Ephesus to Corinth, where his encounter with the congregation ended in personal disaster and his subsequent "letter of tears" (cf. 2 Cor. 2:4). Returning to Ephesus and dispatching Titus to Corinth, Paul

Introduction

eventually traveled to Macedonia to await from Titus the news of a possible reconciliation (cf. 2 Cor. 2:12f; 7:5ff.). Once more, on the heels of Titus, Paul paid his last visit to the city, during which he composed the Romans epistle. From Corinth the apostle sailed to Jerusalem, where he was imprisoned. In all, then, Paul composed four letters to the Corinthians, two of which are lost to us, though attempts have been made to abstract from 2 Corinthians (chaps. 10–13) that third "letter of tears."

The occasion for 1 Corinthians lay in oral reports of the situation at Corinth (brought by "Chloe's people"? cf. 1:11), as well as in a letter of inquiries from the congregation (brought by Stephanas, Fortunatus, and Achaicus? cf. 16:17), and to which Paul responded (seriatim? cf. 7:1, 25; 8:1; 12:1; 16:1, 12). The picture of the congregation which resulted was not a happy one. There were factions (1:11-17). The congregation allowed excesses which pagans did not permit (chap. 5), though some appeared to regard sexual intercourse and marriage as sin (chap. 7). In strife over property, Christians went before pagan courts (6:1-8). They participated in sacrificial meals in heathen temples (8:10), or accepted invitations to meals in which sacrificial flesh was served (10:27). Enthusiasm led women to appear at service without head-covering, against all custom and convention (11:3-16). The Christian agape or "love feast," and its focus in the Lord's Supper, had been transformed into a revel (chap. 11), and there was wild disorder at the worship. Glossolalia, touted as the principal Christian charisma, threatened to displace all other workings of the Spirit (chaps. 12 and 14). Finally, offense had been taken at the Christian teaching concerning the resurrection (chap. 15).

3. Corinth versus Paul

The difficulty involved in an interpretation of the epistle is that the historical details, the congregation's "situation in life" is hidden from us. For Ferdinand Christian Baur, the first great historian of the early church, 1 Cor. 1:12 was the lever of Archimedes by which to move the history of earliest Christianity. He believed that the factions at Corinth proved that at the very beginning Christianity was not unified, but moved out of contrasts toward a unity reached only in early catholicism. Thus, according to Baur, it was dogmatic debate which gave the impulse to primitive Christian history. Accordingly, Baur described the party of Peter and its extreme wing, the party of Christ, as resting on a factual, historical relation to Jesus—a party of "Judaists" or "Judaizers." Conversely, he described the adherents of Apollos as extremists who had altered the universal, law-free gospel of Paul to an enthusiasm sprung from vision and ecstasy. In other words, they had out-Pauled Paul.

Opposition to Baur's hypothesis was at first lightweight, and the degree to which it has ruled interpretation of the epistle (though with modifications) can be seen in Introductions to the New Testament reaching from the latter half of the 19th century to the present. Effective challenge to Baur's scheme occurred with a study by the Greifswald scholar, Wilhelm Lütgert, who contended that the Christ-party was Paul's principal opponent. This party, wrote Lütgert, was composed of Jews, but of a vastly different sort than those addressed in Galatians. The party had emerged from the primitive Christian proclamation of freedom, laid claim to a "pneumatic" knowledge of Jesus and thus to a revelation and perfection which reached beyond faith. These pneumatics scorned submission to law, and extended their canon of freedom to the entire sexual realm. The asceticism often attaching to this party, Lütgert contended, was only the obverse side of its libertinism, both habits of life deriving from an overemphasis on the freedom given with the Spirit and its opposition to the natural or corporeal. The great Tübingen scholar, Adolf Schlatter, agreed that Paul had but one opponent at Corinth, adding that the Christ-party was an export originating in Syria, and that its fanaticism was not irrational but characteristic of Jewish freethinking.

In 1955, Walter Schmithals, critical of Lütgert's "inattention" to the uniqueness of the heresy at Corinth, as well as of Schlatter's

Introduction

derivation of the heresy from Palestinian Judaism, contended that the "Gnosis in Corinth" was "classical" and pre-Christian. This gnosis, Schmithals asserted, rooted in Indo-Iranian mythology, had been altered by Greek thought and later developed in Judaism. Its principal concepts were of the self as heavenly in origin, though sunk in the material world, and of the "redeemed Redeemer" who, in coming down to liberate the soul, by this action freed himself. In this guise, Schmithals argued, the opposition to Paul at Corinth appeared.

Anyone who has read a standard work on that congeries of ideas and worldviews called "Gnosticism" will have little difficulty tracing the similarity between those ideas and those of Paul's opponents at Corinth, or of the apostle himself. Paul's reference to a wisdom of God "hidden" from "the rulers of this age" (2:7-8), as well as from human thought ("what no eye has seen, nor ear heard, nor the heart of man conceived," 2:9), has its analogy in the Gnostic's wisdom as an esoteric possession, unrecognizable to the evil powers of the world. The Gnostic, too, could boast that through his knowledge (8:1) he had been liberated from all external authority, and that for this reason "all things are lawful" (6:12; 10:23). Libertinism, the denial of traditional morality, was as characteristic of the Gnostic as of the Corinthian "pneumatic." Yet, like Paul, the Gnostic could add that it was not only a knowledge of one's true nature, but also steadfastness in the path of that knowledge which was decisive. If the Gnostic's doctrine of salvation reflected a kind of solipsism, in a vision of the "unworldly self" at odds with nature and creation, it also embraced a brotherhood which distanced itself from the this-sided fraternities of antiquity. "Not all things are helpful" (6:12); "not all things build up" (10:23); "when you come together to eat, wait for one another" (11:33), or "make love your aim" (14:1), could as easily have been uttered by a Gnostic as by Paul.

The eschatological aspect was not lacking to Gnosticism any more than to Paul. Paul's words concerning "the appointed time" as having "grown very short," of the shape of "this world" as "passing away" (7:29, 31), have their counterpart in these lines from an old Gnostic fragment: "The times are cut short and the days have shortened and our time has been fulfilled, and the weeping of our destruction has approached us." The Gnostic too had his variation on the theme of the apostle's sufferings in chap. 4 ("to the present hour we hunger and thirst," v. 11): "We go about in hunger [and] in thirst . . . we are ill [and] feeble [and] in pain. . . ."

If at Corinth there were not many "wise according to worldly standards, not many . . . powerful, not many . . . of noble birth" (1:26), it was from the plebs that Gnosticism drew its adherents, and in contrast to the remainder of antiquity which gave no consideration to the social situation of the oppressed and exploited. Paul's word in 7:22, "He who was called in the Lord as a slave is a freedman of the Lord," veiled a promise which the Gnostic *Gospel of Philip* made explicit: "In this world the slaves serve the free. In the kingdom of heaven the free shall minister to the slaves. . . ."

The Gnostic as well as Paul inclined to a "charismatic" understanding of the "brotherhood." For both, the congregation was to rule over its own occasions, establish its own functionaries, and care for its own feasts (cf. 6:18; chaps. 11; 12; and 14). If there is little evidence to prove that the Gnostic underwent such baptism on behalf of the dead as Paul describes in 1 Cor. 15:12, there is sufficient evidence to suggest that, among certain groups such as the Valentinians, the dead themselves were baptized. Denial of the resurrection, despising of the Christ "after the flesh" (cf. 12:3, "No one speaking by the Spirit of God ever says 'Jesus be cursed!' "), the contrast between the first and second "Adam" (cf. 15:45-49)—these easily correspond with the Gnostic creed of the material or corporeal as "filth," and conjure up associations with Gnostic preoccupation with the myth of the "archetypal man," later come to full term in that notion of the redeemed Redeemer.

Gnostic analogies in Corinth or in Paul cannot be denied, and it was particularly to Paul that second- and third-century Gnosticism made appeal. Such Gnosticism, of course, was already

Introduction

"Christian," as its advocates and defenders insisted. For the rest, the origins of Gnosticism are hidden from us—due chiefly to the fact that the writing of history belonged to the temporal, the earthly, thus to the despised. No doubt, the *roots* of Gnosticism lie back of the New Testament, but the question as to the degree of its influence—if any there was—upon the nascent Christian community will always be moot. For this reason, the question as to Gnosticism's "invasion" of Christianity, whether at Corinth or elsewhere, cannot be decided with certainty, any more than can the question of its emergence from out of Christianity. But this only means that the interpreter, as the umpire, must "call it as he sees it."

The thesis of this commentary is that the "heresy" at Corinth was homegrown, that the "pneumatic" tendencies afoot in the congregation had Paul as their author. But that means Paul as misinterpreted, caricatured, and misapplied—more a likelihood than merely a possibility in a society whose members had grown accustomed to thinking of themselves as of the same stuff as deity. What put Paul at odds with Corinth was not an invasion of the congregation from without, but a "Paulinism" which Paul had never advocated, and which was fired by the spirit of the age. To that extent, F. C. Baur's hypothesis stands.

In what may still be the greatest commentary on 1 Corinthians, with its mastery of religious-historical parallels and attention to literary-rhetorical detail, the author, Johannes Weiss, urged his readers to prepare themselves for an understanding of Paul by acquaintance with the Stoic philosopher Epictetus. Weiss's commentary abounds with parallels from Epictetus and the other later Stoics. In his exegesis of the section on the body and its members in chap. 12, Weiss writes that he has no doubt that Paul appropriated the concept from Stoic popular philosophy, though not without altering it in favor of a fellowship "newly arisen, supernaturally created and sustained, held together by the Spirit of Christ." As with Gnosticism, the similarity in language and conceptuality cannot be denied—in this instance a similarity between Paul and a "school" whose historical precedence is obvious. The

Stoic had been on the scene long before Paul. For this reason, those who deny that Paul appropriated Stoic thought cannot, as with Gnosticism, take support from a lack of external, historical evidence, but must argue from the internal evidence of the epistle itself. But this also requires that the umpire "call it as he sees it." The thesis of this commentary is that the striking parallels between Paul of Tarsus (a city celebrated for its Stoic schools) and the popular Stoic philosophy do not derive from intimate acquaintance with Stoicism, but rather from Paul's contact with a society for which Stoic terms and concepts were part and parcel of that "spirit of the age."

4. The Theology of the Cross

Throughout the commentary, the reader will find references to parallels in Gnostic and Stoic literature, in the literature of Jewish "Wisdom" and of apocalyptic. While it is true that conservative scholarship most often attempts to disprove the similarities between Paul and the religious thought contemporary with him, the same anxiety which leads such scholarship to deny the parallels has induced many a student of comparative religions to seek the uniqueness of Paul in the degree of his difference from the sources on which he drew. In other words, for both types, newness—uniqueness—is a fundamental theological category. In some fashion or other, Paul must be first—if not in the content of his ideas, then in his "inwardness." But with Paul, what was first or had recently come upon the scene was not truest, and therefore to be believed. Everything hinged on the acknowledgment of an activity of God to which everything, new or old, Gnostic, Greek or Jewish, Christian or pagan, had to be warped. Paul was not an innovator, and in that sense a "second founder" of Christianity. He was an orchestrator, perhaps best imitated by that "fifth Evangelist," J. S. Bach, who never winced at purloining texts and tunes from a hundred and one composers if they proved serviceable to his theme.

Introduction

But it was not merely in threshing out the language and conceptuality of current religiosity through his own mind and heart that the difference between Paul and his contemporaries can be seen. Nowhere is it clearer than in 1 Corinthians that everything within sight or hearing of Paul was bent to a single event, and that for this reason, not for reasons of genius or creativity or ingenuity, everything suffered qualification. The fracture of contemporary religious thought is apparent on almost every page of the epistle—not because Paul believed there was nothing of truth in it. The relish with which the apostle adopts the language and ideas around him—even those of Corinth!—indicates that for him, at least, something more than a mere temporal quality adhered to "newness." The fracture of systems, concepts, occurred of itself, as if automatically, once attention was concentrated on the crucifixion of Jesus. Not an idea, but an event, an event rooted in time and space, had turned everything on its head: "We preach Christ crucified, a stumbling block to Jews and folly to Gentiles, but to those who are called, both Jews and Greeks, Christ the power of God and the wisdom of God" (1:23-24). What was Jewish or Greek would be abandoned or would be retained, not for its Jewishness or its origins in Greek thought, but for its service to the "Christ crucified."

5. The Unity of the Epistle

In his commentary, Johannes Weiss expressed pique at the willingness of the majority to assume the loss of two epistles rather than a redactional combination of extant fragments into two great letters. Weiss posited three stages within the epistle, each distinguished from the others in form and content. In his investigation of the "Gnosis in Corinth," Walter Schmithals divided the two letters to Corinth into six. These are but two in the long history of attempts at differentiating "fragments" in the epistle from subsequent editing. The fact that so many and diverse hypotheses of partition have been advanced indicates that no final and conclusive argument can be brought against the epistle's unity.

Agreed, the lack of apparent sequence, the repetition, and the sudden alteration in moods which characterize certain sections of the epistle have puzzled more than one reader. But the often curious structure of the letter is as easily explained from occasions within the existence of a man whose days were characterized by breaks and interruptions, than from any one of 100 theories respecting pages or leaves lost and combined willy-nilly.

Despite the "haphazard character" of the series of subjects dealt with in 1 Corinthians, the letter has its center or focus. In the introduction to his commentary on the epistle, Karl Barth asked whether or not the theme of chap. 15 should be regarded as just one among many, or be recognized as the epistle's theme, and answered that the latter is the case. This commentary will attempt to show that chap. 15 is the "authentic commentary" on chaps. 1–14.

Finally, the reader will note explicit and implicit appeal throughout to the comments and studies of Karl Barth, Rudolf Bultmann, Hans Conzelmann, Ernst Käsemann, Johannes Weiss, and, of course, Martin Luther. I make no apology for my dependence upon these great interpreters, on whose shoulders I have stood for a good many years, and from which I have seen further than I could have seen standing alone in my own little "sandpit."

Now, a word from the Jewish poet and thinker, Schalom Ben-Chorin, which will serve to explain (and perhaps also defend) the faults and deficiencies in this book:

> If anyone thinks he has finally confined Paul within the prison of his own book, or gotten hold of him with an idea he has over and again thought through, he disappears once more as he did over the wall of Damascus or from prison.[1]

OUTLINE OF 1 CORINTHIANS

I. Introduction (1:1-9)
   A. Paul, to Corinth (1:1-3)
   B. The Thanksgiving (1:4-9)

II. The Parties (1:10—4:21)
   A. Chapter 1
      1. The Divisions (1:10-17)
      2. The Foolishness of God (1:18-25)
      3. Corinth and the Theology of the Cross (1:26-31)
   B. Chapter 2
      1. Paul's Appearance at Corinth (2:1-5)
      2. Wisdom and the Spirit of God (2:6-16)
   C. Chapter 3
      1. Babes and Milk (3:1-4)
      2. Corinth's Heroes and the Test by Fire (3:5-17)
      3. Reprise (3:18-23)
   D. Chapter 4
      1. The Criterion for Testing (4:1-5)
      2. Paul and Corinth in Contrast (4:6-13)
      3. Conclusion of the Argument Begun at 1:10 (4:14-21)

III. Excesses in the Community (5:1—6:20)
   A. Chapter 5
      1. A Specific Case of Immorality (5:1-8)
      2. Paul—Misunderstood or Caricatured? (5:9-13)

1 Corinthians

- B. Chapter 6
    1. On Settling Disputes before Pagan Courts (6:1-11)
    2. Regarding Immorality (6:12-20)
- IV. Responses to the Corinthians' Questions (7:1—10:33 [11:1])
    - A. Chapter 7
        1. Concerning Celibacy (7:1-7)
        2. Concerning the Unmarried and Widows (7:8-9)
        3. Concerning Divorce (7:10-11)
        4. Concerning "Mixed" Marriages (7:12-16)
        5. "Call" and "Calling" (7:17-24)
        6. Concerning Virgins; the Reason Why; the Unmarried; the Engaged; and Concerning Widows (7:25-40)
    - B. Chapter 8
        1. The Thesis—Negative (8:1-3)
        2. The Confession—Positive (8:4-6)
        3. Weak and Strong (8:7-13)
    - C. Chapter 9.
        1. Opening Salvo—The Claim to Apostleship (9:1-2)
        2. The Rights of an Apostle (9:3-7)
        3. Torah Support (9:8-11 [12])
        4. Levitical Practice and the Word of the Lord (9:13-14)
        5. Paul's Waiver of Rights and Its Purpose (9:15-18)
        6. All Things to All Men (9:19-23)
        7. The Apostolic Discipline (9:24-27)
    - D. Chapter 10
        1. The Sacrament Does Not Guarantee Immunity (10:1-13)
            a. The Story of Israel (10:1-5)
            b. Warnings for Us (10:6-13)
        2. The Cup of the Lord and the Cup of Demons (10:14-22)
        3. Meats Sacrificed to Idols (10:23-30)
        4. All to the Glory of God (10:31-33 [11:1])

Outline

V. Worship at Corinth (11:2—14:40)
   A. Chapter 11
      1. Women's Deportment at the Worship (11:2-16)
         a. Commendation (11:2)
         b. Women without Head Covering (11:3-6)
         c. "Image," "Glory," and the Qualification (11:7-12)
         d. The Appeal to Propriety, Nature, and Custom in the Churches (11:13-16)
      2. The Supper at Corinth (11:17-34)
         a. Chaos (11:17-22)
         b. The Paradosis (11:23-26)
         c. Commentary on the Paradosis (11:27-32)
         d. The Appeal (11:33-34)
   B. Chapter 12
      1. Speaking in Tongues and the Test (12:1-3)
      2. Varieties of Gifts; the Test Particularized (12:4-11)
      3. The Body Analogy and the Necessity for Variety (12:12-31a)
   C. Chapter 13
      1. The Gifts as Nothing without Love (12:31b—13:3)
      2. The Nature and Activity of Love (13:4-7)
      3. The Imperishability of Love (13:8-13)
   D. Chapter 14
      1. Tongues and Prophecy Contrasted (14:1-5)
      2. Illustrations (14:6-12)
      3. Application of the Principle of Verse 12 (14:13-19)
      4. Tongues and Prophecy from the Perspective of the "Outsider" (14:20-25)
      5. Practical Conclusions for Order in the Worship (14:26-33)
      6. Let the Women Keep Silent (14:34-36)
      7. One More Vigorous Word (14:37-40)

VI. The Resurrection from the Dead (Chapter 15)
   A. Introduction and Gospel of the Resurrection (15:1-11)
      1. Introduction (15:1-2)

1 Corinthians

      2. The Credo (15:3-8)
      3. Paul "Last of All" (15:9-11)
  B. The Argument for the Resurrection (15:12-19)
  C. The Reality of the Resurrection (15:20-28)
  D. Return to the Argument: The Corinthians' Inconsistency (15:29-34)
  E. How the Dead Are Raised (15:35-49)
  F. The Destiny of Those Still Alive (15:50-58)

VII. Conclusion (Chapter 16)
  A. The Collection for the Saints (16:1-4)
  B. Paul's Travel Plans (16:5-9)
  C. Timothy's Arrival and Apollos's Delay (16:10-12)
  D. Concluding Admonitions (16:13-14)
  E. Stephanas and His Company (16:15-18)
  F. Paul's Greetings (16:19-20)
  G. The Conclusion (16:21-24)

COMMENTARY

■ Introduction (1:1-9)

Paul, to Corinth (1:1-3)

Paul was not inattentive to tradition in matters of style or rhetoric. That will become clear. Then, as now, occasions for inventiveness in the affair of letter-writing were not infinite—that is, if the author was not intent on founding a "school," or if he wanted first of all to be understood and allowed what he had to say determine how he said it. But it could happen that what an author had to say could not be contained or restrained by whatever custom or habit dictated should be the form into which he should pour whatever he had to say—that when he began to speak or write, those traditional forms began to creak and strain at the seams. The shape of the introduction to our "first" epistle to the Corinthians appears usual enough. There is a superscription (**Paul**), an address (**to the church . . . at Corinth**), and a salutation (**grace . . . and peace**). But already the form is strained by a cluster of modifiers which will not answer to the usual. If the superscription belongs where it is—the ancients had not attained that level of modesty which requires the sender's name below the "complimentary close"—the qualifiers which follow it lay claim to something calculated to fix a gap between sender and reader, unless, of course, the reader had somehow been convinced that it belonged there—**Paul, called . . . to be an apostle.**

This man holds an appointment, thus a title (*apostle* is not yet limited to the Twelve), and he came by it in a fashion that had nothing to do with him—**by the will of God.** However much or little of the Damascus encounter may be reflected in that phrase and others like it (cf. Gal. 1:1; 2 Cor. 1:1; Rom. 1:1), it is certain that it is there. Did the terminology in which Paul describes his Damascus experience help to shape the introductory formulae of his epistles? Later, Paul would describe that calling as his "destiny" (9:16). But if the appointment was fate, it was also freedom from every conceivable human authority. As he wrote earlier, "an apostle—not from men nor through men" (Gal. 1:1). And it was that dialectic of fate and freedom marking Paul's calling which drove him and his readers apart, but at the same time threw them together. *He* was called to be an apostle, and his readers were called to be **saints** (v. 2)—and let none ignore the difference! But what *they* were depended on what *he* was. The same will which had made Paul an apostle and created the difference between him and Corinth, had bent that difference to the service of Corinth. If there had been no calling to be an apostle, thus no distinction, the **church** at Corinth would not have been **the church of God,** but merely one more religious phenomenon gotten up by the like-minded. The appointment, the title, the fate and the freedom of Paul had all been for Corinth—**by the will of God.** That will had determined whose apostle Paul should be—**of Christ Jesus** (the genitive here denotes possession). The sequence of those two names—**Christ Jesus**—may be traditional, and the appearance of **Christ** without the article may be accidental (though Paul had begun to alter it to a proper name), but was their connection, here, at least, a kind of first thunderclap ahead of the storm to come? Do these names in parallel already hint at attempts to break the link between them, between *Christ, Messiah, Anointed One,* and *Jesus,* the crucified man? Does the connection hide the implication that Corinth sought to put asunder what earliest, post-Easter Christianity had joined together when it fixed that title *Christ* to utterances concerning the death of Jesus?

That dialectic of fate and freedom into which Paul's calling **by the will of God** had thrust him, that being owned and possessed by one who had been appointed for death would expose him to solitariness. And more than once the solitariness would find expression in pathos: "Am I not free? Am I not an apostle? Have I not seen Jesus our Lord? Are not you my workmanship in the Lord? If to others I am not an apostle, at least I am to you!" (9:1-2). But that will of God would also give him others whom Christ had made his own, and his life with them would be the truth of his existence between the visible and perceptible isolation and the pathos, the truth of which even that isolation and pathos would be the proof. So he adds **and our brother Sosthenes** (had Sosthenes been that ruler of the synagogue at Corinth who took the beating intended for Paul? cf. Acts 18:17).

Now comes the address: **To the church of God which is at Corinth.** The definite article makes it crystal clear: Even that scattered group with its base at Corinth is the one church of God—**to those sanctified in Christ Jesus, called to be saints.** (The word **sanctified,** in apposition to **church of God,** translates a perfect passive participle, marking an event of the past, the significance of which for the present is undiminished). But when did Corinth become the church of God; when was it sanctified? The answer will appear later (e.g., in 6:11). Enough for now simply to state the fact. And if it is the church of God, if sanctified, then it is **called to be saints** (that noun almost never appears in the singular!). If the apostleship of Paul derived from his call, the "setting aside" of the Corinthians, their sanctification or "sainthood" derived from their call to be such. There lies the indissoluble connection between Paul and Corinth—both were "called"—the connection which the difference between them had to serve, for the sake of which the difference between them had to be maintained. There would be no "church of God which is at Corinth," no sanctification without a call, no Corinth without a Paul to call. And no Paul without a call, no Paul without a Corinth to call!

If in v. 1 Paul had given definition to his apostleship as "of Christ Jesus," in v. 2 he gives definition to the call and sainthood of Corinth as **in Christ.** Libraries have been devoted to the exposition of that tiny preposition **in.** Is it to be construed as local or spatial, the relation between Christ and the believer conceived as mystical, as an absorption, or does it denote a radius of power or sphere of influence? Or, does "in Christ" simply mean "Christian," in service to, in the discipleship of Christ? So far, this much is clear, no allowance is made for a calling or sainthood as a possibility given with existence. The calling and the sainthood are what they are "in Christ." The prepositional phrase raises an exclusive claim.

If the one church of God is at Corinth, it is not coterminous with Corinth, but rather embraces it. So the apostle adds in v. 2b, "with all who in every place call on the name of our Lord Jesus Christ, theirs and ours" (the possessive pronouns are to be attached to "our Lord," etc., and not to "every place"; cf. the RSV). The phrase **who . . . call on the name** is a technical, liturgical expression. Corinth, together **with all those,** together with the totality of the church of God, is conjured up in a vision of the worshiping assemblies, and at the moment of their acclamation of Jesus as Lord (was the epistle begun on a Sunday?). As for the words **in every place,** they read like a line torn from the old synagogue worship which acknowledged the presence of the people of God from Palestine to the Diaspora.

Grace to you and peace from God our Father and the Lord Jesus Christ (v. 3). Neither **grace** nor **peace** refers to some inner condition of soul, and neither is a summons to achievement. Both refer to an act, both to an act of God. "Grace," the favor of God, the "spontaneous, uncaused, and unmerited favor of God" toward his world, become concrete in the life and destiny of Jesus of Nazareth, the one anointed for death, and because of his death exalted as Lord, and for that reason what is said of God may as well be said of him—**from God our Father and the Lord Jesus Christ** (cf. also Paul's reference to the prophets' description of the day of judgment, the "day of the Lord," as "the day of our Lord Jesus Christ," v. 8). The sequence is not accidental. **Grace** is the presupposition, the precondition, the basis, the reason for peace. And if **peace** marks that universal reign of God to come when the hostility between himself and what he has made is declared to be at an end; if **peace** strains toward the future, then no future, no rule of God or end to conflict can be anticipated apart from the favor of God in the one who died. Again, is the link between **grace** and **peace,** here at least, forged for other reasons than the usual? If the Corinthians had tried to break the link between "Christ" and the crucified Jesus, then they had tried to break the connection between **grace** and **peace,** had tried to anticipate the peace, the observable rule or reign of God above, beyond, apart from the grace, since grace was manifest in, had lodged in a death, a death which rendered the grace equivocal because unobservable, a death which made grace give the lie to peace! Then Corinth had tried to fix that peace to something—to an idea, a "wisdom," or to an event, a "sign"— or to someone—to a person, a group or party which could deliver from the ambiguity—which could make of **peace,** or even of **grace** for that matter, more than a word to be heard and held to. **Grace to you and peace!**

The Thanksgiving (1:4-9)

As per the form of the ancient letter, Paul appends a thanksgiving, and again the form begins to creak and strain. The thanksgiving, with its welter of prepositions (11 in all; 6 in vv. 4-5 alone; Paul loved to heap up prepositions!) is more a proemium or introduction to the letter's main theme than a thanksgiving—something akin to the preacher's "talking over God's shoulder." Here are ranged most of the topics that will make up the body of the letter. **The grace of God . . . given you in Christ Jesus; enriched . . . with all speech and all knowledge; the testimony** of (or "about"—the genitive is objective) **Jesus Christ . . . confirmed among you; you come behind in no spiritual gift,** waiting for the revelation **of our Lord Jesus Christ** (vv. 4-6). Not one assertion in this encomium will be left unchallenged; not one parcel of it is without its direct antithesis in the "theology" or "ethics" of someone at Corinth, an antithesis sufficient to draw Paul's fire. "What have you that you did not receive?" (4:7)—grace had somehow come a cropper. "The kingdom of God does not consist in talk but in power" (4:20); "has not God made foolish the wisdom of the world?" (1:20)—so much for being made rich in speech and knowledge. "I fed you with milk, not solid food; for you were not able to take it" (3:2)—so much for confirmation of the "testimony." "If I speak in the tongues of men and of angels, but have not love, I am a noisy gong or a clanging cymbal" (13:1)—and so much for spirituality or piety. And as for waiting for the revelation, "if the dead are not raised, 'Let us eat and drink, for tomorrow we die'. . . . Come to your right mind, and sin no more" (15:32, 34).

Should we set the thanksgiving down to pure irony? Not unless we eliminate vv. 8 and 9: **who** (does the relative clause in v. 8 introduce a sentence from an old credo?) **will sustain you to the end, guiltless on the day of our Lord Jesus Christ. God is faithful, by whom you were called into the fellowship of his Son.** The words reflect the basic mood of earliest Christianity. Their context is eschatological, having to do with "last" and thus ultimate things; with judgment and testing by fire, with the "great assize," the "day of the Lord" (in Greek, "day" can also mean "court"—a nuance carried through the Latin to the Middle High German "Diät"). The implication is that whatever Corinth may be now— the church of God sanctified and called—is not perceptible in the present. The "day" will disclose it (3:13). But the accent in all this talk of future judgment and ordeal is on the promise: **he will sustain you** and it is the promise that will not allow us to set down Paul's thanksgiving to mere irony. The abnormal, the absurd, the aberrant is always fascinating, more fascinating than the good, for which reason the interpreters of our epistle, observing Paul in struggle against party strife, libertinism, the parading of spirituality, and the denial of his gospel, have cast Corinth in the role of a rabble. But rabble or no, Corinth was Paul's, and for Paul that meant Corinth was God's, and to Corinth the promise belonged: **God is faithful, by whom you were called.** And with that Paul has not simply closed the ring, returned to the opening lines in his "introduction" ("called to be saints," etc.), but given everything said till now its reason and support. The apostolic appointment and title; Corinth's call and sanctification, its fellowship with all those who "call on the name"; the "grace" and the "peace," the enrichment and the confirmation; the lacking of nothing and the waiting—all are for nothing without the faithfulness of God.

■ The Parties (1:10—4:21)

Chapter 1

The Divisions (1:10-17)

This section is crucial to an understanding of the situation at Corinth, and thus to an interpretation of the epistle. But the section is sufficiently cryptic to require the interpretation of the body of the epistle for its understanding. The interpreter is thus trapped in a circle, and the decision to fix the arc where the circle begins will always have something of the arbitrary about it. Let the innumerable hypotheses attest to that. As indicated in the introduction,[2] this commentary rests on the decision that the opponents of Paul addressed in 1 Corinthians were neither Gnostic—if by "Gnostic" is implied adherence to a discrete community organized about a discrete worldview—nor were they interlopers come to alienate Paul from the arch-apostles at Jerusalem. They were rather enthusiasts whose behavior reflected more a kaleidoscope of attitudes and opinions than an integrated, settled "position," opinions in part derived from misinterpretations of Paul and in part from religious notions common to the age which would later congeal into systems rivalling New Testament Christianity, all of it converging on the notion that the Spirit of God gave immunity from the conditions of this world, thus a denial of the event which rooted existence in this world as existence for God and the other—the crucifixion of Jesus of Nazareth, the Messiah, proclaimed Lord by his obedience unto death.

The section opens with an admonition in the form of an antithetical parallelism: **I appeal to you, brethren, by the name of our Lord Jesus Christ, that all of you agree** (Greek, "say the same thing") **and that there be no dissensions among you, but**

that you be united in the same mind and the same judgment (v. 10). Reference to the **name** is not an oath calculated to give force to the appeal. In the New Testament, there is nothing of "theurgy," according to which possession of the god's name is equal to possession of his power, so as to compel him to act. Exactly the opposite is true. The name denotes a sphere of power already present and at work. Hence, the words **by the name of our Lord Jesus Christ** (equal to "in the Lord," a phrase which Paul may well have coined), signal the presence and power of the one sent from God, first among those who confess him (cf. 5:4 and 6:11), finally among all who shall confess him (15:25; cf. Phil. 2:9-11), the one who has harnessed Paul to his apostleship, and by whose authority he speaks.

Verse 11 gives the reason for the appeal. From oral report—answers to the Corinthians' correspondence are delayed till chap. 7—Paul has learned that the community at Corinth is torn by **quarrelings** (the noun is in the plural). His informants are **Chloe's people** (*Chloe* in Greek means "sprouting" or "blooming," a cognomen for the Greek or Roman goddess of fertility [Demeter or Ceres], a name given female slaves in the ancient world). Whether or not Chloe was a Christian, lived at Corinth or Ephesus, and was attached to any one of the parties, is impossible to tell. This is Paul's first and last reference to her. Paul next recites what he has heard ("now I say this," or as the RSV translates, **what I mean is**): **Each one of you says, "I belong to Paul," or "I belong to Apollos," or "I belong to Cephas"** (Peter's Aramaic name—restricted to contexts of dispute? cf. 3:23; 9:5; and Gal. 2:11ff.), **or "I belong to Christ"** (v. 12). Attempts to attach to each party a particular stance or posture later attacked in the epistle ("I belong to Apollos" referring to those who despise the "simple" preaching of Paul and strive for a higher wisdom; "I belong to Cephas" to Palestinian-Jewish Christians who had been converted by Peter, come to Corinth from the orient, etc.) have met with little success, for the reason that Paul nowhere addresses the groups, but rather the party spirit as a whole. But it is conceivable that the slogan "I am of Christ" which climaxes the list—at times construed as a gloss by a later hand, or even as a misprint for Crispus(!)—reflects an orientation to the exalted Lord calculated to annul the message of the crucified Jesus, and resulting in that "spiritual" exaltation of the individual against which Paul is struggling throughout the letter. This hypothesis takes support from the verse following, in which Paul describes the absurdity of self-deification by referring to his possible role as savior: **Is Christ divided? Was Paul crucified for you? Or were you baptized in the name of Paul?** (The negative particle prefixed to the question requires an answer in the negative—"certainly not!" The oldest manuscript witness to 1 Corinthians may have prefixed that particle to all three questions, not merely to the last two.)

Why the reference to Baptism here, and what possible connection can it have with the "quarrelings" at Corinth? Have some (the pronoun "each" in v. 12 need not be stretched to include every living soul at Corinth) laid claim to special rank or privilege by virtue of being baptized by Paul, Apollos, or Cephas? Do they believe that the one or the other enjoys a monopoly on deity and its gifts, and that through Baptism by the one or the other they have come to share that monopoly? Paul's demurrer in vv. 14-16 and his later attack on the notion of the sacrament as guaranteeing immunity from the judgment (10:1-13) appear to support the conclusion that the Corinthians construed their Baptism as magic, for which reason the person of the baptizer as conjurer or mystagogue would have been all-important: "I am of Paul; I have been baptized by Paul; he is the medium by which I have acceded to spiritual rank, to oneness with God." Paul writes: "I thank God" **that I baptized none of you except Crispus and Gaius** (v. 14). Paul regarded holding such activity at a minimum as a divine dispensation. Even the reference to Gaius, not a name but a "pronomen," a designation for any freedman under the sun, reflects casualness respecting his role as baptizer (was Crispus the one-time ruler of the synagogue referred to in Acts 18:8?). The casualness is heightened when Paul adds: **I did baptize also the household of Stephanas. Beyond that, I do not know whether I baptized any one else** (v. 16). Following the final clause in v. 15—

1:10-31 *1 Corinthians*

Lest anyone should say that you were baptized in my name—the sentence appears to compensate for the memory lapse in v. 14. Was Paul dictating right off here, in final form? And did not Fortunatus and Achaicus belong to that list (cf. 16:17)?

Verse 17, prepared for in v. 13 ("was Paul crucified for you?"—in the Greek: "Paul was not crucified for you, was he?"), and setting the theme for what follows, draws two sharp contrasts, signaled by the adversative in its first, and by the negatives in its second half: **For Christ did not send me to baptize but to preach the gospel, and not with eloquent** (a word of) **wisdom** (the nouns may be linked to "send" or "evangelize"), **lest the cross of Christ be emptied** (reduced to nothing).

But if sent **to preach the gospel** and **the cross of Christ** constitute a pair, "to baptize" and "to empty" do not. The antithesis in v. 17a is not between baptizing and evangelizing, as though Paul were spurning the role of a mere "liturgist," but rather between the *person* of the baptizer and the proclamation of the gospel. In other words, Christ had not sent Paul to be a party leader. But if the contrast lies here, then the answer to the question, Why the reference to Baptism? deserves further answer.

For Paul, Baptism and cross were linked, inseparable. The Corinthians had been baptized "into the name," into the presence and power, into the body of the Christ who had died, who even now as exalted made his way in the world as the crucified, as Lord in hiddenness, in nonobservability, his reign under the sign of weakness. It was precisely the Corinthians' Baptism which signaled the antithesis between "cross" and "word of wisdom." But once that truth had been denied, then the event had been reduced to a spiritual exaltation of the individual. In face of such a reduction or emptying, Paul exclaims: "I thank God I baptized none of you!"

The Foolishness of God (1:18-25)

No section in the epistle may be better suited to introduce the reader to Paul's use of traditional literary devices than these verses. The section abounds in rhetorical flourishes. Verse 18 contains an antithetical parallel (*folly* **to those who are perishing, but to us who are being saved it is the** *power* **of God**), both clauses ending with the same Greek word. Verse 19 contains another parallel (**the** *wisdom* **of the wise, and the** *cleverness*—behavior resulting from theoretical knowledge—**of the clever**), this time in chiasma (*I* **will destroy the wisdom . . . the cleverness of the clever** *I will thwart*). Verse 20 begins with the threefold repetition of the word *where*, and continues with an antithesis (**has not God made foolish the** *wisdom* **of the world?**), the second half of the verse in Greek ending on the same syllable as the first. Verse 21 contains an antithesis (**since, in the wisdom of God, the world did not know God through** *wisdom*, **it pleased God through the** *folly* **of what we preach to save . . .**). Both clauses in v. 22 end on the same Greek syllable. Verses 22 and 23a contain an antithesis (**Jews demand signs and Greeks seek wisdom, but we preach Christ crucified**). Verses 23b and 24 contain another antithesis (**stumbling block to Jews and folly to Gentiles, but to those who are called . . ., Christ the power of God and the wisdom of God**). Verse 25 forms a chiasma with v. 24b, the beginning of the verse corresponding to the end of v. 24b, and the end of the verse to the beginning of v. 24b (**Christ the** *power* **of God and the** *wisdom* **of God. For the** *foolishness* **of God is wiser . . . and the** *weakness* **of God is stronger**), and, in Greek, concludes with the same words, the same syllables, and the same sounds. And in all this rhetorical display the most striking is Paul's use of the terms *folly, foolishness,* and *wisdom* throughout the section in two altogether different senses. The "folly" of vv. 18 and 23 is the antithesis to the "folly" or "foolishness" of vv. 21 and 25; and the "wisdom" (or "wise man") of vv. 19-22 is the antithesis to the "wisdom" or to what is "wiser" of vv. 24 and 25.

The section takes up and interprets the antithesis first set up in v. 17 (**word of wisdom . . . cross of Christ**) and which will dominate the discussion to the end of chap. 3, giving to 1:18—3:23 its "ring" character (1:18: "Folly to those who are perishing, but to us who are being saved it is the power of God," and 3:19-23: "For the wisdom of this world is folly with God").

What has divided Corinth? It is not race—"Jews and Greeks" (Paul's cipher for all humanity) are both on either side of the divide (vv. 23-24). Let Lucian, second-century Syrian philosopher, speak for the Greek:

> The poor wretches have convinced themselves, first and foremost, that they are going to be immortal and live for all time, in consequence of which they despise death and even willingly give themselves into custody, most of them. Furthermore, their first lawgiver persuaded them that they are all brothers of one another after they have transgressed once for all by denying the Greek gods and by worshipping that crucified sophist himself and living under his laws.[3]

Let Trypho speak for the Jew:

> Whether Christ should be so shamefully crucified, this we are in doubt about. For whosoever is crucified is said in the law to be accursed, so that I am exceedingly incredulous on this point. It is quite clear, indeed, that the Scriptures announce that Christ had to suffer; but we wish to learn if you can prove it to us whether it was by the suffering cursed in the law.[4]

It would be an error, however, to interpret Paul's word of the cross as in antithesis merely to Jewish or Greek expectations of salvation. It is to the Christian congregation at Corinth that Paul's word is opposed. The antithesis is thus between two perceptions, two ways of life among "believers," people of faith, and thus, to judge from history, with no greater prospect of reconciliation than between believers and unbelievers.

Nothing intrinsic has created the division, nothing given with human intelligence or feeling or strength of will which one could claim to possess to greater degree than the other. Something extrinsic has created the division, an event for which neither Jew nor Greek could furnish the occasion. Despite Paul's "concession" to the subjective response to that event in v. 18 (cf. 2:14), the gulf does not lie in the attitude which the one or the other might take toward that event, as though nothing more than perspective or taste or personal judgment lay on either side of the divide, something over which two could violently disagree but in the end achieve a reconciliation, provided each agreed to allow the other's point of view. It is the event itself which divides, which renders every attitude or position taken toward it, every perception of it subordinate, a reflex or reaction. To this event **the word of the cross** gave witness. Did that phrase, "word of the cross," together with, say, Deut. 21:22-23 ("a hanged man is accursed by God") once belong to the arsenal of the argument of the anti-Christian Paul? And does the Christian theology of Paul take the sharpness, the acuteness of its contours exclusively from the background of an earlier polemic against Jesus the crucified, at the "word" about whom he once took irreconcilable offense? Those participles in v. 18, **to those who are perishing, but to us who are being saved,** point ahead to a decision which made that event what it is. Paul's quotation of Isa. 29:14 (LXX) in the verse following is not a proof from Scripture of the vanity of philosophy, but a reference to the initiator of that event: "I will destroy the wisdom of the wise, and the cleverness of the clever I will thwart" (v. 19). Corinth had a love affair with wisdom. Paul's continual reference to *sophia*, "wisdom," throughout the first four chapters of the epistle gives every indication that some (not all—the pronoun in the prepositional phrase, "to us . . . it is the power of God" is not editorial) believed they possessed a knowledge, however they may have arrived at it, which lofted them above the fleshly, earthly, temporal, and historical. Therefore they regarded concentration on the event of the cross which plunged human existence into the conditions of this world as a seduction or temptation to embrace again what they had abandoned, a reversion to a state from which they had been set free. But that division at Corinth was only the reflection in religion or piety of a decision and act which had fixed a gulf within humanity itself. *I will destroy . . . . I will thwart* (v. 19); *God* has **made** (v. 20); **it pleased God** (v. 21), and to those who are "called" **Christ** is **the power of God and the wisdom of God** (v. 24; the repetition of the divine name is not merely for effect). If the subject of the event is ignored for the sake of the division which it creates, then Paul's description of the reversal of wisdom and folly which have come about through the cross—(**Where is the wise man?** . . . **the scribe?** . . .

the debater of this age? [no subtle distinction is to be made between those three] **Has not God made foolish the wisdom of the world? . . . It pleased God through the folly of what we preach to save. . . . For the foolishness of God is wiser than men, and the weakness of God is stronger than men,** vv. 20-21, 25)—is reduced to mere rhetoric, a punning on words. Paul's move from a reference to the subjective appraisal of the action of God in the cross in v. 18, to wisdom and folly's exchange of roles, signaled in vv. 19-20, a reversal carried through to the end of the section, must not be missed. The rhetoric, Paul's use of the words *wisdom* and *folly* in two contrary and opposed senses, has been required by the event which turned wisdom to folly and folly to wisdom. Finally, then, the point is not that God has made to be power and wisdom what the world imagines to be their opposite, as though the section ended with a paraphrase of the Magnificat ("He has put down the mighty from their thrones, and exalted those of low degree," Luke 1:52). The reversal, the standing of folly or wisdom on its head has come about by the fact that God has made his power and wisdom weakness and folly, that is, has deliberately set his saving activity against whatever may be grasped through perception or conception, opposed it to whatever is provable or able to be disproved by appeal to sense or reason (**for Jews demand signs and Greeks seek wisdom,** v. 22).

But did not the incapacity of human wisdom at least furnish the occasion for this foolishness of God? **Since,** Paul writes in v. 21, **in the wisdom of God, the world did not know God through wisdom, it pleased God through the folly of what we preach to save. . . .** The sentence is reminiscent of ancient Jewish speculation, according to which the wisdom of God was hypostasized, given arms and legs, personality and gender, in an attempt to explain what fate it had been forced to suffer in the world. Wisdom, agent of creation, had made her descent, had appeared to the race, but the race rejected her, whereupon she retreated to heaven from which she reappeared, but only to the elect or wise. Chapter 42 in the Similitudes of Enoch reads:

> Wisdom found no place where she might dwell;
> Then a dwelling place was assigned her in the heavens.
> Wisdom went forth to make her dwelling among the children of men,
> And found no dwelling-place:
> Wisdom returned to her place,
> And took her seat among the angels.[5]

Against such a background, v. 21 would imply that the world, created through the wisdom of God, was suffused with wisdom (the phrase **in the wisdom of God** to be construed spatially) so that it was possible, by means of wisdom, to come to a knowledge of God, to relate to God as God. The comment that, of course, Paul would not have allowed that possibility of knowing God to be anything more than an awareness of God as Creator, of God as not-I or not-world, or that the world's not knowing God through wisdom denotes a conscious, active rejection of that awareness, though true, would still not get at the cause for the **folly of what we preach.** It would merely delay the question, "Who or what was the cause of that wisdom by which God could be recognized only as Creator?" The **since,** the causal conjunction at the beginning of v. 21 gets its come-uppance, its qualification, in the verse's second half: **It pleased God**—again, there lies the cause for the folly! If the first half of the sentence has its final interpretation at the beginning of the Romans epistle ("ever since the creation of the world his invisible nature, namely, his eternal power and deity, has been clearly perceived in the things that have been made. So they are without excuse," Rom. 1:20), the second half has its interpretation toward that epistle's end ("for God has consigned all men to disobedience, that he may have mercy upon all," Rom. 11:32).

But what of Corinth? If the decision to act in the Christ crucified lay only with God, if that event was the cause for the division between those who are perishing and being saved, were not at least some in Corinth fated for, doomed to, perishing? If a call, however misinterpreted or misapplied, determined the

Corinth and the Theology of the Cross (1:26-31)

The style of the section is that of the ancient diatribe. Paul is engaging his reader-hearer in dialog, a style of which he will never tire throughout all his correspondence. **Consider your call, brethren,** he writes, "you yourselves are a graphic illustration of my contention:" **Not many of you were wise according to** "the flesh" (the RSV correctly interprets: **according to worldly standards**), **not many . . . powerful, not many . . . of noble birth** (v. 22). The three members of that negative clause then form the scheme for the three clauses following in vv. 27 and 28: **But**—again the antitheses!—**God chose what is foolish in the world** (in the Greek, the neutral plural with the genitive recurring in these verses denotes a plurality of persons) **to shame the wise, God chose what is weak in the world to shame the strong, God chose what is low and despised in the world, even things that are not, to bring to nothing things that are.** To the Greek, nothing could be more trifling than **things that are not.**

The verses are not an argumentum ad hominem. The threefold verb and its subject make that clear. And, again, the accent does not fall on the antithesis or reversal, but on its initiator: **God chose!** The shaming of the **wise** and **strong,** or the destruction of the **things that are** may be the "natural" consequence of the manifestation of God's power in folly and weakness, but they are not the purpose. For what reason, then, had God determined to save through the folly and weakness of the "Christ crucified"? Why this scandal to sense, to those for whom the world must yield some evidence of deity and its intention with the world, at least some "sign" by which that intention could be inferred—a law, a code, or a cultus? Why this affront to reason, to those for whom mind or spirit are somehow linked with deity, so that whatever accords with rationality may be acknowledged to be divine, and whatever does not would be unworthy of it? And why this folly to those for whom deity and its intent can be grasped in a trice, in a sudden "vision" of the self and God as one, and for which the world, history, temporality, the other are an obstacle? The answer to the question has been postponed till now: "For the reason that no flesh (**no human being,** RSV) **might boast before God**" (v. 29). That flotsam at Corinth had suggested it, the correspondence of that ragtag and bobtail crew to the event which had constituted it what it was, had moved Paul to the answer. God had called Corinth out of nothing, and God had fixed his power and wisdom to a nothing, and the connection between these two events was indissoluble. The one nothing was the efficient cause of the other, "that no flesh might boast."

His reflection moves Paul to a confession in v. 30: "You have your source from God" (literally, "from him you are, you exist"; RSV: **He is the source of your life**). That was always true of Corinth, and would still be true, whatever side of the event and its divide it would stand. But God **is the source of your life in Christ Jesus.** That was not always true of Corinth, for Corinth had been given a second birth, **in Christ Jesus, whom God made our wisdom** (note again the "rehabilitation," cf. v. 24), **our righteousness and sanctification and redemption.** Earlier, Paul had described Christ as God's power and wisdom; here he writes that he became such "from God"—the subject of all this activity has never been out of sight! **Our wisdom, . . . righteousness . . . sanctification . . . redemption** (in Paul, the latter term is not to be interpreted literally; no special theory of purchase attaches to it)—are these terms strictly soteriological, limited to the work of Christ who justifies, hallows, and ransoms? If **in Christ** means that Corinth and Paul have been taken up into his history, with the result that whatever may be said of him applies to them as well, the terms are also autobiographical. And if it is true that Paul's anthropology throughout his epistles often thwarts attempts at systematization, the reason does not lie simply in his Jewish heritage or his preoccupation with eschatology, with apocalyptic thought, but in his understanding of faith as making of Christ and the believer one flesh. What creates the confusion is our attempt to regard Paul's anthropological terms as retaining the same sense for existence "in" as well as apart from Christ, as though the structures of that existence were identical in either case. Or, it derives from our attempt to define existence from the perspective of the "I" as self-contained, whereas for the apostle Christ had become the subject of believing existence. For that **in Christ,** let a word from a disciple of Paul serve as its interpretation: " 'For this reason a man shall leave his father and mother and be joined to his wife, and the two shall become one flesh.' This mystery is a profound one, and I am saying that it refers to Christ and the church" (Eph. 5:31-32).

Therefore, the section concludes with resuming the thought in vv. 26-29, **as it is written, "Let him who boasts, boast of the Lord."** The quotation is from Jeremiah:

> Thus says the Lord: "Let not the wise man glory in his wisdom, let not the mighty man glory in his might, let not the rich man glory in his riches; but let him who glories glory in this, that he understands and knows me, that I am the Lord who practice steadfast love, justice, and righteousness in the earth; for in these things I delight, says the Lord" (Jer. 9:23-24).

The quotation is not exact. Further, the sense of the sentence requires the alteration of object from God to Christ (cf. Gal. 6:14). But the alteration does not merely derive from that dialectic in Jewish use of Scripture according to which the "Book" could be regarded as having a single, unequivocal sense by which life was to be regulated, *and at the same time,* since it was God's Word, could be conceived as infinitely plastic, allowing for infinite strata of meaning. The alteration is an exhausting of the prophetic word, pulling it out of shape. For Jeremiah, the object of boasting remained aloof: Yahweh would exercise his mercy, justice, and righteousness from heaven against uncircumcised Egypt and Ammon—and Judah with its "uncircumcised heart." Even the forgiveness which Yahweh would guarantee to the house of Israel and the house of Judah in a "new covenant" would come by way of a surrogate—the Law (cf. Jer. 31:31-34). For Paul, "righteousness, sanctification, and redemption" had taken on flesh and blood in the one whom God had made to be such, in the KYRIOS, the Lord.

Chapter 2

Now Paul turns his readers' attention to the time of his initial appearance at Corinth and the founding of the congregation. In the first five verses, he concentrates on the manner of his appearance, tersely describing the content of his preaching (v. 2). In the chapter's second section (vv. 6-16), he again refers to the content of his preaching (vv. 6-8), but also to the power which attended it. The argument throughout is formal, descriptive, characteristic of the greater part of the first four chapters of the epistle. Chapter 2 also contains a variety of terms which occur for the first time: "mystery" in vv. 1 and 7 (RSV: "testimony" and "secret," respectively); "Spirit" or "Spirit of God" in vv. 4, 10-14; "spirit" as an anthropological term in v. 11; "spirit of the world" in v. 12; "those who are spiritual" or "the spiritual ones" in vv. 13 and 15; "spiritual things" in v. 13; the adverb "spiritually" in v. 14; "those who are perfect" or "the perfect ones" in v. 6 (RSV: **the mature**); "the rulers of this age" in vv. 6 and 8; "the one who is psychic" or "the psychic one" in v. 14 (RSV: **the unspiritual man**), and "the mind of Christ" in v. 16. Whether or not any or all of these terms were in vogue at Corinth, almost every one of them—to say nothing of terms such as "word," "power," and, above all, "wisdom" or "knowledge" used earlier—ultimately became fixed in the nomenclature of that congeries of sects which laid claim to a "wisdom" not available to reason or logic, but acquired in a single, sudden act. And it was Paul to whom those sects later made their appeal, for Paul had spoken of a "mystery" once hidden and now revealed (vv. 1 and 7); a "wisdom" available only to "the perfect" or the "spiritual" who had plumbed the depths of God (vv. 6, 7, 9, 10, 12-16; more than once Paul's quotation from the alleged "Apocalypse of Elijah" in v. 9 would be repeated in oaths and descriptions of the Gnostic's "vision"). Paul had contrasted the "psychic" and the "spiritual" (v. 14—in some Gnostic systems, the "psychic" represented an

45

existence one stage below the "spiritual," and one above the "fleshly"). He had referred to the world as fallen and dominated by Satan and the demonic powers (vv. 6, 8; in Gnosticism, the term translated "rulers" here was often applied to them). He had spoken of those powers as ignorant of what God had "decreed for our glorification" (in Gnosticism the "Redeemer" was a heavenly being who descended unknown and returned again to God). And it was Paul who wrote that what he spoke was not taught by human wisdom, but by the Spirit (v. 13; the Gnostic would insist that his "wisdom" could not be gained through rational-logical means, and thus could not be mediated to others and in turn be rejected or accepted by them through rational or logical means). But, however well Paul may have served his curious successors, he made no party with them, and his distance from them is perhaps nowhere clearer than here.

Paul's Appearance at Corinth (2:1-5)

All the verses in this section, with the exception of the third, contain an antithesis: In v. 1, **I came** is contrasted with "excellence" or "superiority of speech or wisdom"; in v. 2 "not anything" or **nothing** is contrasted with **"Jesus Christ and, indeed, this one crucified"** (the "epexegetical" conjunction and the demonstrative pronoun allow no confusion in identity); in v. 4 "persuasive **words of wisdom**" form the antithesis to **demonstration** (in ancient Greek rhetoric, the term for "proof" or "evidence") **of the Spirit and of power,** and in v. 5 the "wisdom of men" forms the antithesis to the "power of God."

To the composition of the community at Corinth corresponded the speech and appearance of its founder. If at Corinth there were not many wise, mighty, or well-born, there was nothing of superfluity of eloquence or wisdom about Paul. How he spoke had been bent to what he had to speak—the "mystery of God." Some at Corinth may have regarded that mystery as a secret to be kept, disclosed only to the initiated, "the perfect." Some would later be drawn by an irrepressible urge to invent new "mysteries." In the Gnostic *Apocryphon of John*, Jesus after his resurrection appears to the son of Zebedee; reveals to him what is, what was, and will be; charges him to give it to his "fellow spirits" in secret, and concludes with a curse on every one who exchanges it "for a gift or for food or for drink or for clothing or for any such thing."[6] But for Paul, "the mystery of God" was not identical to the revelation of God. There lies the difference between his and anyone else's use of the term, then or now. The "mystery of God" was the object of the revelation, for which reason it could not be hid. If it was a mystery prepared for before the world began (v. 7), hidden from "the rulers of this age" (v. 8), it had now been made manifest in an event set in space, in time, in "Jesus Christ, and, indeed, this one crucified" (v. 2).

It was not a deficiency in the apostle that established the correspondence between him and Corinth. Attempts to compare Paul unfavorably with such possible competitors as Apollos, allegedly schooled in rhetoric and declamation at Alexandria, are wide of the mark. There had been more in his quiver than Paul had strung to his bow at Corinth ("I . . . could not address you as spiritual, but as . . . of the flesh, as babes. . . . I fed you with milk, not solid food; for you were not ready for it . . . ," 3:1-2). And as for those "spiritual gifts," Paul could lay claim to every one in the list of chap. 12—apostles, prophets, teachers, workers of miracles, healers, helpers, administrators, speakers in tongues—and of the latter to greater degree than any at Corinth (or, all at Corinth put together? cf. 14:18). What created the correspondence was a resolution (the verb translated **decided** in the RSV denotes an active, deliberate choice; the old KJV with its "determined" was a better reading). But the resolve was not arbitrary. The suggestion that because Paul had failed with his "fundamental theology" or apologetics at Athens (Acts 17:16-34) he had decided upon another approach at Corinth is also wide of the mark. (Apart from failing to distinguish the hand of Luke in the speeches of Acts, it ignores what in Acts 17 may still coincide with the theology of 1 Corinthians, a preaching determined by an expectation of the end-time and the resultant call to repentance). Paul's resolve, thus the correspondence between his appearance and the form of his preaching with the composition of the Corinthian community, was determined by the event which had effected the reversal of wisdom and folly: "Jesus Christ, and, indeed, this one crucified." Whatever else he would say or write—of "the day of the Lord," the body of Christ, love, the resurrection—it would all be rendered utterable by this event, would never overtake it.

If v. 1 indicates the conformity of the apostle's message, v. 3 indicates the conformity of his appearance to the mystery he preached: **I was with you in weakness and in much fear and trembling.** Paul is not referring to his anxiety in face of possible rejection at Corinth. Corinth here, Corinth there, Paul had nothing to fear from Corinth (cf. 4:21). The two terms are paired elsewhere in Paul's correspondence. To the Philippians he writes: "Work out your own salvation," then adds, "for God is at work in you, both to will and to work for his good pleasure" (Phil. 2:12-13), and in midst of that apparent dialectic he sets the words, "with fear and trembling," signal of the acknowledgment of an "epiphany," of the recognition of the subject in all this "working," the acknowledgment that the autonomy in all this activity has belonged only to One. The same signal is given here to Paul's appearance at Corinth. And if the Philippians' salvation could be called their own, so Paul could call "mine" the mystery of God, that **speech and . . . message** which were **not in** persuasive **words of wisdom, but in demonstration of the Spirit and of power**—not merely since what the preacher preached would have been truncated or amputated if it had not taken on his own flesh and bone, but because he had consented to the necessity of that autonomy, had made it his own.

Still, was there proof, evidence, something higher or greater than the word of the cross, something to warrant its truth— **demonstration of the Spirit and of power?** One interpreter writes: "With words nothing yet is altered of the actual state of our existence. The goal of the apostle lies higher and the gift he brings is greater. The Spirit is active through him, and the Spirit is more than words."[7] But the "persuasive words of wisdom" are not a concession to the paltriness of speech. They are the antithesis to "the word of the cross," and for this reason to "the demonstration of the Spirit and of power." "My speech and my message," the "mystery" had been borne by a power beyond human persuasion, but it was that speech and the message which it bore, and that power was as much a folly as the word it bore. If there was power at Corinth, and a fear and trembling as its concomitant, there was also "weakness" at Corinth (v. 3), again, not a weakness of eloquence or wisdom—the resolve had been to dispense with such (vv. 1 and 4!)—but a weakness to which the power of God had fixed itself, and for this reason to the apostolic "parousia": **That your faith might not rest in the wisdom of men but in the power of God.** Faith, but only faith, would see the power in the weakness.

Wisdom and the Spirit of God (2:6-16)

From this point on till 3:18-23, Paul will not use the term *wisdom* in a dual sense (*antanaklesis*) to mark the act of God as folly, and thus as effecting a reversal in the roles of folly and wisdom. In what follows (with the exception of the irony in 4:10), use of the term *wisdom* without modifiers will signal the reversal as complete: The folly of God has become the true wisdom, its antithesis in the "wisdom of this age" or in "human wisdom" has become folly (3:18-20).

The conceptuality lying behind this section is in part that of the Jewish apocalypse. The wisdom by which the world was created and is suffused is hidden, obscured by evil, accessible only by way of special revelation to the righteous, conscious of their piety and fear of God. Here lies the dualism in the apocalyptic view. The world is a theater of conflict between good and evil, God and the "rulers of this age," a conflict to be resolved only by divine intervention in the destruction of "this age" and the appearance of the "age to come." From this idea of the two aeons in temporal, horizontal succession, it is only a short step to the Gnostic concept of that process as spatial or vertical, of the aeons as layers through which one ascends. And here lies the esoteric character of that worldview—only the "elect" or "righteous" possess such "wisdom"—and the resultant separation of "sinners" from the "righteous" who are not at home in the world and await the future of God in a new aeon. "I'm but a stranger here, Heaven is my home; Earth is a desert drear, Heaven is my home. . . ." And again, it requires only a short step to alter "sinner" to read "psychic" or "fleshly," the one bound or not yet free from the earthly and temporal, or to alter "righteous" to read "spiritual" or pneumatic, for whom the earthly and temporal denotes filth and imprisonment of the soul.

Jewish "wisdom" teaching also has its deposit here, a teaching which finally bred pessimism ending in skepticism. Wisdom's struggle to be heard in face of error and stupidity rendered her homeless. The believer was hard-pressed to find order or meaning in such a chaos. If faith was still faith that God was just and ruled all things, it was more an act of despair. The book of Job, part of the "wisdom" genre, may be a protest or rebellion against the God who crushes the innocent, and for no apparent reason than that he distrusts them, or is intent on humiliating Satan at their expense ("you moved me against him, to destroy him without cause" is part of God's dialog with Satan which Job never hears). Such skepticism could have direct consequences for the manner of life. It could result in bitter hedonism, or in spurning everything earthly. All this, together with Platonism, Hellenistic Greek thought, the "mysteries," cults and gods from the east, oriental syncretism, the condition of the masses and social protest, would congeal into systems which one day would threaten to snuff out the life of the nascent community of Christ. And all of it has its earliest flickerings, in Christian literature at least, in the correspondence of Paul with Corinth. But if it is impossible to state that Gnosticism full-blown had emerged at Corinth or penetrated there—and one of the reasons for the impossibility is that the Gnostic cared nothing for history and so wrote none—what of Paul? Where is the "word and message" of Paul in all this talk of wisdom and its revelation in hiddenness, its accessibility to "the perfect," to the "spiritual"? Where is Paul in this assuming the axiom of "like through like" (**For what person knows a man's thoughts except the spirit of the man which is in him? So also no one comprehends the thoughts of God except the Spirit of God,** vv. 11-12)? And at the center of it lies a piece of profane, secular baggage whose owner has never been traced—**what no eye has seen, nor ear heard** . . . (v. 9).

Paul is where he has always been. The section is a resumption (*epanelepsis*) of the argument in vv. 18-25. It is the language and conceptuality in which Paul has returned to his argument over which his interpreters have tripped. The situation at Corinth required setting the argument in this "secular" form. Paul was not an apologete, but neither was he a purist who hurled words at his hearers under the assumption that all would somehow be rendered intelligible in some mysterious disclosure which freed him from the obligation of struggling to match to the hearer's existence the scene in which the encounter between God and the hearer should occur. Later, he would ask: "If I come to you speaking in tongues, how shall I benefit you unless I bring you some revelation or knowledge or prophecy or teaching? If even lifeless instruments, such as the flute or the harp, do not give distinct notes, how will any one know what is played?" (14:6-7). The gospel was the constant; the "scenery" was the variable, and Paul would not make do at Corinth with what had suited Galatia or would later suit Rome. The reason lay in the gospel itself which called to life for the other—"in church I would rather speak five words with my mind, in order to instruct others, than ten thousand words in a tongue" (14:19).

Yet for all that, the language and conceptuality, the form in which Paul resumes his argument is stranger to its content. The vehicle which the gospel required would not simply represent to his hearers what they had always heard. The message would fracture its medium. Or Paul's hearers would hear what they had always heard, but the "syntax" in which whatever they had always heard it would be so radically altered that what they had always heard would appear as though they had never heard it before. The unease at the disarrangement of what they had always heard would be like that of moving in a gallery from a room strung with Rubens to another with Picasso or Klee. The fracture of the medium is visible at v. 7: **But** (again an antithesis, this time to v. 6) **we impart a secret and hidden wisdom of God** (in the Greek: "a wisdom of God which has been hidden in a mystery"), **which God decreed before the ages for** (the little preposition denotes purpose or result) **our glorification.** The "wisdom hidden in a mystery" is the same "wisdom" and "mystery" to which Paul had referred in 1:23-24 and 2:1-2: "Christ, and, indeed, this one crucified." This was what had been decreed, and in it was rooted the ultimate end and goal of God's activity toward his creation—"our glory." This was what eye had not seen, nor ear heard, had created the divide between "the rulers of this age" and "those who love him." And the event was not a trick. The powers which had held the earth in their grasp did not crucify **the Lord of glory** from out of ignorance (the phrase **Lord of glory** is as august a statement as Paul will ever make in reference to Christ, assigning to him a predicate which Old Testament faith had reserved for God, for describing the "weight" ["glory," Hebrew: *kabod*] of God's appearance, experienced as honor, might, or brilliance). Basilides, the first Christian Gnostic of any importance, was alleged to have taught that the highest God had sent his Christ-Nous (cf. v. 16, **but we have the mind**—the *nous*—**of Christ**) into the world to appear in Jesus, but that Christ had avoided crucifixion by taking on the form of Simon of Cyrene, and, laughing all the way, returned unrecognized to the Father. (Note the similarity with Luther's description of Christ's descent to earth, where the devil finds him like "a worm and no man," swallows but cannot digest him, chokes and is slain, taken captive by Christ.)[8] For the apostle, there was nothing of deception in the "Christ crucified." The event had occurred for all to see, and the "rulers" had killed him because they believed they had apprehended God in their "wisdom." The phrase **crucified the Lord of glory** is an oxymoron, the linking of two mutually exclusive predicates to a single subject, and on it Paul's entire argument in this epistle turns. It was the oxymoron, the "death of God," which the "rulers of this age" denied, and which God had made his wisdom. For those who embraced this "contradiction" (a contradiction not in God; God had not come into contradiction with himself in this event; **before the ages** he had determined to be the God who would set himself, his Godhead, his honor and might in question in this event). Paul reserved the term "perfect" for **those who love him,** a phrase taken from that piece which Origen and Jerome supposed belonged to the *Apocalypse of Elijah* (the thought itself rarely occurs in Paul; it is God's love for us which preponderates, but cf. Rom. 8:28).

The fracture is visible everywhere, and no less in vv. 10-16, with their substitution of **Spirit** for **wisdom.** Why the substitution? Corinth furnished the occasion for it. The concept of "Spirit" had come loose from its moorings. Some have suggested that in his struggle with enthusiasm Paul was forced to develop a doctrine of Spirit, and thus a doctrine of existence from the perspective of the divine, whereas in his struggle with nomism or legalism he shaped his teaching from the perspective of the human, with its accent on sin and justification, and for this reason plunged his theology into an antinomy. This suggestion, however, ignores the fracture signaled in the synonymity of "the wisdom of God hidden in a mystery" in v. 7 (that is, "Jesus Christ, and, indeed, this one crucified") with "the depths of God" traced by the Spirit in v. 10, a synonymity demanded by that substitution of "Spirit" for "wisdom" (the conjunction in the phrase, **for the Spirit searches everything,** *even* **the depths of God**—the terms are nautical—is not copulative, but emphatic: "and actually"). What has been **revealed** through the Spirit and enables understanding (vv. 10-12); what **we impart** and what is **taught by the Spirit** and enables interpretation (v. 13b reads, "comparing spiritual things with spiritual," i.e., interpreting the gifts or revelations we receive with what we already possess, and accordingly judge); what is **spiritually discerned** (v. 14); what defines the **spiritual man** who judges all things but is free of all judgment based on investigation (v. 15)—this has the oxymoron, the contradiction, at its heart and core. It is the embracing of that contradiction which is the work of the one as near to God as self-consciousness to the human person (v. 11 is not an analogy, but a simile; it does not assume Homer's axiom of the god as "bringing like and like together,"[9] in order to identify human self-consciousness with the Spirit of God). Nowhere in Paul is "Spirit" an addendum to the activity of God in Jesus Christ. Nowhere in Paul is the Spirit without Christological shape. And nowhere is that shape anything else than cruciform. For this reason, neither enthusiasm nor nomism may be construed as a cause for the Pauline proclamation, nor his reference to "Spirit" or to justification be set down as provisional, temporary, suited to the needs of the moment. For enthusiast and nomist the offense was the same—the folly of God in the crucified.

So the division between the "psychic" and the "pneumatic" or spiritual, between the one who is able to understand, interpret or judge and the one who is not, does not arise from qualities inherent in the one or lacking to the other, but in the event the one had embraced (**we have received . . . the Spirit,** v. 12) and the other denied (**the** psychic [**unspiritual**] **man does not receive the** things **of the Spirit of God, for they are folly to him,** v. 14): "The depths of God," "Jesus Christ, and, indeed, this one crucified."

But if the pneumatics at Corinth had construed the simile in v. 11 as an analogy, had regarded the characteristics of the human spirit and the Spirit of God as in agreement, and on this assumption raised claim to know "the things of the Spirit of God," then this notion too suffered fracture in Paul's choice of the verb *graced* in v. 12 (RSV: **bestowed**). The term is not used "mystically." It is one more deliberate, calculated, polemical substitution of a term which leaves no doubt as to origins or initiative for another which could suggest an inherent or earned (and thus inherent) superiority. **Now we have received . . . the Spirit which is from God, that we might** know the things **bestowed on us by God,** through the spontaneous, uncaused and unmerited, the sheer favor of God. The language and the conceptuality, whatever their origin, and whatever their future, had suffered fracture through being harnessed, warped, twisted, and forced to a decision of God in an event of God recognized as God's through the Spirit of God—"Jesus Christ, and, indeed, this one crucified."

Chapter 3

The chapter is composed of three sections. In the first (vv. 1-4), Paul resumes his attack on the partisanship at Corinth. In vv. 5-17, he identifies Corinth's heroes from the perspective of their relation to his gospel and the community, and in a series of agricultural and architectural metaphors. In the last section (vv. 18-23), Paul returns to the argument in 1:18-25, applying it directly to his readers.

Babes and Milk (3:1-4)

But I, brethren, could not address you as spiritual men, but as men of the flesh, as babes in Christ (v. 1). Again Paul refers to his initial appearance at Corinth, this time to describe the status of his hearers. Whatever their boast now, the Corinthians *then* were not "spiritual" but "fleshly" (the term takes its definition from vv. 3 and 4—"walking according to what is human" [RSV: **behaving like ordinary men**], in contrast to "walking according to the Spirit;" Paul often uses the term *walk* to denote the orientation of life, cf. Gal. 5:16; Rom. 6:4; 8:4; etc.). More, the Corinthians were **babes,** "unripe." The language is reminiscent of Paul's older contemporary, Philo of Alexandria, who contrasts the last term in Paul's description with the "perfect" or mature (cf. 2:6):

> But seeing that for babes milk is food, and for grown (perfect) men wheaten bread, there must also be soul-nourishment, such as is milk-like suited to the time of childhood, in the shape of the preliminary stages of school-learning, and such as is adapted to grown men in the shape of instructions leading the way through wisdom and temperance and all virtue.[10]

In Philo, "milk" and "wheaten bread" correspond to the "less lofty" and the "topmost," to the "literal" and the "latent," the "suckers" of learning and the "plant of sound sense," or to "sense perception" and "Mind."[11] Did what Paul had "decided to know" at Corinth (2:2) fall under the category of **milk**? Did the "meat" (**solid food**) he withheld correspond to a wisdom which relegated the "word of the cross" to child's fare? Had the incapacity of the Corinthians required standing on its head the word of Jesus:

> I thank thee, Father, Lord of heaven and earth, that thou hast hidden these things from the wise and understanding and revealed them to babes; yea, Father, for such was thy gracious will (cf. the similarity in language and content of 1 Cor. 1:19, 21 and Matt. 11:25-26; Luke 10:21)?

Of the flesh, babes, and **milk, spiritual men,** and **solid food** shadow that religious aggregate (Gnosticism) which would contend for the future of Christianity, with its myriad ceremonies and initiations leading from one stage to another, and a curse on whomever had reached the higher level and told what he knew to those at the lower. The pneumatic alone was capable of tarrying in the realm of Spirit. The "spiritual man" saw with other eyes than the fleshly. The "unripe" was neither able nor permitted to see what he saw—**I . . . could not address you as spiritual men, but as men of the flesh, as babes in Christ** (v. 1). The Ophites or "snake people," named after their principal symbol, would later distinguish initiation into the "small" and the "great mysteries" which required a novitiate: **You were not ready for it; and even yet you are not ready, for you are still of the flesh** (vv. 2b-3a).

If there was more to tell at Corinth, and if Paul had not already begun to tell it—the words in v. 2b, **even yet you are not ready** (sc. to receive it), need not be read to mean that the apostle still refused to give Corinth solid food, but could just as well be construed to mean, "ready or not, here it is"—it would not differ in kind from what he had already disclosed. It would correspond to the **milk** as whatever was built would correspond to the foundation, and other than that foundation no one could lay (v. 11). Thus, whatever of the pejorative attaches to vv. 1-4 attaches less to what Paul preached than to whom he preached it: "Because" (RSV: **while**) **there is jealousy and strife among you, are you not of the flesh, and behaving like ordinary men? For when one says, "I belong to Paul," and another "I belong to Apollos," are you not** human (RSV: **merely men**)? The jibe attaches less to the "milk" than to the sarkic or unripe, for if it was "milk" with which Paul first fed Corinth, the feeding was done with skill (v. 10).

Corinth's Heroes and the Test by Fire (3:5-17)

In face of the sloganeering, Paul proceeds to assign Corinth's heroes to their proper place, and by way of an agricultural metaphor. But their mention is restricted to two: **What then is Apollos? What is Paul? Servants through whom you believed** (v. 5). The omission of Cephas (Peter) does not imply a loftier status for that personage, as though his designation as "servant" would fall under the same tabu as a reference to Christ as one **through whom you believed.** Paul would later contend for his equality with the head of the Jerusalem community (in 9:5, and in 15:5 and 8). Because Cephas had nothing to do with establishing or nourishing the community at Corinth (cf. 4:15), and because what takes the accent is what had actually occurred there, and not anything Corinth might lay claim to (**I belong to Cephas**), mention of Cephas is omitted.

There is no more of self-deprecation over against Corinth in Paul's reference to himself and Apollos as servants than there is in his earlier reference to his appearance there in "fear and trembling" (2:3). The self-designation takes its definition from events which neither Paul, Apollos, nor Corinth had initiated— "and to each as the Lord gave" (v. 5; RSV: **assigned**). The point is driven further home in the metaphor which follows: **I planted, Apollos watered, but God gave the growth** (v. 6; the last verb is in the iterative imperfect, denoting a continuous act in the past), or again, **neither he who plants nor he who waters is anything, but only God who gives the growth** (v. 7). But the metaphor allows for more than one distinction. For all their nothingness, thus their equality over against the God "who gives the growth" (vv. 7-8

Chapter 3 *1 Corinthians*

are parallel), Paul was "the planter" and Apollos "the waterer," and each **shall receive his wages according to his** own **labor** (v. 8). The twice-repeated possessive adjective ("his own") is calculated to serve the distinction between "planter" and "waterer" in respect of their work within or on behalf of Corinth (Paul himself may have introduced that term *labor* into the nomenclature of the Christian community).

The reference to reward (RSV: **wages**) is jarring. It summons up the ancient notion of a day when punishment or bliss would be meted out according to whether the evil or good done in this life had tipped the scales. Verses 10-17 make clear that for Paul that **Day** and **each shall receive his** "reward" were still correlative. But if Paul's notion of reward gave the lie to the accusation that his teaching encouraged libertinism or moral passivity, did it not threaten to mute his accenting the spontaneous, uncaused, and unmerited favor of God apart from human willing and acting? The "eclecticism" in Paul's choice of vehicles to bear his message is beyond question, and it is also beyond question that he found the language and conceptuality of Judaism more compatible than that of paganism. In its anxiety in face of mortality, pagan religiosity erased the distinction between Creator and creature. In an identification of the divine and the human it relegated the historical and temporal—thus the moral—to the accidental. That identification guaranteed the return of the "spirit" to God or its return to indivisibility with God, whether or not its potentiality became actuality. Judaism, however, began with the distinction between Creator and creature, thus with an inquiry into the will of God, with Law and performance. But while "reward" and "Day of the Lord" are retained in Paul as correlates, the idea of requital has been shattered. The "reward" in v. 8 takes its meaning from v. 5: **As the Lord assigned to each** or from v. 10: **According to the grace of God given to me**. . . . What each receives will not be for work construed as meritorious service. Paul's counter to enthusiasm is not law, just as his counter to legalism is not moral laxity, but rather grace which reaches the world in the crucified to seize humanity and make of existence which hears the "word of the cross" one continuous anticipation of love, and to make of love or "labor" the signal that the "word of the cross" is being heard. Grace is the giver, grace the empowerer, but never in the abstract, never in the timeless, always in the temporal, historical, and for this reason spelling "labor," for each to whom "the Lord has given" is never done with doing, since grace is never done with seizing. And if "each will have his own reward" that can only mean that grace is not a possession but a continually being possessed, through a word needing continually to be heard—**for we are God's fellow workers; you are God's field, God's building** (v. 8).

With the traditional coupling of field and structure, Paul moves from the agricultural to the architectural metaphor in vv. 10 and 11: **According to the grace of God given to me, like a skilled master builder I laid a foundation.** . . . But if Paul laid the foundation, it was a foundation which already had been laid (v. 11). The architectural metaphor screens a paradox—Paul's "wisdom" consisted in his consenting to do what had already been done, refusing to allow what occurred through him to be anything else than what had already occurred. For this reason, what he laid could never be renewed: **For no other foundation can any one lay than that which is laid, which is Jesus Christ** (v. 11), and for this reason the warning in v. 10. The grace made *explicit* in the first metaphor (**as the Lord assigned to each**, etc., v. 5) is now implied in the second, and the warning *implicit* in the first ("each will receive his own reward," v. 8) is now made explicit in the second metaphor: **Let each man take care how he builds upon it. For no other foundation can any one lay** . . . (vv. 10b-11).

Paul is not yet done with metaphors. In vv. 12-15, he moves from the figure of the structure to that of its components—**gold, silver, precious stones, wood, hay, straw**—and what was explicit in the second metaphor (**let each man take care how he builds**) is implied in the third, and what was implicit in the second metaphor (**as the Lord assigned to each**, v. 5) is made explicit in the third: **If anyone builds . . . each man's work will become manifest** (vv. 12-13). The third metaphor limps—**gold, silver** and **precious**

stones are scarcely needed for building. It limps by design, since it leans toward the event implied in what the first two figures made explicit, and it reaches its climax in the third, the event for the sake of which durability has replaced value, and toward which each one of the figures has been tumbling: **For the day will disclose it, because it is revealed with fire** [use of the present tense as future is frequent in prophetic speech, hence the RSV **will be revealed**], **and the fire will test what sort of work each one has done** (v. 13).

That event, "the Day of the Lord," described in the four successive clauses of v. 13, had been the target of an ancient hope in God's visible manifestation of himself to rescue Israel and destroy its enemies, but which the prophets had expanded to include Israel's assize and had linked to fire, signal of theophany and divine judgment (this connection threads through the literature between the Testaments and of Qumran to the New Testament; cf., e.g., Amos 5:18ff., the "locus classicus" of Old Testament references to the "Day of the Lord"; Mal. 3:19; 2 Apoc. Bar. 48:47; 49:2; 4 Ezra 13:52; 1 Enoch 61:5; Matt. 24:37-39; Luke 17:24, 30-31). The Dead Sea community described "the Day" as a day of requital, of vengeance on "the sons of darkness," and of deliverance for "the sons of light" (cf. CD 8:2; 19:15; 1QS 10:19; 1QM 1:9, 11; 7:5; 13:14; 15:3, 12; 1QpHab 12:14; 13:2f.; 1Q XIV [Micah commentary] 8:1—10:8f.). The so-called War Scroll, a mini-Clausewitz for the brotherhood at the battle of "Armageddon" when the wicked would finally be put to rout, concludes with a thanksgiving for victory:

> Blessed be Thy name, O God [of merci]es, for Thou hast done great and wondrous things. From of old hast Thou kept Thy covenant unto us; and Thou hast opened for us gates of salvation time after time so that [Thy power might be revealed] through us. And Thou, O God, hast done righteously, for Thy name's sake.
>
> [Verily, Thou hast wrought] wondrously, and the like of this hath not been from of old. Thou it is who determined [this] time for us, and this day [Thy glory] hath shone upon us, [—] and Thy [—] is with us, ensuring perpetual redemption, removing the enemy from us, that he be no more. . . .[12]

But if for ancient Israel, the writers of apocalypses, or for Qumran the "Day of the Lord" was a day of Yahweh's vengeance on Israel's enemies, for Paul it was the day of his own and the community's judgment (cf. 1:8; 2 Cor. 1:14; Phil. 1:6; 2:16). Paul had harked back to that prophetic alteration of the "Day" to include the "house of God." But the similarity between Paul and his predecessors ends there. Unlike them, he did not flesh out the apocalyptic scheme, but reduced it to its bare minimum, crystallizing all future expectation about the person of Christ, so that the day of judgment would be the day of Christ, the revelation of Christ's glory. That Day as "Day of the Lord" had thus lost its terror. For this reason the parallelism of vv. 14 and 15 is disturbed and the entire third metaphor is wrung out of shape in that alien thought of the builder's rescue in v. 15: **If any man's work is burned up, he will suffer loss, though he himself will be saved,** and thus as (RSV **but only as**) **through fire.** So there is a punishment which does not involve the loss of salvation. The idea will occur again, in 5:4-5 and 11:30-32. Where "God gives," where grace is the initiator and empowerer, there is no end to doing, but it is grace, not the doing which saves.

But if the Day of the Lord has lost its terror, it has not lost its urgency: **Do you not know that you are God's temple and that God's Spirit dwells in you? If any one destroys God's temple, God will destroy him. For God's temple is holy, and that temple you are** (vv. 16-17). Ten more times that **Do you not know?** will appear in our epistle (5:6; 6:2, 3, 9, 15, 16, 19; 9:13, 24; cf. the softer, more didactic "I do not want you to be ignorant," in 10:1 and 12:1). The expression belongs to Paul's diatribe style, in which he refers to assumptions shared by him and his readers or establishes contact with them—a style characteristic of his oral delivery and reaching back to ancient rhetoric. The difference between Paul and the ancient Cynic or Stoic, for whom such expressions were common coin, is that the apostle always puts such questions to a specific group in which each should find himself or herself addressed, and not to the ideal or imagined listener of the philosophical preacher.[13] The question resumes the figure appearing at the conclusion of v. 9 (**you are . . . God's building**), but the figure has been nuanced, as though it needed firing in the kiln of vv. 12-15: **You are God's temple.** The figure belongs to Jewish apocalypticism:

> From every land they will bring incense and gifts to the house of the great God. There will be no other house among men, even for future generations to know, except the one which God gave to faithful men to honor. . . .[14]

Paul has altered the metaphor, and in two significant ways. First, what the apocalypticist awaited for the end-time Paul describes as already realized—**you are**. . . . And, what has turned anticipation to realization is the presence of the Spirit (the conjunction *and* in the phrase, **and that God's Spirit dwells in you** is epexegetical; it explains what precedes, and should thus be translated, "that is"). Through that one by whom the crucified Jesus is recognized as the "wisdom of God" (2:10-16), the future has already penetrated to the present—which can only mean that the cross constitutes the apocalyptic event par excellence. Whatever had been awaited, whatever it was which the futurist or apocalyptic writer had drawn from a treasury 1000 years old to describe, had reached its goal in "Jesus Christ, and, indeed, this one crucified." Second, Paul has substituted Corinth for the temple of the end-time—**you are God's temple.** By the same Spirit which worked recognition of what had been anticipated as realized in the crucified, Corinth, and all of Corinth, had become "the house of the great God." As "fleshly" or as childish and oriented to the "human" Corinth might have been (3:1-4), it was still for all that the dwelling of the Spirit, and should thus reflect on its rank!

The urgency threading through the entire section climaxes in the "sentence of holy law" in v. 17 (the sentence is set in a chiasma—**if any one destroys** . . . **God will destroy him**—and employs the word *destroy* in the dual sense of temple profanation and the judgment of God). The "sentence" is reminiscent of the placard excluding Gentiles from the forecourt of Herod's temple: "Whoever is caught is alone responsible for the death which follows." Paul, the charismatic, the prophet, holds up to his readers the panorama of the divine tribunal, setting Corinth before its Judge. The style reflects a stage in primitive Christianity far back of our Gospels and Epistles, and of which only vestiges remain. In that period, Christian prophets announced to a community living in imminent expectation of Christ's return that the "Day of the Lord" was not merely an event of the future which charged the present with urgency, but that the power of the Judge was already in effect. Thus in blessing and curse those prophets called their hearers to decision, setting before them the possibility of escaping eternal judgment. In other words, such "sentences of holy law"[15] or announcements of a quid pro quo, of a punishment suited to the guilt as already effective in the present (**if anyone destroys God's temple, God will destroy him**), were in the service of grace. The precedent for such "sentences," both as to style and content, lay in the Old Testament prophetic utterances, according to which the prophet anticipated the judgment of God through his word.

Reprise (3:18-23)

The section is a recapitulation of the argument in 1:18-25, resumed at 2:6-16. It reflects the same antithetical structure: **If any one among you thinks that he is wise in this age, let him become a fool** (v. 18); **the wisdom of this world is folly with God** (v. 19); **the Lord knows that the thoughts of the wise are futile** (v. 20). It reflects the same reversal of the roles of "wise" and "foolish" as in chaps. 1–2. In the scripture quotation in v. 9, just as in the quotations in 1:19 and 2:9, it traces the cause of that reversal to the same initiative of God. Finally, from the argument it draws the same conclusion: **So let no one boast of men** (cf. 1:29-31).

This time, however, the movement is swifter. The succession of steps required to fix the reversal in chaps. 1 and 2 is made in a single leap, in v. 18: **If any one among you thinks that he is wise** [1:20, 25, 26; 2:13] . . . **let him become a fool** [1:18, 21, 23, 25, 27; 2:14] **that he may become wise** (1:24; 2:6, 7). And what was needed to signal the decision which effected the reversal (1:19, 20-21, 24-25, 27-28, 30; 2:4-5, 7, 9-10, 12, 16) is achieved in a chain quotation with only two small links (Job 5:13 and the LXX version of Ps. 93:11).

Again, as with its counterparts, this section does not give the accent to subjective perception. The modifiers in vv. 18-19, and the chain quotation make that clear. "Being wise" does not spell playing the fool to those who are **wise in this age,** or to **the wisdom of this world.** There is nothing here of a call to sacrifice the intellect. The assertion that in his rejection of the wisdom destroyed by the foolishness of the cross the antiintellectualism of Paul finds classical expression or that Paul's distaste for knowledge drove him to a "second naivete" is false.[16] For the apostle, the "wisdom of God" has not made detour around this "age" in the crucified. Rather, that wisdom has mastered this age, so that whatever does not take its orientation from that event belongs to what God has made folly, futile. But if such an event has deprived the creature of all initiative for giving the orientation to life, for fixing the point which should determine all thinking, willing, and acting, above all, for taking that orientation from itself or another like it (**so let no one boast of men**), in its submitting to that deprivation, in its passivity over against that action, the creature has won the world: **For all things are yours, whether Paul or Apollos or Cephas or the world or life or death or the present or the future, all are yours; and you are Christ's; and Christ is God's** (vv. 21b-23). The verses are reminiscent of one of the most pregnant expressions in Stoicism. Of the "wise man" Seneca writes:

> Free, therefore, from the great anxieties that rack the mind, there is nothing which he hopes for or covets, and, content with what he has, he does not plunge into what is doubtful. And do not suppose that he is content with a little—all things are his. . . . It is only the wise man who has all things, and has no difficulty in retaining them.[17]

But if the Stoic is free because he allows the divine principle which inhabits him and all other things to thrust him out of the material and temporal to pure, unadulterated "spirit," and for that reason owns all things, Corinth is free, has overcome the profoundest contrasts—"life or death, whether the present or the future"—because it belongs to the one whom God made his wisdom (1:30), and thus owns all things. Paul's words are far more reminiscent of a logion contained in Matthew:

> But you are not to be called rabbi, for you have one teacher, and you are all brethren. And call no man your father on earth, for you have one Father, who is in heaven. Neither be called masters, for you have one master, the Christ (Matt. 23:8-10).

In this brief coda or reprise, all the terms, catchwords, cliches, and slogans which Corinth had used are warped to their true meaning. To the oxymoron of the crucifixion of "the Lord of glory" corresponds the oxymoron of Corinth's ownership of the world through its subjection to him.

Chapter 4

With the exception of vv. 14-17, the chapter is a philippic. In vv. 1-5 Paul, attaching to his definitions in 3:5, 9, fixes the criterion by which he and his coworkers are to be judged, denying Corinth's (or his own) competence to apply it. In vv. 6-13 he heaps up antitheses in a biting contrast between the realities into which his office has thrust him and Corinth's imagined superiority. In vv. 14-21, following a brief change in mood, he promises to put the arrogant to the test.

The Criterion for Testing (4:1-5)

This is how one should regard us (v. 1). If earlier Paul had held up the absurdity of matching him against Christ ("Was Paul crucified for you? Or were you baptized into the name of Paul?" 1:13), the tactic was clearly for other reasons than to disavow divinity. At Corinth, none had to be restrained from making sacrifice to Paul (cf. Acts 14:8-18). In, with, and under the quarreling, the apostle had come off badly. Corinth's initial receptivity had cooled, and whatever could be left to inference respecting the waning of Paul's authority in chaps. 2 and 3 ("my speech and my message were not in persuasive words of wisdom. . . . Yet among the mature [perfect] we do impart wisdom," and "I . . . could not address you as spiritual . . . like a wise architect I laid a foundation") needed stating flat outright in a direct and frontal response. If the self-designation in 3:5, 9 had lacked clarity ("servants through whom you believed . . . God's fellow workers"), the nouns in 4:1 remedy the lack. **This is how one should regard us, as** Christ's adjuncts, his aides-de-camp [**servants,** RSV, is too pale], those who execute his will; stewards, masters of the house, privy to the intention and decision of God." While the term *apostle* would have to wait for promotion, those words translated "servant" and "steward" would make do, and with a vengeance. But with all the pique, Paul has not lost his head. There is no confusion of the roles of appointee and appointer, no contradiction of that demurrer in 3:5 ("What then is Apollos? What is Paul?"). The adjunct has a superior, the steward has a master—**servants of Christ**—and the stewardship is restricted. It does not extend to a knowledge of the intention or purpose of deity beyond what deity has disclosed—**the mysteries,** that in which God had hidden his "wisdom" but had now revealed (the use of the plural includes nothing which would not begin or end with that event, but it does include everything which relates to it). Verse 1, then, is not a general statement. However inclusive (at least of Apollos, cf. 3:5-6) the use of the pronoun in the plural—**this is how one should regard us**—is not intended to distract attention from the one whose authority is "on the line."

What should be the criterion? The answer begins maximlike in v. 2, only to slide into the particular: **Moreover it is required of stewards that they be found** faithful. The English "faithful" does better duty than the Greek it translates, *pistos*—a term which, together with its congeners, was always liable to misunderstanding among Paul's readers who would set it in the context of human initiative, whether of mind or will.

Corinth, however, is not competent to apply the criterion to Paul: **But with me it is a very small thing that I should be judged** (the term is juridical and denotes being subjected to an examination at a "hearing") **by you or by any human court** (v. 3a). Even if Corinth were to apply the criterion, Paul would place no value on it. And the reason for Corinth's incompetence did not lie in what it lacked, as though Corinth were "fleshly" now (2:6ff.; 3:1ff.), but could conceivably mature to the point where it would be capable of judging. Not even Paul himself was competent to apply the criterion—**I do not even judge myself** (v. 3b). Paul then turns the coin over in v. 4, best translated to read: "My conscience does not accuse me" (RSV, **I am not aware of anything against myself**). This is not a man who is aware of his "pure intention and sacred activity" (Weiss on the passage), nor a man for whom conscience is not authorized to exonerate, simply because it can only hand down an immanent judgment. The words **but I am not thereby acquitted** (or "justified"), and **it is the Lord who judges me** are not a contrast between the lower, inferior, and the transcendent. They fix the competence for judgment elsewhere—with **the Lord,** not with my "knowing together with" (the Greek term for "conscience"), a function which commences and lodges approval or complaint with the self. The old saw, "let conscience be your guide," would never do for Paul, because it was the self, signaled in that pronoun and always at the center of that function from which one needed to get free. Self-judgment, then, was as impossible as self-redemption.

It is the Lord who judges me. Often enough, that phrase appears trippingly on the tongue. And if Paul's readers should gather that by it Paul intends to avoid examination altogether, v. 5 quickly dispels the notion: "So, do not judge anything **before the time, when the Lord comes.**" Wherever in Paul there is talk of judging or evaluating, such talk finally comes round to that "coming." Wherever there is reference to God's knowing the secrets of the heart, it all comes round to their disclosure on that "Day." In chap. 3 that note had already been struck: "He who plants and he who waters are equal, and each shall receive his own reward" (3:8); "the work of each will become manifest; for the Day will disclose it" (3:13). In our "Second" Corinthians, Paul will write: "For we must all appear before the judgment seat of Christ, so

Chapter 4 *1 Corinthians*

that each one may receive good or evil, according to what he has done in the body" (2 Cor. 5:10). Justification, acquittal, or indictment await confirmation in a final revelation, "on that day when according to my gospel, God judges the secrets of men by Christ Jesus" (Rom. 2:16).

But the eschatology of Paul, his alteration of the ancient teaching that God knows the heart to a future event of disclosure; his linking of justification (or, as in v. 5, "praise") to a final judgment as its sealing or ratifying, is not a mere remnant from the past which he was unable to shrug off. The dogmatism which requires agreement concerning "the last things" as a final test of orthodoxy was alien to Paul. He had abandoned performance and quid pro quo for the sake of grace (3:5, "to each as the Lord gave"; "according to the grace of God given to me," 3:10). He had mulcted the "Day of the Lord" of its terror ("if any man's work is burned up, he will suffer loss, though he himself will be saved," 3:15; note the conclusion to our section: "**Then** there will be praise for each **from God**"). Why not finish the job, give that "Day" a final coup de grace in one, grand announcement of grace without judgment, or at least demythologize the concept in Johannine fashion:

> Truly, truly I say to you, he who hears my word and believes him who sent me, has eternal life; he does not come into judgment, but has passed from death to life (John 5:24)?

Paul's "pupil" would not balk at breaking the link:

> God, who is rich in mercy, out of the great love with which he loved us, even when we were dead through our trespasses, made us alive together with Christ (by grace you have been saved) [!], and raised us up with him, and made us sit with him in the heavenly places in Christ Jesus (Eph. 2:4-6).

Why this clinging to a day of judgment shorn of terror?

The answer lies in Paul's Christology, in what he conceived to be the nature of that "wisdom of God," once hidden and now revealed. What had been revealed was still hidden—"a stumbling block to Jews and folly to Gentiles"—known only to "those who are called" (1:23-24). But if still hidden, that wisdom lunged toward visibility. Still, it was not visibility itself on which everything hinged, but who or what should become visible: "For *he* must reign until he has put all his enemies under his feet" (15:25). The Lordship of Christ, now exercised in its opposite, in weakness and death, in the cruciform, a Lordship apprehended only by faith (1:21) and "through the Spirit" (2:10), pressed toward disclosure in an event at which "every knee should bow, in heaven and on earth and under the earth, and every tongue confess" (Phil. 2:10-11). The particular of Damascus demanded a universal, an unrestricted encounter in which none would stand "speechless, hearing the voice but seeing no one" (Acts 9:7). If it was eschatology that struck down the popular notion of conscience, it was Christology that robbed eschatology of its preoccupation with the damned and the saved, twisting it to the shape of the Lordship of Christ become visible. And if it was the coming of the Lord on which everything hinged, if everything depended on the Lordship of *Christ* become visible, then Corinth and Paul's consciences were incompetent because they were untimely. **Do not pronounce judgment before the time.** The time of the "Day" was to be left with him, and hope, expectation in the face of the demand for signs and the search for wisdom, was the other side of faith. Here lay the fault with Corinth's eschatology, its trading of hope in the visible coming of the Lord for visibility.

But Corinth and Paul's consciences were not merely incompetent because untimely. They were perilous, for if the evaluation lay there, then there was no surety of "praise for each"! Here lay the error in Corinth's enthusiasm, its preoccupation with the demonstrable and the bizarre which rendered praise conditional, questionable, dependent on allegiances, on "gifts" or a "spirit" inherited or acquired. Galatia and Corinth, the legalist and the enthusiast, for all their disparate genealogies, had never occupied separate beds.

It is **the Lord . . . who will bring to light the** hidden things of darkness **and will disclose the purposes of the heart.** When the Lord comes, "there will be praise" (RSV: **commendation**). It was this indissoluble connection between Christology and eschatology which had altered anxiety to hope. But the justification, the acquittal, the praise or the reward—it would all be secondary, subordinate, moved to the wings, giving way to the one to come. Nothing of Paul's past, his language or his conceptuality; nothing of his view of the world or of human existence, of God or religion, of Scripture or tradition, had escaped fracture. Nothing had escaped alteration, qualification, reduction, even elimination in face of the event signaled in the phrase "the Lord"—"and, indeed, this one crucified."

Paul and Corinth in Contrast (4:6-13)

The section begins with a puzzling sentence: "Now these things, brethren, I have given shape as applying to myself and Apollos for your sake, that you might learn from us the 'not beyond what is written' (RSV, **not to go beyond what is written**), **that none of you may be puffed up in favor of one** (teacher) **against another.**" "These things" hark back to the argument begun at 3:5 ("what then is Apollos? And what is Paul? . . .") and concluded at 3:22-23 ("whether Paul or Apollos . . . all things are yours; and you are Christ's; and Christ is God's"), or at 4:5 ("then there will be praise for each from God"). The argument had more than Paul or Apollos in view. Nothing had divided them or damaged their perspective, and for precisely that reason the argument had been given this curious shape (the verb translated **applied** in the RSV means to pour into a form other than the usual or expected). Paul and Apollos illustrated the attitude which should have prevailed at Corinth, and if not every soul at Corinth had joined a faction, the disunity, in Paul's mind, had reached sufficient proportion to suggest that what should have prevailed at Corinth simply did not, or if it did, only among an unidentifiable few, for which reason none at Corinth could serve as illustration. At any rate, the argument had been **for your benefit.** The sentence smacks of arrogance. But it is hardly a match for the apostle's earlier contention that one's eternal fate rested on how one built on what he had laid (cf. 3:10-15)! It was for such "self-understanding" that one author wrote 25 years ago:

> Where, really, does Paul of Tarsus derive the special privilege of thoroughly crushing everyone when and as he pleases, and of forbidding all criticism of himself, even any that is relevant or respectful? Is he immune, is he a tabu, a mimosa, a fetish?. . . This man seems to regard himself as inerrant, despite all the formulae of humility with which he embellishes his letters; a judge of hearts and destinies, of persons and morals, of near and far—HE alone. . . . I love Paul, but would rather not assign him an inerrant teaching office. Jesus of Nazareth is the measure of all things. He and no one else.[18]

Arrogance, perhaps, at least to the well-bred—but let no one judge "before the time"!—though with that author Paul's arrogance had served its purpose, moved him to a confession he could not have made without him.

More than one has described that elliptical phrase in v. 6—"the not beyond what is written"—as totally unintelligible. The fact that it is substantivized by the neuter article suggests a quotation (cf., e.g., Rom. 13:9, "For *the* 'you shall not commit adultery, you shall not kill, you shall not steal, you shall not covet,' and if there is any other commandment, it is summed up in this word, in *the* 'you shall love your neighbor as yourself' "). But if it is a quotation, from what? From the Old Testament passages referred to earlier in the letter (1:19-20,31; 2:9,16; or 3:19-20)? If so, the relative pronoun would require a Gulliver's leap backward to locate its antecedent. (The relative **what** in the phrase, **what is written,** and which appears in the plural in the original, could refer to the **all this** in v. 6, thus to the argument beginning at 3:5, were it not for the fact that **what is written** always involves a quotation.) Or, is the quotation lodged in the clause itself, a slogan, perhaps, by which Paul's opponents disparaged his preaching—"with Paul, everything by the book!"—and which he now hurls back at them? The hypotheses mount with each new reading. The suggestion that the phrase is a gloss which finally crept into the text is too clever by far. (According to this hypothesis, between the clause **that you may learn by us** and the clause **that none of you may be puffed up,** a copyist had inserted the note that he had supplied the negative omitted in some of his manuscripts by writing it over the alpha of the conjunction **that** in the final clause, or over the numeral **one,** in the Greek denoted by the letter *a* hence: The *not* is written above the *a*!)

Whether or not the phrase contains a reference to specific Old Testament texts, to a slogan at Corinth, or to a maxim of Paul, it refers to the norm which Paul and Apollos had observed in their behavior toward each other. In form, the clause is thus analogous to those rules governing mutual conduct (*mishpatim*) which Jewish teachers derived from the Torah, and which eventually found their way into the Talmud. Paul's reference in 11:2 to the "traditions" which he had handed on and which Corinth had preserved is of the same type. And, just as in chap. 11, those traditions are not enumerated but rather interpreted in 11:3 and what follows, so here the "canon" or norm is simply stated, its interpretation already given in what proved to be an illustration from Paul's and Apollos's life with each other ("these things, brethren, I have given shape as applying to myself and Apollos").

The series of three questions hurled at his readers in v. 7 describes the distance between Paul's and Corinth's adherence to the norm: "For who has singled you out [the phrase translated **sees anything different in you** in the RSV means to separate or distinguish, thus to judge to the advantage of one over the other]? Or, what do you have that you did not receive? And if you received (it), why do you boast as though you had not received?" The first question demands a "no one," and the second a "nothing" in answer. The third does not wait for an answer, but cuts it off with the verse following.

Party allegiance, sloganeering, boasting—"on behalf of the one against the other"—had done grace in at Corinth. And at the bottom lay its enthusiasm, whether congealed in a theory or worldview, whether simply the consequence of allegiances on which it had never bothered to reflect, or both. But the effect of that enthusiasm was to create a gulf between Paul and Corinth, signaled in that apostrophe to irony in vv. 8-13:

"You are filled! You are rich! You reigned! [v. 8]. You are wise in Christ! You are strong! You are held in honor! [v. 10]—we have been exhibited as apostles last in rank [antithesis], as sentenced to death, a spectacle to the world, to angels and to men [v. 9]! We are fools! We are weak! We are in disrepute! [v. 10]. We hunger and thirst and are naked, have our ears boxed, no roof over our heads [v. 11], and we labor working with our own hands; when cursed we bless [antithesis], when persecuted we endure [antithesis; v. 12], when blasphemed we comfort, admonish, speak a good word [antithesis—all these senses are contained in the verb translated **we try to conciliate**]; we have been made like the refuse of the world, the scum of everything till now! [v. 13]." The use of temporal adverbs and phrases only heightens the contrast: "*Already* **you are filled!** *Already* you are **rich!** *Till this very moment* **we hunger and thirst** [v. 11], the scum of everything *till now!* [v. 13]." And the pathos cannot be missed in the prepositional phrase and the expression of a wish gone begging at the conclusion of v. 8: "*Apart from us* you reigned; and would that you did reign, so that we too might reign with you!"

If the gulf between Paul and Corinth was to be bridged, the initiative would have to come from Corinth, for it was God who had exhibited those who had been promised first seats as Johnny-come-latelies (cf. Matt. 19:28), had made them a spectacle. It was God who had reduced them to the status of condemned criminals, battling for their execution in the arena, or to that of sacrificial victims whose lives were such a torture they went willingly to their deaths—"**For I think** [the verb translated here expresses more than an opinion] **that God has** made us to be apostles last in rank.... We were made a **spectacle**.... We were made **the refuse of the world**" (vv. 9, 13).

The wise man as spectacle for gods and men in his struggle with destiny was a favorite Stoic picture. Seneca wrote of Cato, who preferred suicide to witnessing the decline of the republic following Caesar's victory over Pompey:

Chapter 4 *1 Corinthians*

> Lo! here a contest worthy of God—a brave man matched against ill-fortune, and doubly so if his also was the challenge. I do not know, I say, what nobler sight the Lord of heaven could find on earth, should he wish to turn his attention there, than the spectacle of Cato, after his cause had already been shattered more than once, nevertheless standing erect amid the ruins of the commonwealth.[19]

But if Cato had resolved to stand erect under whatever fate he himself had provoked, making himself a marvel to gods and men, Paul had no hand at all in his misfortune. Its cause lay with a Jupiter who would not merely turn his head to look, once the spectacle had begun, but had set it all in motion with nailing his apostle to his suffering for the world and all to see (antithesis!).

The list of sufferings in the antitheses of vv. 11-13, but particularly of vv. 12b and 13a ("when cursed we bless; when persecuted we endure; when blasphemed we speak a good word") echoes Jesus' "Sermon" in Matthew and Luke, even to the choice of terms ("Blessed are you when men revile you and persecute you and utter all kinds of evil against you falsely. . . . Pray for those who persecute you," Matt. 5:10-11, 44; Luke 6:22, 28; cf. Rom. 12:14-21, in which the list is reproduced in exhortation). More, v. 11 of that catalog is a tiny passion narrative. Christ's life and death had been replicated in Paul's own existence: "**We hunger** (cf. Mark 11:12) **and thirst** (cf. Mark 15:36 and John 19:28) and are naked (cf. Mark 15:20, 24), have our ears boxed (cf. Mark 14:65), no roof over our heads" (Matt. 8:20). The First Epistle of Peter would summon its readers to an imitation of Christ's passion ("Christ also suffered for you, leaving you an example, that you should follow in his steps," 1 Peter 2:21-22). But for Paul the "imitation" had never been left to a summons, as though a choice or resolve were needed for its achieving. From the outset his life had begun to be hammered into the cruciform. Corinth had resisted that shape for itself; the **already** tells the story—**Already you are filled! Already you are rich!** Corinth had anticipated the "then" in the "not yet," had traded a theology of the cross for one of glory.

Commentary   *Chapter 4*

Conclusion of the Argument Begun at 1:10 (4:14-21)

The section begins with a radical change of tone: "**I do not write** these things to shame you, **but to admonish you** [the verb **admonish** is peculiar to Paul and those under his influence] **as my beloved children.**" Did Paul have second thoughts over having spent all that shot and shell on Corinth? (*epidiorthōsis* is the rhetorician's term for a literary change of heart). Of the later "letter of tears" (cf. 2 Cor. 2:3-4, 9), following his personal disaster at Corinth, Paul would write: "Even if I made you sorry with my letter, I do not regret it" and then would add, "though I did regret it" (cf. 2 Cor. 7:8). Regret it or not, Paul insists that what is occurring between him and Corinth is a family affair: "I write these things . . . as admonishing my beloved children." **Children**—the term is not handed down to the laity from some episcopal height. What Paul was to Corinth needed a metaphor which would carry heavier freight than the earlier "I planted" or "I laid a foundation" (3:6, 10), and which had left open the question of the link between planter and planted, builder and the thing built. A figure was needed to indicate that what Paul was to Corinth no one else could be: "For if you were to have ten thousand pedagogues [the clause expresses a condition, the reality of which is *not* assumed], you still do not have many fathers." Corinth might have had an army of guides, but it had only one father (the term *pedagogue* first denoted the slave or houseboy who protected the son and heir from molesters on his way to school; it later came to denote "teacher" or "guide," as, e.g., in the Talmud, where the term appears untranslated).

But there is more afoot here than Paul's reaching for a figure to describe what he was to Corinth. Something had occurred through the instrumentality of his preaching which demanded the metaphor. But in the *use* of the metaphor, it had come to stand on its own feet, to make its own demands, to disclose a sphere of meaning beyond what "father," "child," or "birth" had ever had in any standard lexicon. The commentator's note that Paul merely intends to state that his relationship to Corinth is not natural is trivial. Who needs the assurance that it did not come by way of natural, biological generation?! The old words had not lost their meaning, but in their *use* a "transfer" (the root meaning of "metaphor") had occurred, and not merely according to likeness. For if Corinth had been a nothing (1:28), then what had occurred with it "through the gospel" had been a being born, a coming into existence. Then Paul was Corinth's true father, and the life into which he had birthed Corinth was that of Christ himself. (Note the same thought in Paul's letter to Philemon: "I, Paul, write this with my own hand, I will repay it—to say nothing of your owing me even your own self," Philemon 19.) This is the meaning which use of the metaphor "father" and "child" or "I birthed you in Christ Jesus" demands. In the metaphor, in the transference of words occurs a transfer of things. For Paul, at least, that is how it was with the "gospel," with "theological speech."

Loosed from its context, v. 16—**I urge you, then, be imitators of me**—can only be a summons to imitate Paul's fatherhood. (Note the use of the imperative in place of an infinitive or purpose clause—in keeping with Paul's preference for direct speech.) But the verse faces in two directions: Backward to v. 6, to the rule of conduct put in the negative, and forward to v. 17, to its positive application to Corinth in the sending of Timothy. "Imitate me," that is, "apply to yourselves what I had poured in a form as applying to Apollos and to me, and prove the constancy of your love, as I do in hurrying Timothy off to you."

Timothy and Corinth had a common ancestor—Paul had birthed them both (**my beloved . . . child,** cf. v. 14), and into the same existence (**in the Lord,** cf. v. 15). Paul adds the word **faithful** (**my beloved and faithful child**), not so much to contrast him with Corinth (though Corinth would not miss the comparison) as to present him as a genuine surrogate: "He will **remind you of my ways** which are **in Christ** Jesus, **as I teach them everywhere in every church.**" The expression **my ways** is odd, but tethered to the final clause can only denote Paul's teaching, synonymous with those "traditions" later referred to in 11:2. The call to Corinth to imitate, then, was not a call to replicate the outward circumstances of Paul's life, to imitate his action or hearken to the will of God in every conceivable situation.[20] Those circumstances were not accidental and therefore were incapable of repetition. They were a given, the shape of his apostleship ("God has exhibited us . . . we were made," vv. 9, 13). Timothy would remind them, and who would not need reminding, party affiliate or no, since the gospel of the cross violated every canon of sense or conception? But if Timothy had been sent before the letter was completed, he would arrive following the letter's reception at Corinth—no doubt on foot, and a grueling trip if it meant detouring the Aegean, swinging northward from Ephesus, crossing the sea at its narrowest point (at Troas?) and dropping down to the isthmus. The term "faithful" screens a passion not only for Paul's "ways," but for the apostle himself.

In v. 18, Paul sharpens his tone to secure the proof of his affection against misinterpretation: "**Some are** puffed up" (in the original, the verb appears in the passive, as with most verbs having to do with emotional or affective states) **as though I were not coming to you.** Clearly, the reason for arrogance was not that some would be left to their shenanigans in the absence of Paul. **Some** were puffed up *as if* Paul would not, or *because* they maintained he would not come, but dared only treat through emissaries. Had the taunt been made public—"Why doesn't Paul come?" "He is afraid to come!"—so that Paul had report of it and reproduced it here? In v. 19, Paul rebuts the challenge: "**I will come to you** quickly," then adds the qualifier, "**if the Lord wills.**" The natural urge to save face had been subordinated. This was the way with Paul; his "spring of action" had nothing of autonomy about it. Even such a commendable and explicable action as arriving at Corinth for the sake of extricating the gospel of God from alien entanglements was subordinated. Not merely natural, human projects were given second seat, but even motives which could be called purely religious, "on God's behalf." What Luther had written of the purpose for Romans, viz., to allow the human to be nothing and God everything, was true also of its author. Everything hinged on God—everything had to wait on God's will,

Chapter 4 *1 Corinthians*

even the good. It was precisely this conviction which rendered him and his behavior capable of misinterpretation—as due to cowardice (here) or to historical accident ("we hunger and thirst and are naked, have our ears boxed, no roof over our heads . . ." v. 11). But Paul did not allow the misinterpretation to alter his behavior. He insisted upon another reading of his intent. Precisely for this reason, being "all things to all men" (9:22) could not have applause for its aim. The rule was: "the one who judges me is the Lord" (4:4).

And how would Paul know if it was the Lord's will that he come to Corinth? By deduction or inference? Those references to his first appearance "in demonstration of the Spirit and of power" (2:4), to his having received "the Spirit which is from God" (2:12), to having the "mind of Christ" (2:16), point in a quite different direction. Paul was a charismatic—God would make known his will directly, and the decision would not read, "after much prayer and deliberation, I have come to the conviction that. . . ." "When I come," Paul adds, "I'll not attend to what 'some' say, but to whether or not they can lay claim to a 'demonstration of the Spirit and power' accompanying what they say! So, go to! Let us match 'power' with 'power'—mine is of God . . . and theirs?!" The verse conjures up associations with Old Testament history—Moses and the magicians of Pharaoh; Elijah and the priests of Baal. And what will constitute the difference is the "kingdom of God" as consisting "not in word, but in power." Does this mean that words are detachable from what they signify? a mere copy of the thing itself; a mere vehicle for the idea, the concept, the notion? The great freethinker of the 17th century, Baruch Spinoza, had written that truth could not be mediated by words; that God could not make himself known through words or "any kind of external sign." Religion, therefore, dependent upon words and dogmas, concerned with obedience and not with truth, was to be separated from reason or philosophy, that rational knowledge of God which alone yielded happiness. But for Paul a chasm lay between "word" and "word of the cross" (1:18), between "word" and "my speech and my message . . . in demonstration of the Spirit and of power"!

Excesses in the Community (Chapters 5 and 6)

Chapter 5

In this portion of the letter, Paul responds to what he has heard of sexual abuses at Corinth. If "Chloe's people" (1:11) had furnished him with information, the opening verse in chap. 5 suggests that they were not the apostle's sole informants. The clause which the RSV translates **it is actually reported . . .** should rather read "it is generally heard" or "noised abroad." Apparently, the abuses at Corinth were an open secret.

At first sight, there appears to be no real connection between this part of the epistle and what precedes. Paul seems to have leaped into the discussion without preliminaries. And from this point onward, the apostle reflects the type of literature which Judaism characterized as "Responsa," that is, answers and instructions pertaining to doctrine or praxis without links between. But if the "wisdom" or enthusiasm at Corinth meant identification with deity (*enthusiasm* is merely the transliteration of a Greek compound meaning "to be filled with the god"), an identification which immunized against the historical conditions of this life, and in opposition to the "word of the cross" which summoned to embrace those conditions, then such enthusiasm could find expression in either of two classical shapes—libertinism or asceticism. Then the move from chaps. 1–4, with its accent on "wisdom" and "word," to chaps. 5–6 with its attack on libertinism, is not as abrupt as might appear.

A Specific Case of Immorality (5:1-8)

"It is noised abroad **that there is immorality among you,** and such immorality which (does) not (exist) among the Gentiles." As any standard lexicon will indicate, the term translated "immorality" was applied to a wide variety of sexual practices which the ancient world considered aberrant or perverse. Paul's concern is with "someone who has his father's wife" (literally translated; note the veiled form in the reference to the offender—"someone"—

Chapter 5   *1 Corinthians*

a device used throughout the epistle, cf. 1:15; 3:4; 5:11; 8:2; 11:16; 14:38; 15:35; 16:11, 22). The reference is to a man's cohabiting with his stepmother, an action which apparently persisted till the time of writing (the present tense of the verb "to have" denotes duration). The offense was in face of unequivocal biblical teaching which demanded the death sentence for both parties (Lev. 18:18; 20:11). According to the Mishnah, such a sentence was to be carried out by stoning.[21] It is no secret that the Old Testament regarded adultery principally as an offense against the husband, whose wife was considered his chattel, for which reason the indictment in Leviticus for the offense cited here by Paul reads, "he disgraces his father."

The anonymous "somebody" had not merely offended against Old Testament teaching. The phrase "and such immorality which (does) not (exist) among the Gentiles" reflects an act beyond a mere breach of Gentile propriety in a violation of law. But if a violation of law, then the offense also involved the woman in bigamy, since it was at that point that Roman law drew the line.[22] If the offense was bigamy, then the man's father was still alive. (Interpreters who insist that the man's father was dead ignore the fact that in Judaism and thus for Paul, the burden of guilt always lay with the male, cf. Matt. 5:28, 32). In one of his briefs on behalf of a certain Cluentius, Cicero expresses horror at the marriage of his client's mother to her former son-in-law:

> And so mother-in-law (Sassia) marries son-in-law, with none to bless, none to sanction the union, and mid nought but general foreboding. Oh! to think of the woman's sin, unbelievable, unheard of in all experience save for this single instance. To think of her wicked passion, unbridled, untamed![23]

In any event, whether or not the father was dead or alive, and if alive had deserted or divorced his wife (or she him), what raised Paul's ire was not merely that Corinth had allowed the perpetrator to remain in the community, but had trumpeted that permission as a badge of its freedom: "And you have been puffed up, and did not rather mourn, so that the one who did this deed be removed from your midst?" (Note again, the veiled form both as to doer and deed; the use of the aorist in the phrase "who did this deed" does not clash with the use of the present tense in v. 1; the aorist here is "constative," summing up the affair as a whole.) Paul had expected excommunication, not reception, much less celebration (the final clause in v. 2 echoes Deut. 13:6 and 17:7).

In vv. 3-5, Paul sets about putting the matter right. The construction of the verses is troublesome, but may be translated as follows: "Now I, **absent in the body** though **present in the spirit,** have, as present, already judged the one who did such a thing [v. 3], so that when you are gathered in the name of our Lord Jesus Christ, **and my spirit is present, with the power of our Lord Jesus** [v. 4], **you deliver** [the infinitive here functions as an imperative] such a one **to Satan for the destruction of the flesh, in order that** the **spirit** might **be saved** on **the day of the Lord** [v. 5]." The reference is to a judicial process which has its consequence or result in the action described in v. 5, in the excommunication of the offender. The initiative for the action lies with Paul ("I have already judged"), though its execution must take place at Corinth ("deliver such a one to Satan"). But neither Paul nor Corinth act independently of each other. Paul is present with Corinth in his initiation of the judgment ("absent in the body though present in the spirit," v. 3), as well as in its execution ("when you are gathered . . . and my spirit is present," v. 4). The accent, of course, lies on the initiative, and on Paul's presence "with the power of our Lord Jesus." Grammatically, the latter phrase could be linked to the opening clause, "when you are gathered . . ." thus not restricted to the presence of Paul, though in light of Corinth's neglect and its boasting, the alternative reading has the greater probability. In any event, the action is shared by Paul and Corinth. (For this reason, there should be no full stop between v. 2 and vv. 4-5, as in the RSV, suggesting two distinguishable events, the judgment and its execution.) Paul, for all his initiative and empowering, and Corinth, for all its neglect and boasting, are conjoined in a single event.

Chapter 5   *1 Corinthians*

How can Paul be present though **absent in body,** and how can he and Corinth share the excommunication of the offender? Paul does not say. If restricted to his presence, the clause **with the power of our Lord Jesus** need not refer to the "how" of his presence at Corinth, but rather to his empowering by the Lord to see the action through to the finish. Again, in light of Corinth's truancy, the latter reading would appear the more probable. Does Paul conceive his "spirit" as existing independently of his "body"? Such an inference would be ruinous to the argument threading throughout the entire epistle, that is, that the existence which Christians share must eventuate in concreteness, corporeality. The "word of the cross" spells return to, not liberation from, earthly life and history. This was the point of 4:8-13—no reigning before the parousia (return of Christ), and therefore "we hunger and thirst and are naked, have our ears boxed, no roof over our heads"! It is the point of the chapters to follow, and in the next to last, Paul will thrust it home. No "spirit," no willing, intending, no "I" without corporeality, without the "body." The answer to the question of Paul's "presence" must lie elsewhere, in that concept signaled in chap. 6, developed in chaps. 10 through 12, and climaxing in chap. 15, the concept of the Lord as present in those who are his, and thus the presence of those who are his with each other. It is such a "presence" which renders Paul's absence "in the body" irrelevant. But the irrelevance of Paul's bodily absence does not render his bodily presence irrelevant. Paul, absent from Corinth "in the body" now, though present "in the spirit" (and behind that phrase lurks the idea of the "Spirit," the present Lord himself, without which the anthropological term would mean little to Paul) will soon be present at Corinth in both "body" and "spirit." "Presence," if not simultaneous with the physical, the spatial, the temporal, must still issue in it, conclude with it.

The perpetrator's punishment is described as a handing over to Satan **for the destruction of the flesh.** The phrase "hand over to Satan" is formulalike, and appears once more, in the Pastoral Epistles (1 Tim. 1:20). Though evidence of its use as a formula in Judaism is late (the 3rd cent. A.D.), Paul could scarcely have been its inventor. The term **destruction** in the prepositional phrase is used by the LXX in its pronominal form to describe the "angel of death" which slew Egypt's firstborn (cf. Exod. 12:23; 1 Chron. 21:12; and Heb. 11:28). In light of the references to Passover in vv. 6-9, it is most likely that v. 5 hides an identification of Satan with the "Destroyer," and is in harmony with Jewish teaching between the Testaments. Most striking, however, is that Satan is shorn of independence. He functions as the executor of the divine judgment, and since that judgment is anticipated in the action of the apostle and his community, Satan is the lackey of Paul and Corinth. "All things are yours . . . whether life or death" (3:21f.)! Since there is no getting loose from the "flesh" without getting loose from the "body"—for Paul the Christian is not oriented to what is "fleshly" or hostile to God, but cannot escape existence "*in* the flesh"—being thrust from the community can only mean the man's death.

But what gives Paul or Corinth the right to such anticipation? The right to the anathema or "God damn" does not automatically attach to being a charismatic. The answer can only be that the eschatological judgment of God mediated by Paul and Corinth is linked to an event on earth by which human destiny is decided ("Jesus Christ and, indeed, this one crucified"), and thus to what serves that event as its sole medium—"the word of the cross."

Again, as in the "sentences" in chaps. 3, 14, and 16, the ultimate purpose of the action is rehabilitation, rescue of the offender's "spirit." Paul holds out no hope for the earthly existence of this man, but he does still hope—he, his "spirit" will be spared at the resurrection (cf. 3:15; 11:30-32).

Did Paul believe the excommunication would result in the man's death? And did the man die, or did he live to sneer at his judgment? Who cares? The possibility of giving temporal, historical shape to the presence of the Lord had been lost to him. He had lost what it was to which the "word of the cross" had called him, existence in the world for the world. He had lost corporeality, or whatever for Paul went by that name.

Chapter 5   *1 Corinthians*

After deciding the offender's case, Paul turns to the truant community: **Your boasting is not good** (in v. 2a he had written, "and are you puffed up?"). Then the apostle takes up a figure which has had a life for two millennia, even among those who have never opened a Bible: **Do you not know that a little leaven leavens the whole lump?** That "don't you know?" will often signal a contradiction between what is and ought to be, between what Corinth knows and does—not, however, a contradiction "in the cards," a paradox, something inherent in the nature of things and about which Corinth can do nothing. It refers to an *intolerable* contradiction, to something which Corinth should never have allowed to occur since it need never have occurred (cf. 6:2, 3, 9, 15, 16, 19). And it was not merely that Corinth should not have allowed it, that it tolerated the offense as a single case, an exception which meant nothing for the condition of the remainder of the community. It took pride in its toleration. The declarative statement, **your boasting is not good,** thus precedes rather than follows the "don't you know?"

As if the figure of the **lump** in v. 6 had a life of its own, taking Paul wherever it pleased, it changes shape in v. 7 and summons up all those old associations with the apostle's Jewish past. (The figure had already hinted at its target in v. 5, in that identification of Satan with the Destroyer, the "angel of death".) Now the comparison of Corinth with the purging out of the leaven at Passover flows automatically from Paul's pen. Was Corinth familiar with the strict prescriptions for the Passover feast in Exod. 12:19 or 13:7 ("Unleavened bread shall be eaten for seven days; no leavened bread shall be seen with you, and no leaven shall be seen with you in all your territory")? Or did the interpretation precede the "text"? Would Paul's hearers or readers, Greeks and Romans, immediately understand the allusion, or did they first hear that Christ, "our Passover," had been sacrificed, and then hunt for the relevant passages in the Old Testament? Sin and the leaven, Christ and the passover lamb—the comparison was "second nature" to a man who had grown up with the Torah.

Commentary *Chapter 5*

"Cleanse out the old leaven, that you may be a new lump, as you are unleavened; for indeed, Christ our Passover has been sacrificed!" The RSV inserts the adverb really—as you really are unleavened—and commentators begin the age-old discussion of the "imperative" as "growing out of" the indicative, as if the summons were to "be in reality what you are in principle," or "be in actuality what you are potentially," or, "wed to your consciousness of redemption the feeling of responsibility." In v. 7, new lump and unleavened are synonymous, identical. Therefore, the relation between the subjunctive that you may be and the indicative you are cannot reflect a gap which somehow needs bridging. Putting an end to the intolerable which Corinth had tolerated did not require an adjustment of praxis to theory, an alignment of doing with knowing. Corinth had been made new, and that meant it had been seized by a dynamic which would inevitably hasten toward its goal. So the summons to Corinth was not to supplement what it had been declared to be or "imputed" to be, if that declaration were merely a judgment uttered in the heavenly forum. The summons was to hear that it had been made what it had been declared to be: "You are unleavened; for indeed, Christ, our Passover, has been sacrificed!" There is no understanding of the apostle apart from the recognition that the beating heart of his "imperative" is promise, good news, because his "speech" and his "message" effect what they say. It was this presumption of Paul, that the "word of the cross" was bringing to naught the things that are, and calling into existence the things that are nothing which made it a folly and stumbling block—above all to the religious, to the godly, who could not believe that a word and its hearing could make new, or that if it did, that its dynamic could not be amenable to investigation. There was no observable, tangible newness in that "lump" of Corinth. Quite the contrary! But Corinth's "cleansing," the "actualization" of its newness would never come by the application of a standard or rule deduced or inferred from its understanding of self. That newness would not be achieved in an action, but in a "passion," in a hearing what it had been made to be. And for this reason, it needed a word to hear, and needed it again and again: "So, let us keep the feast, not with the old leaven, and not in the leaven of badness and evil, but with the unleavened bread of purity and truth" (v. 8). The pairing of "badness" and "evil," "purity" and "truth" has long induced scholars to attempt some distinction between the members of each pair, the first allegedly referring to behavior toward others or toward God (hence the RSV **malice** in the first pair), and the other to some interior state. Neither term in the pair requires sharp distinction from the other, and all take their definition from the word, "Christ, our Passover, has been sacrificed," in allowing or not allowing that word to be heard, to be what it is. Note the similarity with Paul's argument, e.g., in Romans 6, where the sequence is reversed:

Rom. 6:10: "The death he died he died to sin . . ."	(a)
Rom. 6:11: "Consider yourselves dead to sin . . ."	(b)
Rom. 6:12: "Let not sin therefore reign . . ."	(c)
1 Cor. 5:7: "Cleanse out the old leaven . . ."	(c)
"As you are unleavened . . ."	(b)
"Christ our passover . . ."	(a)

Here, in 1 Corinthians, the argument is not as fully developed, but it is the very same: An event in which believers have been made to share ("Christ, our Passover, has been sacrificed" = "we were buried with him . . . made sharers of his death . . . our old man was crucified . . . we have died with Christ," Rom. 6:4-6, 8), has established a new existence characterized by a dynamic which propels it toward its goal.

Paul—Misinterpreted or Caricatured? (5:9-13)

Most agree that Paul's attack on Corinth's permissiveness furnished him the occasion for correcting a misinterpretation of an earlier letter: **I wrote to you in my letter not to associate with immoral men; not at all meaning the immoral of this world, or the greedy and robbers, or idolaters, since then you would need to go out of the world** (vv. 9-10). (The verb translated **to associate**—as ambiguous as was once our English "to have intercourse with," and in the context of Paul's use of the Passover metaphor—echoes all those Old Testament strictures against cultic impurity or fraternization with foreigners which threatened Israel's status as the people of God.)

It is possible that Paul's earlier injunction, repeated and expanded here, was honestly construed as a prohibition against trafficking with all such persons as he describes, thus, in effect, as a summons to asceticism. If, for example, the "catalog of vices" in vv. 9-11 belonged to the instruction of persons who had received Baptism and become members of the Christian community, and if it rooted in a "primitive holiness code" such as Leviticus 17–26, which called for radical separation from the impure, then it is possible that when Paul cited a similar catalog in his earlier letter Corinth had understood him to mean cultic separation from the world.[24] In that case, the enthusiasm at Corinth reflected both "classical" extremes (cf. 5:1-8, with the attitude assumed to be reflected here in v. 10). But it is also possible that Paul is rebutting a deliberate caricature of his position. He had written, "do not associate with immoral persons," and some at Corinth had reduced that injunction to the absurd ("to observe that rule, we would have to get off the earth!") for the sake of allowing the incestuous person to remain in the community. In that case, Paul would not be addressing a misunderstanding, but a direct challenge to his authority. But the challenge was absurd. Paul's authority did not reach to the entire inhabited globe: **What have I to do with judging outsiders? God judges those outside** (vv. 12, 13a). Paul's authority extended only to the church, for which reason his injunction prohibiting "intercourse" with the immoral or greedy or idolatrous or blasphemous or besotted or rapacious had only to do with whomever "called himself a brother" (v. 11), **not at all** with **the immoral of this world** (v. 10). Paul adds, **not even to eat with such a one.** Had the offender been invited to table, or to participate in the Supper? The rules for table fellowship had been vastly altered with Paul. On the one hand, neither ethnicity nor religious persuasion furnished a criterion for inclusion in or exclusion from table fellowship (cf., e.g., 10:27: "If one of the unbelievers invites you . . ."). But, on the other, the rules had been intensified, since not merely actions but intentions (the intention to get the better of one's neighbor cannot be subtracted from the term **greed** in v. 11) were made a criterion. The rule had been intensified precisely because the ethnic-religious criterion had been abandoned.

Corinth had been derelict—**is it not those inside the church whom you are to judge?** (v. 12b; the question requires an affirmative answer). But Corinth had been more than derelict. It had not only allowed one who should have been outside to remain inside, but had wrapped its liberalism in malice, had deliberately misapplied Paul's word concerning those inside to those outside. And as for the offender himself, he had been only an occasion, had only served to illustrate a "principle." Paul was intent on saving the man: **Drive out the wicked person from among you** (v. 13 is a quotation from the LXX of Deut. 17:7; cf. Deut. 19:19; 21:21; 22:21, 24; 24:7; cf. also Deut 17:12 and 22:22). The offender would become an outsider, beyond the reach of Paul or Corinth, but not beyond the reach of God, who will **judge those outside.** And if not beyond the reach of God, then still with the prospect of rescue—"that his spirit may be saved on the Day of the Lord" (v. 5). Who was the liberal?

Chapter 6

In chap. 6, the apostle addresses further crises at Corinth, again, presumably, on the basis of oral report. The first section concerns the settling of disputes before courts chaired by unbelievers (vv. 1-11), concluding with a catalog of vices, and the second illicit intercourse (vv. 12-20). The first section is thus related to the theme of judgment immediately preceding in 5:12-13, and the second to that of immorality reflected in the case of incest (5:1-8), and in the misapplication of Paul's teaching (5:9-11).

On Settling Disputes before Pagan Courts (6:1-11)

When one of you has a grievance against a brother, does he dare go to law before the unrighteous instead of the saints? The phrase translated **go to law** is a technical term for lodging a formal complaint before a magistrate. The question reflects Paul's ire at the individual's transgressing the Christian community's right to arbitrate by initiating legal suits. Jews in the Diaspora had never expected justice from non-Jews, and thus had established their own courts. The appeal to strange judges was expressly forbidden, and could result in excommunication. Paul's impatience, however, does not derive from habituation to an ancient pattern, from Corinth's offense against the logical assumption that Christians would get justice only from Christians. The plaintiffs and defendants had committed lése majesté, had arrogated to themselves a right which belonged to the community as a whole. For this reason, Paul opens his attack with the jarring **does he dare . . .?** But instead of countering this rampant individualism with an appeal to Corinth as the body of Christ, he harks back to a tenet of apocalyptic thought, which explains the alteration of the distinction between those "outside" and "inside" in 5:12-13 to that between the "righteous" and "saints": "Do you not know that the saints will judge the world?" In the Aramaic and Hebrew Book of 1 Enoch, in its completed form from the first century B.C., the seer writes: "Fear not the sinners, ye righteous; for again will the Lord deliver them into your hands, That ye may execute judgment upon them according to your desires,"[25] and in the Qumran midrash on Hab. 1:12-13, God is described as giving to his elect the judgment on all the nations.[26] "Now," writes Paul in verse 2b, **if the world is to be judged by you** (in prophetic speech the present tense is substituted for the future), **are you incompetent to try trivial cases?** The form of the question is the old, familiar *qal wa-ḥomer*, "the easy and the hard" (in classical rhetoric the argument *a minore ad majus*, from lesser to greater), used by Jewish teachers to press an argument by moving from the easily comprehensible to the more difficult, or the reverse. "If you will do such a great thing, can't you do the least?" The adjective is not Paul's personal evaluation of the disputes at Corinth, but results from his use of the eschatological measure—**the saints will judge the world.** Corinth was engaged in activities incompatible with its hope.

Chapter 6   *1 Corinthians*

The form of v. 3 is identical to that of v. 2, again from the "hard" to the "easy": **Do you not know that we are to judge angels? How much more** "bodily things" (RSV, **matters pertaining to this life**)! Paul raises the ante. The saints will not merely judge the cosmos, that is, all humanity whose "wisdom" has set it in opposition to God (cf. 1:20-21; 2:12; 3:19; 4:9,13; 5:10), but even the most privileged creatures belonging to that world. The idea of God's judgment as extending to angels appears in Isa. 29:12ff. (In 1 Enoch, the apocalypticist describes the judgment of national guardians as well as of fallen angels),[27] and it reappears elsewhere in the New Testament (cf. Jude 6, and 2 Peter 2:4). That the "saints" will judge angels is nowhere explicitly stated, but an inference which Paul draws from their ownership of the cosmos by virtue of their belonging to Christ (cf. 3:21b-23: ". . . whether . . . the world or life or death or the present or the future, all are yours. . . .").

Verses 4 and 5 repeat the thought of vv. 2 and 3: **If then you have such cases, why do you lay them before those who are least esteemed by the church? Least esteemed** is a synonymn for the "unrighteous" in v. 1, and, again, results from the same eschatological measure: The "unrighteous," "the despised" are given authority over the "saints" (there is never room for grey in the distinctions of apocalyptic discourse); persons from whom one could expect nothing in any other circumstance are accorded a status above the future judges of the world.

The first four verses are replete with rhetorical devices. Taken together, they reflect that *a b b a* pattern of argument occurring so frequently in Paul: *(a)* "Dare any of you go to law before the unrighteous?" *(b)* "Don't you know that the saints will judge the world?" *(b)* "Don't you know that we will judge angels?" *(a)* "Do you seat those who are despised in the church?" The entire section is freighted with antitheses: "unrighteous" and "saints," "saints" and the "cosmos" (v. 2); "those who are despised" and "the church" (v. 4); "brothers" and "unbelievers" (v. 6); allowing injustice and doing injustice (vv. 7b-8), etc. In addition appear all those nuances of expression we encountered earlier in the epistle—the heaping up of prepositions ("against," "before," "among," "in," "to," "between," "with"); anaphora (the phrases "before the unrighteous" and "before saints" in v. 1 begin with the same word), and *homoioptaton* (the phrases end on the same vowels); climax (from cosmos to angels in vv. 2-3); parallelism of members (judging the cosmos, judging the angels); chiasma ("the saints will judge the world . . . the world will be judged"), the argument *a minore ad majus*, etc. The style is Hellenistic, similar to that of the Stoic or Cynic preacher (i.e., to the diatribe), but whenever these devices appear in such clusters, are we to see a reflection of the apostle's oral delivery? Did Paul use all these devices consciously, or were they "second nature," a habit resulting from training?

The suggestion that Paul is not struggling against Roman civil law and its norms is correct, if by "struggle" is meant resistance. But if Paul is alarmed at the Corinthians' inability to decide matters "pertaining to bodily existence," it is clear that he does not acknowledge the right of the state to arbitrate between Christians. But if the right of the state to arbitrate in "bodily" matters is not acknowledged—and what could possibly be excepted from such?—what remains is the state reduced to a mere forum in which Christians suffer wrong and waive their rights (the terms in v. 7b belong to legal nomenclature: **Why not rather suffer wrong? Why not rather be defrauded**—in court? This is a perspective in light of which Romans 13 is seldom read). In an ironic turn of phrase Paul continues: **Can it be that there is no man among you wise enough to decide between . . . the brotherhood?** (an ellipse for "between brother and his brother"). Then he adds, **but brother goes to law against brother, and that before unbelievers** (vv. 5-6). The spectacle of saints, brothers, future judges of the cosmos and of angels, unable to decide the "least," hailing one another before the "unrighteous," "despised," before "unbelievers," moves Paul to a harsher reproach in v. 7 than he had made in v. 5 (**I say this to your shame**). The cluster of particles at the beginning of the verse allows only a clumsy paraphrase: "Already, then, it is altogether a defeat for you that you have suits with one another" (the RSV translates the adverb **at all,** and sets it in the wrong place: **To have lawsuits at all with one another is defeat for you**). For the Stoic, that term **defeat** denoted moral failure, a loss of dignity and personal honor. Does Paul have in mind a logion of Jesus such as Matthew records in the fifth antithesis of the "Sermon" ("You have heard that it was said, 'An eye for an eye and a tooth for a tooth.' But I say to you, Do not resist one who is evil," Matt. 5:38-39)? Socrates could only bring himself to describe the suffering of injustice as a lesser evil than the doing of it, both to be avoided.[28]

Verse 8, framed in antithesis to v. 7b, serves as transition to what follows in vv. 9-10 (the disjunctive conjunction *or* in v. 9, omitted in the RSV, makes a connection with what precedes). The charge that Corinth was doing injustice to brothers before pagan courts suggested the reservation stated in v. 9a—or, **do you not know** (!) **that the unrighteous will not inherit the kingdom of God?**—and its explication in the catalog of vices in vv. 9b-10. The idea of "inheriting the kingdom" belongs to the same treasury of thought as that of the saints' judging the cosmos and angels, in vv. 2 and 3. Beginning with Yahweh's promise to the patriarchs that their seed would take permanent possession of Canaan (cf. Gen. 17:8; Exod. 6:4, 8), the concept grew to Israel's possession of the earth. In the book of Jubilees 32:19 the Lord appears to Jacob and says:

> And I shall give to your seed all of the land under heaven and they will rule in all nations as they have desired. And after this all of the earth will be gathered together and they will inherit it for ever.[29]

But the concept was not confined to the promise of the earth. It came to embrace an aeon to come, and in this form was fixed in the literature between the Testaments:

> For that which will be in the future, that is what one will look for, and that which comes later, that is what we shall hope for. For there is a time that does not pass away. And that period is coming which will remain forever. . . . For those are the ones who will inherit this time of which it is spoken, and to these is the heritage of the promised time.[30]

Against this background New Testament utterances concerning "entering" or "inheriting" the kingdom take their shape (cf. Matt. 25:34), an inheritance in which Paul included the Gentiles by virtue of their union with Christ (cf. Galatians 3 and 4; Romans 8; etc.).

Verses 9b-10 yield the negative requirements for the inheritance, and expand the catalog of six in 5:9-10 (**immoral,** greedy, robbers, **idolaters,** revilers, drunkards) to ten, adding **adulterers,** active (pederasts) and passive (effeminate) homosexuals and thieves (in the RSV translated **robbers,** a term which Paul reserves for those who take by force rather than by stealth). With one exception (thievery) the vices added all concern sexual abuses.

It is obvious from Paul's question in v. 9a, as well as from his response to the misunderstanding or misapplication of his teaching in 6:9-13, that vv. 9b-10 together with 5:10-11 contained nothing strange to Corinth. The catalogs had belonged to its instruction. Whether or not they hark back to catechetical materials later used by Paul, or reflect instruction prior to or following Baptism, or both (the question is moot), Paul applies the catalogs to those who have already become Christians. In other words, whatever their origin or intent, they emerge here as "rules of the house" (*Haustafeln*).

Such catalogs are legion in the New Testament and in the literature of the postapostolic period.[31] The lists have their counterparts in the literature of antiquity, in intertestamental Judaism, Qumran, and Rabbinism,[32] in Greek and Latin authors,[33] and in the literature of Gnosticism.[34] Scattered in the museums of Europe and the Near East are counters used in an ancient game resembling our checkers. One side of the counter contains a number, the other a noun or adjective—"are you . . . ?" Many of these counters offer striking parallels to the vices listed by Paul.

Obviously, then, Paul did not invent the catalogs, but he gives them a radically different orientation. In contrast to those in Judaism which (with some exceptions; e.g., Judaism in the 5th century B.C. appears to have confessed its sins on Yom Kippur

93

in catalogs of vices) describe Gentile, pagan excesses which Israel must eschew, in Paul the catalogs are applicable to both Jew and Gentile, since faith involved not merely turning from paganism, but from one's former life in Judaism as well. Further, in contrast to the apocalypticist's (and Gnostic's) strict differentiation between the good and the evil, a differentiation rooted in nature, for the apostle the difference roots in an historical event in which the believers participate through their Baptism (**but you were washed,** v. 11). Again, as Paul contended in 5:9-11, the catalogs do not reflect a call to monkish existence, since the purity of the congregation is not constituted by cultic separation but by its incorporation into Christ (**you were sanctified . . . in the name of the Lord Jesus Christ and in the Spirit of our God,** v. 11). Next, in contrast to the Stoic or Greek tradition, the catalogs are not addressed to the individual, but to the community:

> Paul knows nothing of a lone, isolated man. How can the Greek arrive at this idea? The . . . reason is that his gods mean nothing to him. . . . The Greek "lived for himself". . . . The Greek does not need [society] in order to gain content for the question as to what he would or should do. . . . He needs it in order to achieve the result which makes his moral performance worth desiring.[35]

Finally, and most important, for Paul, Christian existence results in a relativizing of authorities and powers which was unheard-of in antiquity. For the apostle, Christianity was not a new moral doctrine; it was the same God whose will was being done. What was new was the believer's relation to the world. "All things are yours," Paul writes, (3:21) and in one blow the *form* of anything good, moral, natural, ethical has been neutralized, desacralized. But its *use* has been radicalized: " 'All things are lawful,' but not all things are helpful. 'All things are lawful,' but not all things build up. Let no one seek his own good, but the good of his neighbor" (10:23-24). Paul left intact whatever Judaism or Hellenism regarded as good, moral, natural, and ethical; the only criterion was its usefulness for the other—a more radical critique than any of his contemporaries had advanced.

That move in v. 11 from "once" to "now," from what Corinth had been to what Corinth had become, is characteristic of Paul: **But you were washed, but you were sanctified, but you were justified.** . . . (In the Greek, the adversative is repeated; the antithesis between "now" and "then" could scarcely have been more sharp.)

But if Paul could say this of a community he had just subjected, and would yet subject, to a series of blistering attacks, then it meant that whatever the difference between Corinth and any other group, whatever constituted it new was not something in its "nature," or in its idea of its nature, but in something which rendered the difference between it and any other community with a bit of moral scruple imperceptible. (Paul would have regarded the denial of moral sense to the unbeliever, the description of the unbeliever's good as a "shining vice" as a denial of the presence of God in the world.) Faith characterized Corinth's existence, and precisely this faith identified Corinth as "justified" with Corinth as observable, tangible, palpable. The Corinthians, the impious, the ungodly were the justified, and the mark of their existence hiddenness. But if faith characterized Corinth's existence, what established that existence as by faith was the event in which God had confounded the world—"Jesus Christ and, indeed, this one crucified." Justification, then, leagues away from a mere tool of apologetic in Paul's mission practice among Jews or nomists, was nothing but the reverse side of his gospel of the cross, which shattered the visibility of apocalyptic, ruined the Stoic's notion of the idea as visibly achieved in a moral progression, robbed the enthusiast of his substitution of the "then" for the "now," and thus removed all reason for boasting or self-praise: "Therefore, as it is written, 'Let him who boasts, boast of the Lord' " (1:31). But if the cross established Corinth's existence as by faith, thus as hidden, if it identified the observable Corinth with the justified Corinth, that hiddenness was no obstacle to growth; it gave no reason for omitting the summons reflected in these catalogs. Quite the reverse! Not the reverse because that hiddenness had somehow to eventuate in visibility; not because

Chapter 6   1 Corinthians

Corinth must become in reality what it had been declared to be—**washed, sanctified, justified.** The reason for the summons lay in Paul's conviction that the event which established Corinth's existence concealed a dynamic. What was hidden, what was imperceptible was at work, and it was essential to make that clear! The imperatives which Paul addresses to his readers are not sprung principally from anguish over the gulf between what is and ought to be, but from the confidence that the one to whom his readers have been joined is at work in them to close the gap. When this, to all appearances sanguine and "optimistic," aspect of the Pauline "ethic" is overlooked, the beating heart of his imperatives—"all are yours; and you are Christ's; and Christ is God's" (3:22b-23)—is missed, and the conviction that God's will will be done is traded for a summons to moral exercise.

Regarding Immorality (6:12-20)

Till now, Paul had addressed the question of immorality in the context of the community's boasting of its tolerance (5:1-8), its misinterpretation of Paul's teaching (5:9-13), and in his list of negative requirements for inheriting the kingdom (6:9-10). Now the apostle focuses on the topic as such, and in what must have seemed to him its most virulent form, though assumed by Greeks to be the right of every sound, young man—consorting with prostitutes. Aside from his earlier use of the term "immorality" or "immoral person" (5:1, 9-11; 6:9), the argument appears to lack connection with what precedes, unless we are to see a sequence from bad to worse, from tolerating evil in the affair of the incestuous person, or from falling prey to it in pleading for justice before pagan courts, to deliberately engaging in it.

Paul introduces his argument with a phrase in vogue at Corinth: "Everything is permitted to me" (the RSV, **all things are lawful for me,** weakens the assertion, which denies the existence of any norm applicable to behavior). If the slogan was Corinth's invention, the sense it conveyed was not. The slogan expressed the Cynic-Stoic ideal of freedom, given classic formulation by Epictetus, the common man's thinker, born in the decade Paul lived and wrote: "He is free who lives as he wills, who is subject neither to compulsion, nor hindrance, nor force, whose choices are unhampered."[36] But Paul himself could have fathered the phrase. If, as he wrote in chap. 3, "all things are yours" (3:22), then the assertion that there was nothing to hamper the Christian's choice was only the logical deduction to be drawn from it. Or again, if the Christ of God had died by judicial decree, then law, statute, and ordinance had made an incredible blunder ("which none of the rulers of this age knew; for if they had known, they would not have crucified the Lord of glory," 2:8), had utterly failed where the "ends of justice" were clearest. But if the law had collapsed where those "ends" were clearest, it had lost all title to ordering existence where those ends were less clear. The death of Christ spelled the end to law for those who acknowledged that death as the "wisdom of God." Paul's "dying to the law" (cf. Gal. 2:19), his freedom from the law (cf. 9:21) was in essence a Christological statement, a witness to the radical alteration of existence through the death of Christ. And how much would it have required for Corinth to construe that freedom as freedom to do what it pleased?

" 'Everything is permitted to me,' but not everything is useful. 'Everything is permitted,' but I will not be mastered by anything" (v. 12). In a parallelism whose members begin with the same phrase (anaphora), Paul states the thesis of the argument to follow. The repetition of the phrase "Everything is permitted to me" signals Paul's agreement with the slogan—"nothing till now conceived as norm or criterion, as an ethic or rule of law, is applicable to my behavior; I am free, and everything is allowed." In the second member of the parallel, set off from the first by the repetition of the adversative (**but not . . . but I will not . . .**), Paul distances himself from the sloganeer: "Not everything is useful (RSV, **helpful**). . . . I will not be mastered by anything." The negative clauses yield the definition of freedom. First, freedom is not an abstraction, but exercised in the concrete, bent to use. The radical alteration of ethical perspective in Paul can scarcely be missed. Law, heteronomous law, constraining and exacting

Chapter 6   *1 Corinthians*

pressure from the outside, its distinction between right and wrong, sacred and profane derived from mere decree, has been jettisoned for whatever serves "the common good." "Use," then, not judicial decree gives definition to the vices cataloged in chaps. 5 and 6. Those vices are what they are from the perspective of what serves the other. If God's "wisdom" appeared under the sign of "folly" in the cross of Christ, and if by embracing that wisdom one came to share the life of the crucified, then that meant that the same ambiguity which attached to Christ now marked the existence of those who are his. Then existence had assumed the shape of the existence of Christ in which use for the other was all. Paul will hammer away at the theme in 10:25 and 12:7 (cf. 7:35), and to another community will write: "Let each of us please his neighbor for his good, to edify him" (Rom. 15:2). Later, some Christians would assert that by faith existence had been radically transformed, but would deny the ambiguity of that existence, and attempt to give it definition according to visible norms.

But if others (e.g., in the Stoa) could not exclude advantage to the self in that use for the other, the second negative in the parallel with its positive explication in vv. 13, 15, 19, and 20 eliminates anyone or anything from mastery, including the self—anyone but one: **The body is . . . for the Lord . . . your bodies are members of Christ . . . your body is a temple of the Holy Spirit . . . you are not your own; you were bought with a price.** In the years to follow, others would assert the ambiguity of believing existence, but assume that since such existence could not be distinguished by visible means the transformation it had undergone was only in "theory" or "in principle." In the end, neither the one nor the other interpreter of Paul would be able to live with the parallel. By resuscitating law in the application of external criteria to Christian existence, the one would abandon the first member of the parallel for the sake of the second—"not everything is useful . . . I will not be mastered by anything." By lodging Christian existence in an "imputation" construed as mere formal declaration, the other would abandon the second member of the parallel for the first—"everything is permitted to me." In the end, both would deny the presence of Christ in those who are his, driving a wedge between the empirical person and the justified person, and thus abandon Paul's concept of freedom. If nothing is right or wrong in itself, nothing in itself sacred or profane, nothing good or evil, but only its use, use for the other, that use takes its direction from the one who has mastered and is at work in me—the Lord.

In v. 13, Paul takes up in chiasma yet another Corinthian slogan, a crude refraction of an idea with a long history: "Meats for the belly and the belly for meats." One hundred years after Paul's death, Marcus Aurelius would give it polish: "Things do not take hold upon the mind, but stand without unmoved."[37] Paul agrees with the slogan. Eating does not contaminate the person (note the word of Jesus in Matt. 15:11, 17), and some day there will be no use for ingestion or the organ it requires: **God will destroy both one and the other.** The phrase is twin to that in 15:50: "Flesh and blood cannot inherit the kingdom of God," and fixes the initiative hidden in the passive voice in 15:42ff., "what is sown is perishable. . . ." But if the Corinthians went on to draw an analogy between ingestion and sexual intercourse (an analogy common to Cynic teaching), whether that analogy derived from the notion that "things do not take hold upon" the center of consciousness, or whether it footed on the assumption that the future held no prospect for corporeality (the phrase, "and God will destroy both," would have met with some agreement at Corinth), for which reason then desire could be given its head, Paul flatly opposes the analogy. The symmetry of the argument, "meats for the belly, and the belly for meats . . ." and retained up to the phrase "and the body" in v. 13b, is suddenly ruptured by the clause which follows—**not . . . for immorality, but for the Lord.** Paul opposes the analogy because he refuses to acknowledge the perishability of "flesh and blood" as spelling an end to corporeality. He does so, not because he cannot conceive self or personhood or the "I" apart from corporeality. Who is to say what Paul could or could not conceive? The notion of "Judaism" as requiring the "body" for persistence beyond death assumes a

Chapter 6 *1 Corinthians*

uniformity in Judaism which never existed. If Gnosticism in its earliest recognizable form drew on the Judaism of the apocalyptic mode, that mode did not uniformly require corporeality for life in the hereafter. Paul's argument is that the Lord stands as guarantor of the body—**the body is not meant for immorality, but for the Lord, and the Lord for the body.** The Lord stands as guarantor, not merely because he has an "interest" in corporeality—admittedly, an assertion which the Gnostic, with his description of the Creator as a laughable, deluded, blind creature of the thought of the highest, unknowable God, would never concede. In v. 14, Paul reaches for a sentence in the old credo which gives the reason. Behind the guarantor and his guarantee stands the one who **raised the Lord and will also raise us up by his power.** Who **raised** and **who will raise**—this is God's name, this is how he is to be denominated (cf. 1 Thess. 1:10; Gal. 1:1; 2 Cor. 4:14; Rom. 4:24-25; 6:4; 10:9; and 2 Cor. 1:9; 5:15; Rom. 6:9; and 8:11). The assertion that Paul's relationship to corporeality was problematic (a relationship which some interpret as consistent with a certain bodily malformation) is as wrongheaded as the assertion that he could not conceive personhood apart from the body. For Paul, the relation of the self to corporeality was an issue having to do with God, not with anthropology. That is, unlike the Greek who viewed the body from the perspective of its limitation in form and shape, and thus as "individual," for the apostle the body denoted communication, participation, orientation to the other, to the claim of the Creator, in expectation of the resurrection, in the possibility of obedience and self-surrender. Coming to consciousness is the presupposition for everything specifically human, but it is also the cause of immeasurable tortures, since consciousness is continually in danger of absolutizing itself, of identifying itself with the "self," which for Paul can only be a self in participation with another. Hence, the enthusiast or mystic knows nothing of fellowship or participation, does not see that the "I" becomes an "I" only through the "Thou," the other. For this reason it conceives the "I" and deity as substance.[38] And if "belly and meats," "flesh and blood," if perishability should render the connection between "raised" and "will raise" an affair of hope, then hope in this God "who raised and will raise," with whom the one deed embraces the other, occurs for the sake of the other: "He died for all, that those who live might live no longer for themselves but for him *who for their sake* died and was raised" (2 Cor. 5:15).

Body, then, corporeality, not because existence cannot be conceived apart from it, but corporeality because of God. Verse 15, and its like in v. 19, mark a progression from v. 14: "Body," corporeality, not only because of God or due to God, not only because visibility, concreteness attaches to the name or the action of God (however odd or capable of misinterpretation!), but also and for that reason corporeality as the essential characteristic of existence with God: **Do you not know** (!) **that your bodies are members of Christ? Shall I therefore take the members of Christ** (the construction in the original is odd, but cf. Luke 5:25) **and make them members of a prostitute? Never!** The question contains an almost blasphemous oxymoron—"members of Christ," "members of a whore." The substitution of the term "members" for "body" in v. 15 is deliberate, calculated to accent concreteness in deeds, acts, but Paul's purpose is also to indicate where the head of this body is located. "Or, don't you know that the one joined to the prostitute is one body [the RSV adds, **with her**)? For, it says, 'the two shall be one flesh' " (v. 16). The terms "body" and "flesh" in this verse are virtually synonymous, use of the term "flesh" controlled by the biblical quotation from Gen. 2:24 (cf. Matt. 19:5) and thus without prejudice (cf. 7:28; 2 Cor. 12:7; Gal. 4:13f.). But since the subject is unchastity, the term "flesh" may also connote hostility to God (its most frequent signification in Paul), for which reason the apostle may have chosen precisely this passage. If body because of God, if corporeality as the means of life with God, then corporeality with only this one in view.

But if with only this one in view, then unchastity—in this instance, whoredom—plunges the member of Christ into an intolerable contradiction, because it expresses the rage to be for oneself, when the Lord has established that the criterion for ex-

Chapter 6   *1 Corinthians*

istence with him shall be use, life for the other (v. 12). Paul does not discourse on whoredom as a sin which more than any other taints the self—which may be true—nor does he describe clinging to a prostitute (in the middle voice, the verb translated **join** denotes duration, and may be a reminiscence of Deut. 10:20 and Ps. 72:28 LXX) as a spurious relationship since it is merely a reflex of a desire to do the impossible—to be for oneself, alone. As the accent on the "members" as denoting action makes clear, the apostle is eminently practical: The contradiction, the impossibility, the oxymoron occurs at the point of use.

In v. 17, Paul gives his argument a new inflexion, signaled in the citing of the Genesis passage in v. 16. Immorality—prostitution—belongs to the category of "flesh"—not body or corporeality, but "flesh," an orientation of life to the "wisdom of this age" (2:16), to what is ready-to-hand, to thought and judgment and their concretion in action as established or approved by this age, by what God has made foolish (1:20). And "flesh" is at war with "spirit": "But the one joined to the Lord is [not, as in the RSV, **becomes**) one spirit." Paul could have written, "the one joined to the Lord is one body," and for all practical purposes does so in v. 15. (The clauses, "members of Christ" and "joined to the Lord" in vv. 15a and 17 are parallel to the clauses "members of a prostitute" and "one flesh with her" in vv. 15b and 16.) If by use of the term "spirit" Paul intended to describe of what sort that "bodily" union with Christ is, a union mediated by the Spirit (cf. 2:10-12), then he did so only incidentally. The point is that "flesh," life as oriented to this age (not "in" this age; how could Paul escape it—cf. 4:9-13!) and "spirit" are at war, neither conceding to the other, and that Corinth has been caught in the crossfire. **Shun immorality,** Paul writes, and then adds: **Every other sin which a man commits** (or better, "whatever other sin a man might commit"—the clause does not express a fact but an eventuality) **is outside the body; but the immoral man sins against his own body** (v. 18). The sentence appears to contradict the logion of Jesus which does not limit what defiles to unchastity (cf. Matt. 15:15-20), but if the thesis is formulated only ad hoc, that is, in reference to the specific case of prostitution, then the contradiction is only apparent. But why the reference to sinning against **his own body** rather than against the **members of Christ?** Immorality, "flesh," collides with "spirit" because it marks an existence oriented to this age, an orientation which ultimately is to the self (for where else does this age finally make its home but in the self, or in that notion that there is a self which is self-contained and free of the other?). But then why should concern for the self, for "one's own body" yield the criterion for shunning immorality? The answer is given in question form in v. 19: "One's own body" is the body which is Corinth. The verse begins (for the sixth time in this chapter!) with the familiar **Do you not know,** in every instance of its use till now a reference to a tradition earlier handed down, and is a virtual repetition of 3:16. The clauses there which describe *what* Corinth is ("you are God's temple"), *who* it is that has taken up residence in it ("and God's Spirit . . . dwells in you"), and *from what source* or by whose initiative ("God's"), correspond exactly to the clauses in our passage here—**your** (plural!) **body is a temple of the Holy Spirit within you,** whom (not **which**) **you have from God.** . . . As reflected in the manuscript tradition, the church was puzzled by the use of the singular **body** in this verse, in contrast to its use in the plural in v. 15 (**your bodies are members of Christ**). The difference lies in the fact that in v. 15 the term **members** as denoting deeds controls the number of the noun (**bodies**), whereas here the one body which the Corinthians are together with Christ receives the accent. The question in v. 19 concludes with the words, **you are not your own,** the reason given in v. 20, **you were bought with a price** (the same clause repeated in 7:23), the chapter concluding with the summons: **So glorify God in your body.**

You are not your own. The words merely state in the negative what had been positively stated in 3:23. Whether in reference to party strife or misuse of the body in ignorance of freedom, the argument is the same: Corinth is Christ's, and Christ is God's, thus Corinth is God's, not by virtue of inborn divine reason or a mystical indwelling, but by virtue of an event—**you were bought with a price** (the ransom metaphor is not to be stretched; its intent is only to indicate that Corinth has a Master). But if Corinth is God's, then its existence as determined by God does not lead away from but rather into the body, corporeality. It does so, not because of any inherent nobility in the body—if there is no despising, neither is there a deifying of the corporeal in Paul—but because God has attached a promise to it: He **will also raise us up by his power;** it does so because "corporeality is the end of the ways of God." For this reason, because the body has been promised union with Christ in his resurrection, freedom from all legal, external constraint, reflected in that Corinthian slogan, "I can do everything," lies in union with Christ in his death, in life for the other. Then, "I can do everything," being interpreted, means, "use is all," use for Christ and the other. It is the cross which gives to freedom its definition, spelling humanness, reconstitution of the self, of the "I" as "member of Christ," as "one spirit with him," as "temple from God," never alone or self-contained, never without the other, without the other in view. **Glorify God in your body!** Use is all, and for the other.

■ Responses to the Corinthians' Questions (7:1—10:33 [11:1])

Chapter 7

Paul now moves from responses occasioned by oral reports to answers to questions from the community conveyed to him in written form. With the possible exception of vv. 29-31, which serve as the hub, chap. 7 appears to lack all logical sequence. First, Paul counsels celibacy, though conceding marriage because of the temptation to immorality (vv. 1-7). Next, he addresses the unmarried and widows, again conceding marriage in view of their lack of self-control (vv. 8-9). Third, he includes a word to married persons respecting divorce, to which he attaches his own proviso (vv. 10-11). Fourth, he gives advice regarding "mixed" marriages (vv. 12-16). In vv. 17-24, he expands his counsel to "disengagement" to include the circumcised, uncircumcised, and the slave. Following this, he addresses virgins (vv. 25-28), briefly reverting to a word to the married (v. 27a). In vv. 32-35, he contrasts the disadvantages of marriage with the advantages of celibacy. He then addresses himself to engaged persons (vv. 36-38), and concludes with a word to the woman or widow contemplating remarriage (vv. 39-40). Attempts to render each section next of kin to what precedes or follows in only loose fashion or merely under the general topic of celibacy or marriage lead to frustration.

The reason for the chapter's unusual shape cannot lie solely in the sequence of questions put to Paul and to which he responds seriatim. There is a "that reminds me" character attaching to the whole (cf. 1:13-14, 17 with 1:16) which characterizes normal, oral discussion. It may even be that interruptions during the apostle's dictation account for the lack of sequence in this portion of his letter, requiring his return to themes treated earlier, and on second thought qualified or expanded. Of what sort those interruptions were, no one will ever know, but the assumption that there were such, and that they thus account for the chapter's curious structure—though each section has its own inner logic and in several instances rhetorically honed to a fine point—seems less out of touch with the vagaries of everyday human existence than the hypothesis of leaves scattered, misarranged and supplemented with glosses and marginalia by later revisers.

Concerning Celibacy (7:1-7)

It is important to note that throughout the chapter Paul distinguishes his counsel from a command of the Lord. In v. 6 he writes, **I say this by way of concession, not of command**; in v. 7, **I wish that all were as I**; in v. 8, **it is well for them to remain . . . as I do,** and in v. 9, **it is better to marry than to** "burn." In v. 12 the section opens with the words **to the rest I say, not the Lord.** In v. 17 Paul writes, **this is my rule,** and in v. 21, **if you can gain your freedom. . . .** Verse 25 opens with the statement, **I have no command of the Lord,** and v. 26 with the words, **I think . . . it is well.** In v. 37 the apostle writes, **whoever is firmly** established in his heart . . . will do well, and in v. 38, he who marries . . . does well; and he who refrains . . . will do better. Finally, v. 40 concludes the argument regarding remarriage with the word, in my judgment. . . . These expressions are in contrast to the word in v. 10, not I but the Lord, a charge repeated in v. 39.

All the expressions cited above refer to Paul's counsel (cf. v. 25: I give my opinion; v. 26: I think, and v. 40: in my judgment). Of course, Paul's counsel is no mere prejudice (for which reason the RSV's opinion in v. 25 is too imprecise) but derives from his charism as apostle (cf. v. 25: As one who by the Lord's mercy is trustworthy, and v. 40: I think that I have the Spirit of God). Further, that counsel is for the Corinthians' welfare (cf. v. 28: I would spare you; v. 32: I want you to be free from anxieties, and v. 35: I say this for your own benefit).

Verse 1 states the thesis: Now concerning the matters about which you wrote. It is good (RSV: well) for a man not to touch a woman. How good is "good" can only be derived from the context. Paul does not assign the term a single, discrete signification, unlike the Greek, for whom the word represented the ideal. As any lexicon will tell, the phrase to touch a woman (or "wife"—the word is used to denote the female, whether single or married) is a reference to sexual intercourse, and not a euphemism (cf. Gen. 20:6; Prov. 6:29).

Simply put, the thesis reads: celibacy is best. Does it reflect assent to a position adopted by some at Corinth? Since there is no union which is not ultimately rooted in union with Christ and thus subordinate to him, had some concluded that "touching a wife," like unchastity, threatened that oneness? According to Paul, marriage could threaten the believer's relation to Christ, but "could" was still a length from "would," and he restricted himself to wishing that all were as he (v. 8). So he writes, but because of the temptation to immorality, each man should have his . . . wife and each woman her own husband. (Reference to the male assumes first position, but the force of that phrase her own husband, that is, her very own and no one else's, should not be overlooked). Marriage, then, represented a concession—**because of the temptation to immorality.** As is evident from the manuscript tradition, the plural in Greek, "unchastities," puzzled the church. Paul, however, is thinking of evil in lumps, not in lump-sum. It is clear: there is nothing here of the joys of marriage. (Luther had made the same concession: "The marriage state . . . is like a hospital for the sick, lest they fall into more grievous sins.")[39]

The concession made, Paul in v. 3 instructs each partner in the marriage to give what is due the other in regard to matters of sex, and in the verse following gives the reason: **The wife does not rule over her own body, but the husband does; likewise the husband does not rule over his own body, but the wife does** (v. 4). With all this conceding or reduction of marriage to a lower rung, Paul will not allow the notion of marriage as surrogate for unchastity. Mutuality in sexual intercourse, use for the other, not thievery or tyranny, must characterize the relationship. (Unlike the bachelor Paul, the young Luther was much more wary about giving advice in such matters: "I will keep silent about what more use or pleasure there may be in [marriage] . . . lest someone stuff my snout and say I am talking of something I know nothing about.")[40] For this reason, the only activity which Paul will allow to interrupt cohabitation is that of prayer, meditation, contemplation: **Do not refuse one another** (do not refrain from sexual intercourse), **except perhaps by agreement for a season, that you may devote yourselves to prayer; but then come together again** (resume intercourse), **lest Satan tempt you through lack of self-control** (v. 5). In a wedding sermon preached in January 1531, Luther interpreted this fifth verse in curiously different fashion: Following a quarrel, husband and wife "should make up with one another again, and be reconciled, lest their prayer together be hindered."[41] Paul's view is more realistic—prayer is not assisted by sexual intercourse.

The demonstrative **this** in v. 6—**I say this by way of concession, not of command**—refers to the word in v. 5. The verse following which concludes the section makes that clear: **I wish that all were**

as I myself am (v. 7a). The counsel and the concession have to do with the entire affair of marriage. The verse contains Paul's first personal reference since chap. 5 (vv. 3, 4, 6, 11, 12), and obviously to himself as unmarried.

If Corinth could not infer from Paul's statements in vv. 3-5 that he refused to identify sexual intercourse in marriage with unchastity, the conclusion to v. 7 should have left no doubt that his concession was not to "nature" or the natural order of things. If Paul would never concede that "nature" rendered refraining from unchastity an impossibility, neither could he concede the impossibility of celibacy on the ground of natural desire. (Luther once had written that it is "impossible that the gift of virginity is as common as there are cloisters.")[42] Of course, the same tyranny of self-love threatened marriage as was lodged in unchastity (cf. vv. 3-5); the same possibility of division lurked in marriage as adhered to immorality (cf. vv. 32-34 with 6:15!). **But,** as Paul writes, **each one has his own special gift** (charism) **from God,** "the one this, the other that." The assertion that Paul's word in v. 7 may not be pressed, as though he would have evaluated marriage positively and thus described it as a charisma (cf. Lietzmann, Wendland on 7:7), ignores the realism in the apostle's differentiation between the "good" and the less good among the gifts of God. If Paul did not regard marriage itself as a charism, he certainly regarded whatever induced one to enter upon it as such. Nor did this inhibit him from describing celibacy as good or better. The same realism is reflected in Paul's ranking prophecy above uninterpreted tongues in chap. 14—both of them gifts from God. It is precisely because Paul regards as a gift from God what to others may simply appear as the natural order of things that he is forced to set down what he wishes as "counsel" and not as command. According to synoptic tradition, Christ himself had refused to give such a command:

> The disciples said to him, "If such is the case of a man with his wife, it is not expedient to marry." But he said to them, "Not all men can receive this saying, but only those to whom it is given. . . . He who is able to receive this, let him receive it" (Matt. 19:9-12).

Commentary *Chapter 7*

(In his sermon of 1531, Luther had written that "violence and injustice is done the estate of marriage, when it is called a worldly estate; it must really be called a divine and spiritual estate.")[43] For Paul, neither celibacy nor marriage was an option to be selected at will. And yet this did not prevent him from distinguishing between excellencies in gifts. Celibacy was preferred; it constituted what Luther would call "die hohe Gnad" or sublime grace,[44] but not because marriage marked a concession to nature. Further, the rank assigned to either charism derived from the eschatological situation, discernible in the "present distress" (v. 26). The "footsteps of Messiah" as precursor of the "day of the Lord" involved a testing which marriage could only render more severe.

Concerning the Unmarried and Widows (7:8-9)

To the unmarried and the widows I say that it is good (RSV: **well) for them to remain single as I do. But if they cannot exercise self-control, they should marry. For it is better to marry than to** burn (RSV: **to be aflame with passion,** i.e., to be consumed by sexual desire). Again, it would appear that the concession is merely to "nature." And again, Paul does not deny the natural desire, but as the context of v. 7 makes clear (**each has his own** charism **from God**), he does not regard that desire as detachable from what God gives. Nowhere does Paul recognize "nature" or the natural order of things apart from the divine willing (cf. 12:18; 15:38; on this verse Luther wrote that "St. Paul will not have precious virginity where it is forced and involuntary"; "priests, monks, and nuns ought to abandon their vows where they find that God's work of sowing and increasing is good and strong in them").[45] If that desire were detachable, unchastity and marriage would be indentical. (Because they appear to be so, Luther argues, the papists denigrate marriage, but "the noblest skill which only Christians or those who want to be Christians possess is that they know how to distinguish marriage from whoredom.")[46]

Concerning Divorce (7:10-11)

To the married (who are still married) **I give charge, not I but**

109

the Lord, that the wife should not separate from her husband [or "man"—the word is used to denote the male, whether single or married] (**but if she does** [the reference can only be to a separation which earlier occurred], **let her remain single or else be reconciled to her husband)—and that the husband should not divorce his wife.** There is no "counsel" here (v. 6), no expression of a desire (v. 7), no distinction between the "good" and the less good (v. 8, cf. v. 1), no reference to what is "better" (v. 9). The word of the Lord—**I give charge, not I but the Lord**—settles the matter. From a comparison of these two verses with the tradition of Jesus' sayings concerning divorce as deposited in the Synoptic Gospels, it is clear that Paul and the evangelists have drawn from a common source. With one exception, however (Mark 10:12), that tradition assumes the male as initiator of a separation or divorce (cf. Matt. 5:32-33; Luke 16:18). In other words, the tradition is shaped against the background of Jewish law (cf. Matt. 19:3-9). Paul then, as did Mark later, altered the tradition to suit the circumstances prevailing in a non-Jewish context, the context of Greek or Roman law, according to which the woman possessed the right to divorce her husband. The words **I give charge, not I but the Lord** are thus not a slip of the tongue and its correction, but the sovereign application of the necessarily restricted Jesus-tradition to the new and altered circumstance on the part of the apostle and charismatic, Paul. The **I** and the **not I, but the Lord** are a single authority.

Concerning "Mixed" Marriages (7:12-16)

The theme of the section is similar to that of vv. 10-11: "Do not seize the initiative for detachment" (the same theme underlies vv. 1-9: "Do not remain celibate, if you have not the charism for it," but whereas in vv. 1-9 single existence is regarded as "good," here it merely *may* be such, since the prior condition of marriage was inferior to the "good"). The move from v. 11 to v. 12 may be a logical one, since the divorce referred to in v. 11 may have occurred earlier. Or, had some at Corinth assumed that an unbelieving spouse belonged to that former existence which conversion to Christianity required should be abandoned? Paul's counsel (**to the rest I say, not the Lord**) is that the decision to separate should rest with the unbelieving, not the believing, partner: **If any brother has a wife who is an unbeliever, and she consents to live with him, he should not divorce her. If any woman has a husband who is an unbeliever, and he consents to live with her, she should not divorce him** (vv. 12-13). The counsel is radical—an unbelieving husband or wife does not belong to the catalog of vices! **For,** and now emerges the rationale for that **I say** in v. 12, **the unbelieving husband is consecrated through his wife, and the unbelieving wife is consecrated through her husband. Otherwise, your children would be unclean, but as it is they are holy** (v. 14; note the chiasmic structure of the verses— "brother . . . unbelieving wife," v. 12; "wife . . . unbelieving husband," v. 13; "unbelieving husband . . . wife," v. 14a, and "unbelieving wife . . . husband," v. 14b; the sequence is *ab cd dc ba*). Does Paul imagine that the sanctity of the one partner is somehow transmitted to the other, or that the one is open to the influence of the other? (Clement of Rome quotes with approval the adage, "cleave to the holy, for they who cleave to them shall be made holy.")[47] Such influence could hardly be identified with the action denoted by that verb **is consecrated.** The point of view is neither magical nor pedagogical; nor is it proleptic, anticipatory of a situation yet to be. Use of the perfect **is** (or "has been") **consecrated** makes that clear. Paul has in view an action of God which has set the unbelieving partner and thus the marriage out of the range of forces threatening it. If an unbelieving spouse does not belong in the category of vices, neither is that spouse an occasion for demonic attack. To the children of such a mixed marriage, Paul continues, the same applies. They too are the objects of the divine activity, not magically, nor by virtue of parental influence, nor proleptically—"*now*" (RSV: **as it is**) **they are holy**—but together with (or, "through the instrumentality of"?) the believing parent. The accent in v. 14 is thus on an action of God, for only God can hallow, and on its occurring in the here and now.

Chapter 7   *1 Corinthians*

Verse 15 states what has erroneously been called the "Pauline privilege." **But if the unbelieving partner** ("man," "husband"—the substantive is masculine) **desires to separate, let it be so; in such a case** (or, "to such people"?) **the brother or sister is not bound. For God has called** you (some manuscript witnesses read **us,** as does the RSV) **to peace.**

First, the "separation" of the unbeliever has often been interpreted as "malicious desertion," that is, abandonment of the spouse without visible means of support. But the injunction, **let it be so** may as well be interpreted as a counsel to submit to the inevitable, malicious or no. Next, the repeated use of the term **unbelieving** in vv. 12-15, use of the term **consecrate** or "holy," together with the reference to the instrumentality of the believing spouse, indicate that the grounds for separation or divorce are neither physical, psychological, or economic, but have to do with faith. Verse 15, then, is the obverse side of the coin turned up in v. 14. God is able to keep a mixed marriage free of attack, but that "consecrating" is not magic. It does not occur without consent (**if any brother has a wife who is an unbeliever, and she consents** . . .). Where there is dissent, where the unbelieving spouse does not agree to live within the sphere in which that hallowing occurs, "let him depart." Finally, the phrase **the brother or sister is not bound** indicates that the believing partner has voice in the matter. This was the reason why the question respecting divorce was put to Paul (the **charge** in vv. 10-11 can scarcely have been news to Corinth). Paul thus assumes the believer has the power to keep the marriage intact, but again, as in vv. 12 and 13, the initiative for action lies with the unbeliever. The notion of "privilege" does not apply. (Luther drew a distinction between Christians who were obliged to observe the biblical injunction regarding divorce, and those who could or would not. Of the 18 papal grounds for prohibiting or dissolving a marriage, he recognized only one as legitimate—impotence. He himself recognized three grounds: impotence, adultery, and the refusal of sexual intercourse. To these he added a fourth, incompatibility, but only on condition neither spouse remarried. None of these "legitimate" reasons, however, applied to the Christian, who should endure all.)[48]

The section closes with a question addressed to the believer: **Wife, how do you know whether you will save your husband? Husband, how do you know whether you will save your wife?** (v. 16). The question is elliptical. The sphere or means (denoted by the prepositional phrases in v. 14, **through** [or "by"] **his wife; through** [or "by"] **her husband**) is to be inferred here. Obviously, the "hallowing" does not automatically issue in being saved. The mixed marriage is out of reach of destructive powers (a comfort to the questioner), as are the children of that marriage. But there is a difference between consenting to live within the sphere in which that "hallowing" occurs, and embracing that activity by faith. There is thus no collision between vv. 14 and 16, between an ancient, primitive notion of holiness, transferrable in a purely external fashion, and a conception according to which intent or conviction dominates (Weiss on 7:16). This difference renders the situation in the mixed marriage problematic, hence Paul's question: **How do you know . . . whether?**

"Call" and "Calling" (7:17-24)

The section is constructed in two strophelike structures (vv. 18-20, 21-24), each concluding with a similar refrain. Verse 17 states the thesis of the section: "Otherwise, to each as the Lord gave, each as God has called, thus let him walk. And so I order in all the churches" (RSV: **Only, let every one lead the life which the Lord has assigned to him, and in which God has called him. This is my rule in all the churches**). The imperatives which follow in vv. 18-24 (seven in all), belong together with vv. 1-9 and 12-16 as apostolic counsel, the reason for which Paul will give later in vv. 26, 29, and 31. The difference between this section and what precedes is that it embraces "walks of life" apart from marriage. The phrases **already circumcised, uncircumcised,** and **a slave** in vv. 18 and 21 are not descriptive of external conditions or "states" in which the believers were called, and thus distinct from that call itself. (Cf. the RSV of vv. 20 and 24, **in the state**

Chapter 7   *1 Corinthians*

... **in whatever state.**) While v. 20 (literally, "each in the calling in which he was called, in this let him remain") most approximates our modern definition of "calling" as the outward, temporal station in life, and thus argues for the distinction, the verses surrounding it do not. They rather indicate that for Paul the Christian's call included a station in life as given from God. It was Luther who drove a wedge between the "call" of God and one's "calling" or state as external condition, in opposition to the medieval application of the term "calling" (*vocatio*) to the clerical orders (cf. the Augsburg Confession, articles 16, 26, and 27).

"Was anyone called while circumcised, let him not pull it over" (the verb is a technical term for surgery performed on the foreskin and undergone by Jewish athletes who competed nude in the arena; in his *Antiquities*, Josephus refers to certain Jewish apostates who petitioned Antiochus IV [Epiphanes] for a gymnasium at Jerusalem, and upon his consent, "concealed the circumcision of their private parts";[49] note the prudery of the RSV translation, **let him not seek to remove the marks of circumcision**). "Has anyone been called in uncircumcision? Let him not be circumcised. Circumcision is nothing, and uncircumcision is nothing, but rather keeping the commandments of God" (vv. 18-19; cf. RSV). Those terms, **circumcision** and **uncircumcision** mark the two types as well as the division between the two types of humanity in Paul's world. He could have written, "Judaism is nothing, and Gentile origin is nothing. . . ." He had already done so in Galatians (cf. chaps. 3 and 4), and would do so again in Romans (cf. chaps. 4 and 9). Some at Corinth may have identified Judaism with salvation, for whom circumcision denoted membership in "the people of God" and on this account deliverance. Again, some at Corinth may have identified distance from Judaism with salvation. Jewish literature between the Testaments often assumed the former, while Gnosticism would assume the latter. For both, these words fix a gulf between **called** and **keeping the commandments of God.** Not that God is indifferent to "calling" or station in life. Paul's casual reference to "calling" as ordered by the Lord in v. 17 will reach its climax in Romans 1 ("to the Jew first," v. 16), and in his address to the Gentiles in Romans 11 ("it is not you that support the root, but the root that supports you," v. 18). There was an advantage attaching to the Jew's call over against that of the Gentile, but that advantage would belong only to the *horizon within which* God would choose what is foolish to shame the wise, and not to that choice itself. The "firstness" of the Jew would no more compensate for regarding the Christ crucified as a stumbling block than the lastness of the Gentile for regarding him as folly. The perspective here is soteriological. The "nothing," the indifference of God is in reference to "calling" as *guarantee of safety*. And as for **keeping the commandments of God,** let Gal. 5:6 or 6:15 stand as its definition: "For in Christ Jesus neither circumcision nor uncircumcision is of any avail, but faith working through love," "a new creation" (cf. Rom. 2:28-29).

Paul continues: **Were you a slave when called? Never mind,** then adds a clause which the modern reader could only describe as insensitive: "But even if you are able to be free, make use of it," that is, "make use of your slavery." Not merely the rules of grammar—the antecedent object of the verb "make use" is most probably the noun "slave"—but the entire context suggests this construction (the RSV here is incorrect: **But if you can gain your freedom, avail yourself of the opportunity;** cf. RSV note: "make use of your present condition instead"). In face of the prospect of freedom, Paul's injunction to the slave reads: "Do not seize the initiative for disengagement." Not even Epictetus with his summons to endure and renounce disparaged manumission.

Whence this piece of cruel advice? The answer, in part, is that Paul's "ethic" does not derive from a view of things, acts, or impulses which are reckoned to be good or bad in themselves, but are what they are in relation to the other. The Stoic, however, was not asocial; he too regarded "virtue" as in relation to the other. For the Stoic the movement in that relation was from self to the other—the urge for self-preservation led him to strive for what was "natural" or in harmony with the order of the world and the insight derived from it, and on that account toward a community of persons which could insure mutual regard. For

Chapter 7   *1 Corinthians*

Paul, however, the answer to the question, What shall I do? was first served up by the other. Use for the other, then, profit for the other—and in this instance who else but the owner, the master?— determined good or evil. Further, for the Stoic goodness or virtue was static, since the order of the world to which the urge for self-preservation was fixed was itself static. Virtue or goodness lay in approximation to an existence in harmony with the unchanging (or ever-emerging as the same) world order (though like Paul, the Stoic could also distinguish the "good" from the "better"—cf. vv. 1, 8 and 9—and in this sense allow for gradation). For the apostle, however, each condition or action ultimately derived its character from a nonrepeatable event in the future. The difference between Paul and the Stoa thus lay in their conception of God. For the one, God and the world order, the law or order of the world and the law of God, were identical. (From this identification happily derived the Stoa's shattering of myth.) For the other, for Paul, God and the world were not identical, and thus God was free. But if the difference lay in the conception of God, then it also lay in the conception of the human. In the Stoa, the urge toward self-preservation could lead to good or evil. For this reason, goodness could be taught, that is, good and evil could be separated from whatever lay beyond human capability (cf. Epictetus: "For if it is one of the things which are not under our control, it is altogether necessary that what is going to take place is neither good nor evil.")[50] According to Paul, the human was not free; humanity had a penchant for evil. Not even the Christian was free, but had a Kyrios, Lord (**he who was called in the Lord as a slave is a freedman of the Lord. Likewise he who was free when called is a slave of Christ**, v. 22; cf. Rom. 14:7-8). As to suffering, privation, or want, both Paul and the Stoic could summon to endure and renounce; both could deny the characterization in Shakespeare's *Much Ado about Nothing:*

> For there was never yet philosopher
> That could endure the toothache patiently,
> However they have writ the style of gods,
> And made a push at chance and sufferance.[51]

And still, neither may be interpreted to enjoin passivity or despair. But whereas for the Stoic such posture meant detachment from all external fate and the separation of all human feeling, willing, and acting from unrestrained impulses and effects, for Paul it meant embracing suffering for the neighbor's, and thus for Christ's, sake—"make use of it!"

The first half of v. 23 (**you were bought with a price**) repeats 6:20a, and the second half (**do not become slaves of men**) is the obverse side of the summons to "glorify God" in 6:20b. Verse 24 gives the refrain of the second strophe (cf. v. 20): **So, brethren, in whatever state each was called, there let him remain.** Then Paul adds, **with God.** The "call" affects, shapes, determines the Gestalt of the "calling"! By virtue of the "call," the "calling" of the circumcised, uncircumcised or slave is what it is in the presence of God. **With God** the "calling" is identified with the "call." To the summons to life for the other Paul attached only one restriction: **Do not become slaves of men** (v. 23), and thus challenged the ancient ethic which summoned to disengagement once an activity could not be identified as good, whether in reference to external law or to a conception of virtue as single, unitary. Paul saw "calling" as for the purpose of use "before God," something that sets one free of considerations respecting advantage or disadvantage to the self (**with God** is synonymous with the "I can do everything" in 6:12 and 10:23), and thus in regard to the slave reflects a dialectic of servitude and freedom. This was unthinkable to the Greek. But if the apostle's counsel falls far short of encouraging the abolition of slavery, by the mere fact of its address to the slave within a society which gave no thought to the conditions of the oppressed and exploited, it does not deserve to be classified with social conservatism.

Concerning Virgins; the Reason Why; the Unmarried; the Engaged; and Concerning Widows (7:25-40)

Repetition of the words **now concerning** in v. 25 suggests that Paul is dealing with yet another topic in response to the Corinthians' questions. In 7:1ff., following the discussion of marriage,

Chapter 7 *1 Corinthians*

Paul refers to the unmarried and widows, whereas in 7:25-28 and 36-38, he appears to have only virgins in mind, perhaps also persons who had agreed to a "companionate marriage," that is, to living together as husband and wife without consummating their union. But why include all the unmarried in v. 34, or with some slight variation repeat the word to widows (vv. 8-9) in vv. 39-40? In this section, Paul has more in view than the groups referred to in the Corinthians' query. He intends to disclose the perspective in light of which he gave his earlier advice, and for this reason relates all types of persons to it, whether earlier discussed or not.

Concerning Virgins (7:25-28) **Now concerning the unmarried** (lit., virgins) **I have no command of the Lord, but I give my opinion as one who by the Lord's mercy is trustworthy** (v. 25). Once again, Paul distinguishes his counsel from a "charge" of the Lord (cf. vv. 6, 10 and 12), but that counsel is not a negligible item. It deserves a hearing, since he gives it as one called to be Christ's servant and steward of God's mysteries. And, in accordance with its requirement, he has demonstrated himself to be faithful by laying as a "wise architect" the only foundation possible. (Cf. 4:1-2, 10ff.; the terms "faithful" and "wise" in this context are synonymous; use of the term "mercied" in place of "called" reflects Paul's acknowledgment that his call had occurred by virtue of God's compassion, cf. 15:8-10.) The apostolic counsel thus enjoys an integrity distinct from mere suggestion (cf. the phrase, "this is my rule in all the churches" in v. 17; the phrase, "who has been shown mercy" [RSV: **by the Lord's mercy**] is twin to the phrase in v. 40, **and I think that I have the Spirit of God**; the two comprise the frame for the remarks made between, and thus add force to the counsel).

But the story does not end there: "Therefore" (for the reason stated in v. 25, or for the reasons about to follow?; this word is untranslated in the RSV), I believe this is good due to the present distress, that it is good for a person to be such" (v. 26; cf. RSV). "To be such" may refer to what immediately precedes and thus equivalent to "to be a virgin," or it may refer to the entire argument beginning at 7:1 (exclusive of vv. 17-24), and thus equivalent to "to be unmarried." The verse yields the perspective from which Paul gives his counsel. It indicates why he regards one condition as "good" in contrast to another, and why that counsel, though not identifiable with a "charge" of the Lord," demands a hearing. But it also indicates why Paul's counsel cannot simply root in the fact that he gives it. If that were so, in his subsequent argument he would not attempt to buttress his position with reference to Scripture, custom, or nature (as, for example in 9:6-12 or 10:4-16), but would simply state, "since I say so, the matter is settled." It is "the reason why" which gives Paul's counsel such force, a reason lodged in something which Paul perceives as an act of God, and in the perception of which he regards his service or stewardship as faithful (the reason had already been hinted at in 1:8; 3:13; and 5:5). What the apostle sees is **the present distress**—a "fate," a "necessity." But the fate he sees is not an immanent world principle, something belonging to the sine qua non of existence such as death, or the physical and material in opposition to the psychic and spiritual, according to the cosmic dualism of the Hellenistic world. On the other hand, Paul appears to share with his contemporaries the idea of "fate" as compulsion, as something withdrawn from one's power to act, and thus as hemming one in.[52] He can speak of "necessity" as "laid" on him (9:6), or will approach the pagan view of fate as immanent necessity when referring to the hardships he endures as privations which "come with the territory" (cf. 2 Cor. 6:4-5 or 12:10).

The similarities are superficial. In the Old Testament, the Hebrew equivalent of "fate" is used of God's executing punishment on the wayward (cf. Ps. 107:10-19). In early Jewish religion, that activity came to be described as the "Day of the Lord," a mixture of historical, political events and cosmic catastrophes through which God would judge the heathen. As noted above (cf. pp. 60-61), the prophets asserted that the Day of the Lord would bring judgment on Israel (cf. Amos 5:18ff.; in the LXX of Zeph. 1:15, the Day of the Lord is described as a "day of tribulation and of fate"). Following the exile, the ancient popular notion reappeared, but was altered to a description of events taking place at "the end of days," when God would finally deliver Israel (Joel 3; Isaiah 12ff.). In Jewish apocalyptic literature, this political-historical expectation was transformed into a transcendent event of world renewal ushered in by the Messiah. And since that "Day" was never identified with a calendar day, its content and duration could be variously described, and the "fate" depicted as events immediately preceding the great world judgment, as "woes" or "footsteps" of the Messiah (a fixed concept in Jewish apocalyptic and rabbinic thought). In this form the concept makes its appearance in the Synoptic Gospels (cf. Luke 21:23, in which the term "fate" is used for the "woes"), but crystallized about the person of Jesus (cf. Luke 17:24). Paul "sees" the "footsteps of the Messiah" as the prelude to the "Day," to the revelation of Christ's glory and judgment. And it is this which moves him to his counsel in chap. 7. "The Day is at hand; the 'necessity' announces it. For this reason my evaluation of celibacy as 'good'; for this reason my 'concession,' my 'desire,' my 'ordering,' my 'counsel.' " (Despite what the later church may make of it, this is the first statement respecting celibacy as an existence with meaning, and not a senseless deprivation.)

Are you bound to a wife? Do not seek to be free. Are you free from a wife? Do not seek marriage. But if you marry, you do not sin, and if a girl (Greek: "the virgin") **marries, she does not sin** (the verbs appearing in the aorist tense denote future condition). **Yet those who marry will have worldly troubles** (lit., "tribulation in the flesh"), **and I would spare you that** (vv. 27-28). Clearly, the reference is to marriage, not to a pledge to preserve virginity as in a "spiritual betrothal." The verses themselves are reminiscent of the synoptic account of Jesus' prediction of the "woes":

> For in those days there will be such tribulation as has not been from the beginning of the creation which God created until now, and never will be. And if the Lord had not shortened the days, no human being would be saved; but for the sake of the elect, whom he chose,

he shortened the days [Mark 13:19-20; Matt. 24:21-22; cf. Luke 21:23, with its reference to the "necessity," or to "that Day" in 12:34. The sombre mood in 1 Corinthians 7; Mark 13; and Matthew 24 is balanced by the logion in Luke 21:28, "Now when these things begin to take place, look up and raise your heads, because your redemption is drawing near"—a variation on the beatitude in Luke 6:22-23].

Again, the logic reads: "Do not take the initiative for engagement or disengagement."

Reference to "tribulation in the flesh" is a second indication that Paul's counsel rests on his eschatological perspective. The phrase as translated by the RSV (**worldly troubles**) suggests the normal, natural sufferings flesh is heir to, heightened, perhaps, by the marriage state. But the term "tribulation" (used more than 20 times by Paul) does not refer to suffering conceived as immanent, but to an act of God. In the New Testament (with the exception of Mark 3:9 and Matt. 7:14) it always has this connotation. Again, like "necessity," "tribulation" appears in the Old Testament, in a Jewish prophetic-apocalyptic context (cf. again the LXX translation of Zeph. 1:15, in which the term "tribulation" appears in tandem with "necessity" or "fate"—as of course it does elsewhere without apocalyptic connotations, cf. Job 15:24; Ps. 25:17; 107:6, 13, 19, 28; it is used in a historical-political sense in Joel 2:2, cf. Matt. 9:27). And, as with the term "necessity," "tribulation" is applied not only to the "nations" but also to Israel (in a suprahistorical, transcendent sense in Dan. 12:1), a feature reflected in apocalyptic and rabbinic Judaism,[53] and finally warped to the parousia of Christ (cf. Mark 13:19). Unlike the term "fate," however, "tribulation" accents the human situation arising from that activity of God, and may thus be applied to the existence of the Christian community, victimized by the world's hostility to its attachment to Christ. Paul can even describe the Christian's suffering as the "sufferings of Christ." That is, the mode of the risen and exalted Lord's appearing in those who are his assumes the shape of tribulation, persecution and death (cf. 2 Cor. 1:5; Phil. 3:10; 2 Cor. 4:10f.)—and all of it set within the context of the "end of days." Thus, far from intending to spare the Corin-

Chapter 7 *1 Corinthians*

thians "worldly troubles" deriving from marriage as such, Paul seeks to lessen the extent or degree of their tribulation, a tribulation occasioned, though not caused, by marriage, since its cause lies elsewhere. The "fate," the "tribulation" are an inevitability, marriage or no.

If the "necessity" or "tribulation" has its origin in God, and is thus inevitable, its severity can be lessened by heeding the apostle's word. The little phrase, **I would spare you** in v. 28 reflects a self-consciousness scarcely matched by anything else Paul writes in defense of his person or office. A prophet could speak in the name of the Lord, could promise escape from God's judgment, but only on condition the inevitability of that judgment merely appeared to be so. And whether or not the prophet actually believed his word would be heard and heeded, thus the inevitable rendered evitable, did not at all affect his understanding of himself as merely speaking in God's stead, as announcing what God would or would not do, but never as part or component of that action or omission himself. Paul sees the "necessity," sees it as inevitable, unavoidable, holds out no prospect of avoiding it, but conceives himself as capable of lessening, attenuating, lightening, easing the inevitable. Aside from whatever inferences may be drawn respecting the psychology of such an assertion, the explanation with which Paul leaves his readers is that he regards himself, his office, his apostleship, as part and parcel of the eschatological event culminating in the visible revelation of the glory of Christ. Together with the "necessity," the "tribulation," the "woes" and "footsteps of the Messiah," Paul regards himself as a phenomenon of the "end of days." (The history of theology yields at least one parallel to this massive self-understanding—Luther's self-appraisal contained in his 1545 preface to Daniel. Commenting on the prophet's unfulfilled prediction of the end of Antiochus IV in 11:44—"but tidings from the east and the north shall alarm him"—Luther writes:

> Jan Hus was a forerunner of this time, when he preached to them in the Spirit and said, "You are going to roast a goose [Hus means goose], but a swan is coming after me, and you won't roast him."

Commentary *Chapter 7*

And so it happened. He was burned in the year 1416 [sic]. The present conflict began with indulgences in the year 1517. . . . This is the last time, our time, in which the gospel has filled the place with sound. . . .)⁵⁴

The counsel of the apostle is thus attended by a dialectic. Distinct from a word of the Lord, it is not to be set down as mere advice, since uttered by one who is not mere prophet or seer, but sign of the end. This is the dialectic veiled by what appears to be merely self-deprecation, modest comment in 7:25 ("I give my opinion as one who by the Lord's mercy . . ."), or 7:40 ("and I think that I have the Spirit of God"). It is not sufficient to state that Paul's understanding of himself and his mission are rooted in apocalypse. He believed himself to be a sign of the end.

The Reason Why (7:29-31) **I mean, brethren, the appointed time has grown very short; from now on, let those who have wives live as though they had none, and those who mourn as though they were not mourning, and those who rejoice as though they were not rejoicing, and those who buy as though they had no goods, and those who deal with the world as though they had no dealings with it. For the form of this world is passing away.** The verses are replete with rhetorical devices. In the Greek of vv. 29b-30a, each clause begins and ends with the same word (the rhetorician's symplectic—"having," "mourning," "rejoicing"). From v. 29b onward, each clause contains an antithesis ("having" and "not having," "mourning" and "not mourning" etc.). There is a heaping up of the conjunction ("and . . . and . . . and," etc.); use of paranomasis (**deal** and **no dealings** in v. 31 belong to the same word-stem, but are assigned separate meanings), and rhythm (e.g., dactylic tetrameter in vv. 29b and 30a). The verses are a relief, worked out from the surface surrounding them. The instances of such carefully honed pieces are many and varied in Paul's letters. This renders all the more surprising Paul's own disparagement of his rhetorical gifts, as well as that of his detractors (1:17; cf. 2 Cor. 11:6, "Even if I am unskilled in speaking," and 2 Cor. 10:10, "For they say, 'His letters are weighty and strong, but his bodily presence is weak, and his speech of no account' "). The criteria for judgment, whether of Paul or his detractors, cannot have been matters of form or style. Paul's omitting to speak "with eloquent wisdom" had nothing of the quality of a counsel of despair, of transforming a necessity into a virtue, but reflected a conscious decision ("I decided to know nothing among you . . .," cf. the remarks on 2:2). His lack of skill obviously did not prevent his achieving some measure of equality with his competition: "I think that I am not in the least inferior to these superlative apostles. Even if I am unskilled in speaking, I am not in knowledge; in every way we have made this plain to you in all things" (2 Cor. 11:5-6). And as for his opponents' estimate of his rhetorical skills, Paul flatly refused to concede it, and responded: "Let such people understand that what we say by letter when absent, we do when present" (2 Cor. 10:11). Such statements no doubt reflect a certain amount of pique, and the irony in his self-appraisal can hardly be missed, but if the Corinthians were wise enough to perceive it, the criterion for judging his powers of speech should have lain in Paul's deliberately distancing himself from the rhetors of his time, even from those of his own religious persuasion, whom he dubbed "peddlers of God's word" (2 Cor. 2:17)—a judgment similar to the Stoic's attack on the sophist, with pretty speeches hallooing and hawking his lack of conviction from every porch or forum in the Graeco-Roman world. From the perspective of the Corinthians, impressed by such peddlers, Paul appeared as "a shallow worldling."

In these three verses, the apostle sails as close to a fundamental principle in Stoicism as anywhere else in his epistles. **Let those who have wives live as though they had none,** reads like a page torn from Epictetus's handbook for beginners. All throughout that little "catechism," the old Phrygian bachelor urges the novice to disengagement (*ataraxia*), to a refusal to allow his peace of mind to be disturbed by things under his control, and to ignore such as are not:

> Just as on a voyage, when your ship has anchored, if you should go on shore to get fresh water, you may pick up a small shellfish or

little bulb on the way, but you have to keep your attention fixed on the ship, and turn about frequently for fear lest the captain should call; and if he calls, you must give up all these things, if you would escape being thrown on board all tied up like the sheep. So it is also in life: If there be given you, instead of a little bulb and a small shellfish, a little wife and child, there will be no objection to that; only, if the Captain calls, give up all these things and run to the ship, without even turning around to look back. And if you are an old man, never even get very far away from the ship, for fear that when He calls you may be missing.[55]

The Stoic has often been maligned, accused of a lack of sympathy for his fellow creatures. True, the "cosmopolitanism" of the Stoic was more or less a Greek affair; he could never completely own that not merely the Greek but also the barbarian could be a neighbor, the "other." But with that restriction noted, the obverse side of his disengagement read: "Don't be a burden to others" (*apatheia*—impassibility). It was disengagement in mutuality, in community, that spelled virtue. The difference between the Stoic's and Paul's calls to disengagement is that for Paul it is required by the **present distress,** by the "tribulation" preceding Christ's appearing, all sharpened in that word **time** (*kairos*)— God's time, the time set and appointed by God in which faith and unbelief are possible, a time to which God has set the terminus (**the . . . time has grown very short,** literally, "has been shrunk"). Or, as Paul concludes this little reprise, **the form of this world** (better translated the "shape" or "form of appearance of this world," in contrast to the phenomenon itself as expressed in the shape, and for which Paul and the Greeks reserved the term "form") **is passing away** (cf. 1 John 2:17).

So the reason for all this counsel is that tomorrow is here; the "woes," the "footsteps of Messiah" are discernible in the here and now; the Day of the revelation of Christ is as close to the present as God's finger to Adam's in Michelangelo's ceiling of the Sistine Chapel. The time within which faith, hope, and love are possibilities for the world is shrunk, and Paul sees it all, because he is part of it all. Perhaps, tucked away in that reference to the world's losing its shape Paul expresses hope for the world, since the world as such, the world as God's, the "form" of the world, the worldness of the world is not passing away, but whatever gives expression to the worldness of the world is fated for replacement.

Concerning the Unmarried (7:32-35) The verses are composed of two times two antithetical double-lines or dystichs: **The unmarried man** is contrasted with **the married man;** the one **anxious about the affairs of the Lord** with the other **anxious about worldly affairs.** For the one, those **affairs** spell life or service for the sake or pleasure of the Lord, for the other for the sake or pleasure of his mate. Such a "divided" man is then contrasted with **the unmarried woman** or virgin whose concern for **the affairs of the Lord** is undivided—her goal that she be **holy,** dedicated to God **in body and spirit**—and in turn contrasted with **the married woman** who is concerned **about worldly affairs,** that is, how she might **please her husband.** The reference to the married man or woman is not merely descriptive but prescriptive, pejorative. The phrase **how to please** (vv. 33-34)—already hinted at in vv. 3-5—constitutes preoccupation with **worldly affairs,** and thus creates division (v. 34). All this Paul sets under the rubric of "care," and from which he would set his readers free (v. 32; cf. Matt. 6:25, 27-28, 31, 34; Luke 12:22, 25-26). Following the double antithesis, Paul further states his intention: **I say this for your own benefit** (v. 35). The term translated **benefit** appears frequently in Paul, and is always used in reference to the life of the community, thus better translated "common good." It is not a good for which the community takes the initiative (cf. 12:7; once more a reflection of Paul's self-consciousness as participant in the divine activity?). At the conclusion of v. 35, Paul further defines that "benefit" as **good order** and **undivided devotion to the Lord.** Let the translation "good order" stand. It is a Stoic term denoting decency, decorum, manner, etiquette—something Paul never regarded as superficial, to be set down to mere habit, but as signal of one's attitude toward the world and the neighbor, the other (cf. 14:40). But the translation "undivided devotion to the Lord" limps and falters. The phrase belongs to that context to which "necessity," "tribulation," the "time" and the reference to the cosmos's losing its shape also belong, and thus gives the reason for such harsh prescriptive statements in vv. 32-34. It should be translated "constant waiting for the Lord." So then, the imminent parousia of the Lord necessitates nonalignment. The **form** ("shape") of the cosmos—to which the state of marriage belongs—"the things of the world" are "passing away" (cf. Luke 20:34-36). Any other posture courts dividedness, and as for "good order," the implication is not that marriage is indecent, indecorous, an offense against good manners. Paul had already stated that those who marry do not sin (v. 28; he will state so again in v. 36), and writes once more that his counsel is not tantamount to a command from the Lord ("not in order to throw a noose about you," v. 35, is twin to the concession in vv. 2, 7, 9, etc.). "Good order," decorum, marks the external and outward shape of the community's incessant attendance upon the Lord's appearing. It is the appearance of the Lord imminently awaited which determines the mode or how of existence. Use, then, spells virtue for Paul; use for the Lord and the other, the neighbor, matched to the Lord's appearing. And whatever appears to match it Paul will embrace—Jewish, Greek, pagan (cf. 9:19-23)—and run the risk of being slandered as taking his agenda from the world. The little result or purpose clause in v. 35 puts the case clearly and succinctly: "Good order," use for the other, and incessant waiting for the Lord—the one in the service of the other, the other in control of the One.

Concerning the Engaged (7:36-38) This section has been subjected to several curious interpretations. According to one, the subject of the activity described is not the virgin or the betrothed, but the young woman's father, resulting in the following translation of v. 36: "If a parent supposes he behaves in unseemly fashion toward his virgin daughter by preventing her marriage, and she is too obviously a candidate for it [i.e., 'overripe'], let him do what he will, he does not sin, let him give her in marriage"

Chapter 7   *1 Corinthians*

(the imperative "let them marry" thus altered from the plural to the singular). In vv. 37-38, then, the parent who is moved to a contrary action is described as doing as well or better than the parent described in v. 36. In another reading, the subjects of the action are the man who is unable, and the man who is able, to keep the vow of mutual virginity with his betrothed. The one does not sin; he "does well" by cohabiting with his partner, but the other does better by keeping his pledge. The first interpretation depends upon a strict differentiation between two Greek verbs for "marry," according to which the one in the active voice implies its object ("to give [or 'offer'] someone in marriage"), while in the passive it does not. The distinction cannot be maintained. The second interpretation appears to be influenced by a reading of v. 27 ("are you bound to a wife?") as referring to "spiritual betrothal" or "companionate marriage" (cf. the NEB translation of vv. 36-39). The questions arising from this interpretation (e.g., Whom shall the man referred to in v. 27 marry, his "spiritually betrothed"? Whom shall the woman marry? Would Paul suggest that the man give his spiritually betrothed to another?), and which have led some to elect the first interpretation, are resolved if we keep to the simplest, least troublesome reading: The man in v. 27 is a married man; the man in verse 36 is betrothed (cf. the RSV), and the references to his **wishes** or **desire** in vv. 36-37 are to sexual desire.

Verse 36 reiterates the concession in vv. 2, 7, 9, 11, 12-13, 15, 28 (with the exception of vv. 2 and 7, the concession is introduced by the conjunction "if" and the indicative or subjunctive mood, in the first instance assuming the reality of the premise, in the second a hypothetical condition). Again, it is clear on which side of the issue the apostle stands. The contrast between the engaged male (behaving "shamefully" toward his "virgin" who is "overripe," and constrained to marry) and the engaged male, **determined . . . in his heart,** under no constraint (**being under no necessity**—the latter term used in a noneschatological sense here), **his desire under control,** is obviously to the advantage of the latter. The former does not sin if he marries. In face of his lack of constraint he **does well.** (The contrast between this apparent word of approval and the total lack of encouragement in v. 2, "because of the temptation to immorality, each man should have his own wife . . ." is occasioned by the fact that here a pledge to marry is involved; cf. Luther's remarks concerning the man pledged to a woman, and who takes another to bed; if that pledge was not made behind his family's back, it remains in force.)[56] On the other hand, the man who keeps his fiancee as **his betrothed** (literally, "his own virgin") does **better,** the only proviso that he do so **in his heart,** that is, through clear reflection—a phrase used twice of this man (nothing is said of the woman's decision in the matter), thus accenting the proviso. If the fiance who marries is prompted to do so for reasons which appear only human and "natural," but which Paul will not detach from the activity of God (cf. v. 7), the clear reflection of the fiance who does not marry must involve an assessment of his charism—the action of either occurring in light of the imminent future.

Concerning Widows (7:39-40) Here Paul apparently addresses himself to the woman whose mixed marriage has become so intolerable that she contemplates divorce. Paul writes that she is **bound** until her **husband dies,** sharpening what he had written in vv. 8-10. In the event of his death, the apostle consents to the widow's remarriage, provided it be with a Christian (**only in the Lord**), but again gives higher status to singleness, nonengagement, nonalignment. The chapter ends with the frame or inclusion, **and I think that I have the Spirit of God** (cf. the remarks on v. 25).

Chapter 8

Most probably following the Corinthians' "sheaf of questions," Paul advances to the further problem of eating meat offered to idols. The question is moot whether or not every meat market in the ancient world received its products from temple sacrifice. (In Rome, the market adjoined the sacred precincts; was that true also of Corinth?) But wherever such was the custom, the heart,

Chapter 8 *1 Corinthians*

lungs, and other portions of the viscera, in which the "spirit" of the animal was thought to reside, were reserved for Zeus, Hera, Aphrodite, and the other occupants of the pantheon, while the ribs, rump, shoulder, and other cuts were left to human consumption. The question seems to have evoked hot debate in Corinth, accompanied by considerable sloganeering, at least on the part of those who laid claim to a "knowledge" which rendered harmless banqueting on flesh once offered to idols. The slogans are not too difficult to detect. Paul recites them: **all of us** (i.e., all the 'enlightened') **possess knowledge** (v. 1; cf. vv. 10-11); "there is no idol in the world" (cf. the RSV: **an idol has no real existence**) . . . **there is no God but one** (v. 4)—each preceded by that familiar phrase **we know.** The term used in v. 9 and usually translated "authority" or "power" (RSV: **liberty**) may also refer to a slogan opted by the "liberal" party. In addition, the term **weak** (cf. vv. 7, 9, 10, 11, 12) may not have been Paul's choice at all—his choice being **the brother** (v. 11)—but rather an epithet hurled by the enthusiasts at individuals on the wrong side of the argument (Paul retains the epithet for his own purposes also in Romans 14-15). The reference to the man of "weak conscience," who is **encouraged** by the example of the liberal to eat meat offered to idols (v. 10), suggests that the problem did not arise among Gentile- and Jewish-Christians or "Judaizers" who continued to observe the dietary laws, since the latter would scarcely trade an injunction of Moses for aping pagan practice, whether done by Christians or not. Yet, it is not inconceivable that some Jews, once having come to faith, completely broke with their tradition and ranged themselves on the side of the "strong" (note that the description of the "weak" in Romans 14 is also not applicable without remainder to Jews).[57] If the account of the founding of the Corinthian community in Acts 18, however scanty, deserves credibility, the congregation was multiracial. More, contrary to popular opinion, in the earliest Christian communities, two Jews, armed with knowledge of the Law and the Prophets were the equal, if not the superior, of 200 Gentiles, lately converted from a paganism whose variety equals the multiplicity of sects in the modern world. Not all Jewish Christians were nomists, and not all Gentile Christians antinomians. Corinth was not Galatia.

The Thesis—Negative (8:1-3)

Now concerning "sacrificial flesh" (**food offered to idols**): **we know that "all of us possess knowledge."** Suddenly, Paul joins hands with that vocal minority in Corinth which had preened itself on its knowledge, its *gnosis* and *sophia,* and which he had leveled in 1:18 through 4:21 with the announcement that God had turned the tables and rendered such *sophia* of no account by his own *moria* or folly, the message of the Christ crucified, and whose inconsistency reflected in practices which belied its wisdom he scorned with that incessant "don't you know? . . . don't you know?!" It is the first time Paul unequivocally takes the part of the party of the "strong" (unless 1:5 can be interpreted in the same fashion). Till now, reference to his allegiance has only been oblique: "All things are lawful for me" (6:12; cf. 10:23). Of course, this declaration of allegiance is freighted with irony. The mood reflected in chap. 4 is on him again, but it will not mar the argument to follow: **"Knowledge" puffs up, but love builds up.** Despite the character of the phrase as maxim or slogan, it cannot be used in a portrait of Paul as an enemy of reason, or of his fixing the criterion for truth in subjective feeling. Paul was not a despiser of the mental processes—at least not the Paul who would later write, "Finally, brethren, whatever is true, whatever is honorable, whatever is just, . . . think about these things" (Phil. 4:8), gathering up into that summons everything that commended Graeco-Roman learning and culture; nor the Paul who plundered that culture for its virtues and, in harmony with the old tradition he had inherited, assigned to reason the capacity for deducing the power and deity of God, to abuse which capacity he described as guilt (Rom. 1:18ff.), nor the Paul who could describe the world as held together, engulfed by the wisdom of God (1:21a).

Verses 8:1b and c (**we know that "all of us possess knowledge." "Knowledge" puffs up, but love builds up**) do not comprise an antithesis. The contrast is between a knowledge which leads to arrogance, that is, a knowledge of God as one, of idols as nonexistent, a knowledge which reckons the eating of flesh offered to such nonexistent things as a badge of liberation from superstition, thus of superiority, and that very same knowledge in the service of love. If till now Paul has counseled the Corinthians not to take the initiative for entanglement or alignment, at this point his counsel will be quite the reverse—"engage, align!"

If anyone imagines that he knows something (the verb is in the perfect tense—has known and still knows, owns what he knows) **he does not yet know as** "it is necessary" (RSV: **he ought to know** [v. 2]). Note the exhausting use of the word **to know.** Again, this is not a jibe at rationality, nor does it hide a claim to a higher *gnosis* which sets Paul apart from even the elite at "Corinth," as does perhaps 2:6ff. Again, the subject is the *use* of knowledge, the shape which reasoning takes in relation to the other, the neighbor—"he does not yet know *as, how, in what manner* it is necessary to know!" The comparative conjunction receives the accent.

How then is it "necessary to know"? It is necessary to know, not that one knows, but that one *is* known—**but if one loves God, one is known by him.** Should not the sentence read, "If anyone loves God, he knows what he needs to know," or, "love is the 'how' of reason"? Was it not, after all, the "practical," the "moral" or "religious" stage at which everything that Kant wrote aimed, a stage prepared for in his description of the limits of reason? Reason in the service of love! But surely nothing higher or even more durable than love; nothing that love could be in the service of; nothing that could antedate or supersede love? "As for knowledge, it will pass away," but love "abides," is "the greatest of these" (13:8, 13)! Love for God and the neighbor—the heart and core of the Law and the Prophets (Mark 12:28-31; Matt. 22:35-40; Luke 10:25-28; Rom. 13:8-10, etc.)! Paul makes it clear—love is no more without derivation, dependence, or origin than reason with which God suffused the cosmos. "But if any one loves God, he has been known by him." The perfect tense here—"is known" or "has been known"—is not a mere substitute for the present. If in v. 2 it denotes a knowing already acquired and still possessed, so also here in v. 3. That one who loves God has already been and is still known by God. There is something higher than love, something which antedates love, from which love takes its origin, in which love is rooted, or it cannot "build up," cannot be the superior of a knowing which leads only to arrogance. Love "builds up" and love "abides," not because it has eternity in itself, but in God, in God's knowing before ever there could be love, in God's knowing as its spring or source.

The contrast in these initial verses is not between knowledge and love. If Paul is not an enemy of reason, neither is he a romantic. The choice, for him, is not between knowing and loving, between Kant, Hegel, and Goethe. The contrast is between two kinds of knowing. The one kind needs an object, something outside itself, something already there, already in existence—the world, things, other persons—waiting to be known, qualified, listed under categories ("weak" and "strong," "wise" and "foolish"). It is dependent (no "I" without corporeality, without the world and the other). It may be tempted to imagine that it is the actor, subject or initiator of its knowing. But that is only because it assumes it was there before whatever was waiting for it to know existed. For the other kind of knowing, there is nothing that already had to exist before it could know it; nothing waiting to be known, waiting to summon up its knowing. It needs nothing separate from itself to jar it into awareness of itself, to an awareness of the difference between itself and what it knows. Quite the reverse, this kind of knowing creates what it knows. The one kind of knowing is human; the other is God's. And just as human knowing needs something already in existence which can serve as object of its knowing, so human love needs something already in existence which can attract it to itself, needs an object which possesses some quality, some goodness to commend it. Such a love renders the lover merely passive, a reactor, a reagent ("We love, because he first loved us," 1 John 4:19). But God's love is an active thing. It needs nothing with some quality to commend

Chapter 8   *1 Corinthians*

it. It runs ahead of, precedes, is prior, antecedent to what it loves, makes it out of nothing: "But God shows his love for us in that while we were yet sinners Christ died for us" (Rom. 5:8). For this reason, love has its source in God's knowing, in God's loving—with God, to know and to love are the same; Paul could as well have written, "if anyone loves God, he has been loved by him"—or it is not love. Love is merely another name for God. And it is not only that God's knowing or God's loving is distinguished from human knowing or loving because it creates an object for that knowing or loving. If the knowledge or the love of God needs no object to arouse it, summon it up, if it creates what is to be known or loved, once what is known or loved by God is created it does not then become an *object* of God's knowing or loving, somehow separate from that knowing or loving, but rather a sharer of his life. There is no object with God, no separation between himself and what he knows and loves, so that he could identify himself apart from what he loves or knows. Not because he is identical with what he knows or loves. How could he be if he created it? But because God is love, and will not be a subject with an object, will not allow separation between himself and what he knows or loves. He will rather endure the threat of a negation in himself before he will make an object of what he has created to know and love. He will divide *himself* into subject and object, to be one with what he knows and loves. "But when the time had fully come, God sent forth his Son" (Gal. 4:4).

So, "it is necessary to know, not that one knows, but that one is known, and for this reason, on this account, love God." And how can one know such a thing; how can one know that one is known and thus love God? "It pleased God through the folly of what we preach to save those who believe" (1:21). It is faith in the word of the cross by which this God, this being known is disclosed, or through which love for this God becomes possibility, faith which gives shape and content to love.

The Confession—Positive (8:4-6)

Hence, as to the eating of food offered to idols, we know that "an idol has no real existence" and that "there is no God but

one" (v. 4). After stating in negative fashion that thesis or principle in light of which the problem or question should be viewed, Paul now proceeds to state it in positive terms, drawing on a confession of faith. But before doing so, once more he joins hands with the libertarian party, repeating its slogan: "We know that 'there is no idol in the cosmos . . . there is no God but one.' " The phrase has a catechetical ring. Could the libertarian party merely have mouthed a phrase from prebaptismal instruction of Gentiles? "There is no idol in the world"—the expression is odd, but it is a thoroughly Jewish invention. The Jew used the term "idol" not only to designate the image of a deity, but also to designate that deity itself. Hundreds of times, the LXX uses the term to denote an entire series of pagan deities. The word reflects a deduction from the presence of images in heathen rites and cultus to the total absence of reality in such worship. It is weighted with scorn and contempt: The pagans worship idols; these idols are truly their gods, which means they have no gods at all. Not even Greeks who abandoned their gods had such a comprehensive term for what the Jews called *eidolon*, No-God. "We know there is no Zeus, no Hera, no Athena, no Isis, no Osiris, no Serapis—none at all—there is no God but one" (cf. Deut. 6:4, etc.). Paul now moves to the confession proper:

For although there may be so-called gods in heaven or on earth—as indeed there are many "gods" and many "lords" . . . (v. 5). The first part of the sentence is easy enough to grasp. There are suns and stars and Caesars which are *called* gods (**although**— the reality of the premise assumed), and all the way from Assyria, Babylonia through Brutus's and Antony's conqueror, Augustus, who first stamped *divus* on his coins, to Paul's own time. But in the second part of the sentence, Paul seems to take with the right hand what he had removed from the left: **as indeed there *are* many "gods" and many "lords."** The phrase hides a concession, if not to the existence of pagan deities, then to those who still imagine they exist. (Note the use of *kyrios*, "lord," in Paul's designation of heathen deities.) But before he addresses himself to

Chapter 8 *1 Corinthians*

the plight of those "believers," he plays a variation on the theme struck in v.4:

Yet for us there is one God, the Father, from whom are all things and for whom we exist, and one Lord, Jesus Christ, through whom are all things and through whom we exist (v. 6; note the symmetrically constructed parallelism in the verse). This confession has its parallels throughout the New Testament (cf., e.g., Rom. 4:25; 11:36; Acts 17:22ff.; Eph. 4:5f.; 1 Tim. 2:15; Col. 1:16f.; Heb. 2:10, the songs in Revelation 4–5, etc.), its counterparts in the Old Testament, and its roots in the worship of the Jewish and Christian communities. It was worship, and confession as its integral part, which first welded fact or historical occurrence (the journey through the sea, the return from exile, the event of Christ) to its interpretation, and so intimately that the one could never again be without the other—the first prohibiting the interpretation from dissolving into myth, and the second prohibiting the fact from dissolving into naked data. It was worship, Israel's and the church's, which explains the peculiarity and uniqueness of the biblical genre developing from it, and which has thwarted attempts to detach the one from the other with any degree of certainty. Paul here draws on the content of worship and its confession, perhaps among Christians converted from paganism, though the term **Father** is the Greek equivalent of an invocation first used among Jewish Christians—"Abba," later appropriated by Gentiles (cf. Rom. 8:15ff.). He uses a portion which applies to his argument vis-à-vis paganism, i.e., the confession of the one origin of all that exists (**from whom are all things**), and of the one mediator by which all that exists came to be (**through whom are all things**). There can be no mistaking this credo's allusion to the participation of the preexistent Christ in the creation of the world. But if Paul is at all responsible for identifying such mediators in Jewish (or Greek) speculation as the "Word," "Wisdom," "Spirit," or the archetypal "Man" with the Messiah Jesus, it was not the consequences for cosmology resulting from such identification that interested him. In his hands, Philo's "Word" or the Stoic's "World-Reason," "Wisdom," or "Spirit," that "artificer of all things" in Wis. 7:22, had all been hammered to the shape of the crucified.

Thus, first of all, the mediator is referred to according to his historical, saving activity—**Jesus Christ**—and according to the title he received at its completion: *Kyrios*, **Lord** (cf. Phil. 2:9ff.). Secondly, in addition to gathering up his Corinthians on both sides of the argument in that initial **yet for us,** he adds a phrase designating God as the destination of the believers' life—"and we for, to, towards him" (so the Greek at the end of v. 6)—and designating Jesus Christ as the means of their present existence: **and through whom we exist.** The citing of the confession and Paul's additions are not "filler." The extract from the confession reiterates (though this time in positive fashion) the slogan of the Corinthian "scientists," with which Paul agrees, and the supplements (again, in positive fashion) create the context within which the question raised by the community respecting eating sacrificial meat must be set: "We have a common destiny, and we are all held together by the same Lord." The scene is set. The thesis, negatively, and in the words of the libertarian party; and the confession, positively, in the words of the worshiping community but warped to the Corinthian setting, have fixed the context within which Paul engages the problem.

Weak and Strong (8:7-13)

"But there is not knowledge among all; rather, some because of custom till now of the idol [RSV, **through being hitherto accustomed to idols**] eat [meat] as offered to an idol, and their conscience, being weak, is bespotted." How can one be a Christian, and acknowledge the existence of other gods? How can a conscience, informed by the word which declares that there is but one God, and that any other deity is nonexistent, be besmirched or endangered by eating flesh sacrificed to a nothing? Did the libertarians raise such questions, in which case their *gnosis* (**knowledge**) had its "orthodox" side? If the libertarian party was represented not merely by Gentile Christians but also by Jewish Christians, this is not impossible. But it is more probable that these Corinthians derived their practice with respect to eating sacrificial meat less from any fixed theological position regarding the nature of God than from notions of the world and everything in it, hence of the corporeal as indifferent, of no consequence, a tenet of that "wisdom" they had gained. Paul's argument, then, is not an apology on behalf of monolatry, i.e., worship of the one God despite recognition of a host of other gods. It is a defense of the "weak," of Christians lately arrived from paganism, for whom such banalities as eating and drinking could still become an occasion for reverting to their pagan past. Significantly, Paul makes no reference to the apostolic decree reported in Acts 15, in which Gentiles are enjoined to abstain from "pollutions of idols and from unchastity and from what is strangled and from blood" (Acts 15:20). Either he did not know of it, or intentionally avoided it.

"But meat will not cause us to stand [RSV, **commend us**] before God. Neither if we do not eat do we lack, nor if we eat do we abound" (v. 8). This little sentence contains a cluster of anaphoras and epiphoras. **Commend** in the RSV has juridical overtones, so that the clause could be translated, "exculpate before the judgment." Paul will repeat the argument in Rom. 14:3-4, and explicitly in the context of the final judgment:

> Let not him who eats despise him who abstains, and let not him who abstains pass judgment on him who eats; for God has welcomed him. Who are you to pass judgment on the servant of another? It is before his own master that he stands or falls.

Then he will conclude, "for the kingdom of God is not food and drink" (Rom. 14:17). But unlike Romans, in which both parties to the dispute are addressed, here Paul speaks only to the "strong."

Only take care lest this liberty (literally, "authority") **of yours somehow become a stumbling block to the weak** (v. 9). **This liberty of yours**—with that little demonstrative following the possessive pronoun, Paul distances himself from his addressees as sharply as he had done in 4:8ff. (Cf. the same usage in the mouth of the elder son, and the response to it in the mouth of the father, in Luke 15:30 and 42.) The warning is not merely against temporarily disadvantaging the "weak," but against furnishing the occasion for their reversion to paganism. Who would suppose the mere business of eating could have such fateful consequences? **For if anyone sees you, a man of knowledge, at table in an idol's temple,** "will not his conscience, which is weak, be encouraged [literally, 'built up'—the term used ironically] to eat what has been sacrificed to idols?" (v. 10). Paul is heating up his argument. He intentionally names the most serious case imaginable, that of eating sacrificial meat in a temple, and not merely in a private home. Further, he has moved from the first and second person plural "we" or "you" (vv. 1, 4, 6, 8, 9), or from the indefinite pronoun "anyone" (vv. 2, 3, 7) to the second person singular—"you." The move is a device for capturing the hearer, who till now has imagined that he could hide in the crowd of addressees, or that nothing said so far has applied to him. This device, too, belonged to the style of oral argument in Paul's day, and is used frequently in his letters (cf., e.g., the second person singular address in Romans 2, following the liberal use of the third person plural in the description of the debaucheries of Gentile paganism in chap. 1: "Therefore, you have no excuse, O man, whoever you are . . ."). The addressee is not only trapped, but roughly handled—his own slogan is hurled into his teeth: "You who have knowledge." If the term **weak** is not Paul's but a concoction of the Corinthians, and if that word translated **encouraged** (but better rendered "built up") is borrowed from the Corinthians' training program for the "weak," the irony in Paul's question is trebled. There is a further move here. The reference is not simply to eating flesh once sacrificed to pagan gods but to alimentation while reclining **at table** in pagan temples. Among the Jews, participation in pagan sacrificial meals was strictly forbidden as 'Aboda Zara, a type of idol worship. Even the consumption of wine which might conceivably be brought to the sacrifice of libation was forbidden. In orthodox Judaism, the prohibition has been retained till now. Of the Gnostics, Irenaeus wrote that

Chapter 8   1 Corinthians

> the "most perfect" . . . make no scruple about eating meats offered in sacrifice to idols, imagining that they can in this way contract no defilement. Then, again, at every heathen festival celebrated in honour of the idols, these men are the first to assemble.[58]

The reference to "weak conscience" occurs three times in this chapter (vv. 7, 10, 12). Whether from the Corinthians' or Paul's perspective, the definition of "weak" is given in v. 7a: "Because of custom till now of the idol" (**hitherto accustomed to idols**). That is, **some** at Corinth are unable to translate what they share with the "strong"—the knowledge that there is no God but one, and that the pagan deities are a nothing—into actual practice, into the eating of sacrificial flesh, without damage to **conscience.** Why Paul should be concerned for **conscience** arises first of all from his understanding of existence as governed by norms or criteria according to which actions are approved or disapproved (**conscience** is derived from the verb meaning "I know together with," i.e., together with the norm). That norm may be autonomous, derived from a person's own observation of the world. It may be utterly selfish, relating to whatever gives one pleasure or pain. The norm may be something imposed upon the person from without and submitted to—custom, convention, the habits of society, laws. The norm may not even be unitary, integrated, comprehensive, but a congeries of criteria, in which case, judged by the norms according to which others behave, a person may be said to have "blind spots" respecting race, color, sex, etc. When a community of persons finds itself in the circumstance of agreeing to a norm, for whatever purpose and however derived, a self-governing society is born, committed to act in accordance with the common criteria such as "life, liberty, and the pursuit of happiness." In the course of time, that common norm may demand reinterpretation or application. Thus "legislation" arises, and its concomitant in a body of judges established to determine whether or not such reinterpretation is in harmony with the letter or spirit of the norm. Such "happy" societies did not exist in Paul's day. The societal norms of his day were heteronomous, imposed—Caesar, the *pax Romana*. But if this spelled lack of consent or agreement required of a democratic state or republic, it did not spell the absence of norms. The ancient world was aswarm with moralists, calling their audiences to embrace in common criteria which should guarantee wholesome, happy existence. To "act against conscience" thus meant to offend against the norm by which one's action could be approved, and to suffer a "bad conscience" meant to carry about the disapproval of that action in one's consciousness. In this one, formal respect, in respect to human intention or action as functioning according to a norm, as a "knowing together with," Paul did not differ one whit from his pagan contemporaries, though he may have differed from some who conceived "conscience" as a material substance, together with "heart," "mind," or "spirit" comprising the parts of which the individual was the sum. The difference between Paul and his contemporaries was material in nature, having to do with the *source* or *origin* of those norms or criteria according to which persons behave. For Paul the source was not "nature" or "nature's God"—a phrase in the American Declaration of Independence which would have thrilled the heart of a Stoic—but the God of Abraham, Isaac, and Jacob. And whether or not the norm was expressed in codified law such as the Torah of Moses among the Jews, or consisted merely of intuitions of good and evil as among the Gentiles, it was this God who had revealed his will in such "knowing together with" and by it would judge all flesh (Rom. 2:12-16). In essence, it was at this point that Paul differed from the party of the "strong" at Corinth. By warning the "strong" and taking up the defense of the "weak," he categorically denied the right of any person to establish his own criterion for approving good or evil, and whether by precept or example (**for if anyone sees you . . .**) to impose that criterion on others. If the "strong" were "strong in conscience," that strength had come from God; if the "weak" were "weak in conscience," the weakness was a refraction of what had come from God, and required to be borne by the strong till the refraction was altered to a true reflection. It is not merely that Paul advocated a Christian humanity which allowed the other to be what he is, or that he did not conceive conscience as setting one before an ideal norm (Conzelmann on the passage). Paul's charity was sprung from a recognition of God as the author of conscience and from what that God had done.

For by your knowledge this weak man is destroyed, the brother for whom Christ died (v. 11; note the parallelism: **destroyed/died; weak/brother; by your knowledge/for whom Christ died**). What was implicit in the credo of v. 6, and into which Paul gathered both weak and strong, is now made explicit in the phrase, **for whom,** on whose account, **Christ died.** That saving historical activity upon whose completion Jesus was acknowledged as Lord, consisted in his death (the fact), a death "**for** . . ." (the web of interpretation about the fact). It was by means of this event ("through whom," v. 6b) that all should share a common destiny in God ("for whom," v. 6a), and thus exist not as weak or strong, but as "brothers." To deny the relationship of brother by acting as master of another's conscience, i.e., by playing God to the other, meant denying the universality of the condition which required that event—who needed to die for the strong?! ("for the word of the cross is folly to those who are perishing," 1:18)—denying the commonality in destiny achieved through it, and finally denying the event itself and its author.

Thus, sinning against your brethren and wounding their conscience when it is weak, you sin against Christ (v. 12). **Therefore, if food is a cause of my brother's falling, I will never eat meat, lest I cause my brother to fall** (v. 13). The Greek has a double negative in v. 13, coupled with the phrase "for ever." Semitic or not, in translation the words can only be done justice in their repetition: "I will never, never, not ever eat flesh. . . ." The section in vv. 7–13 is infinitely harsher than in Romans 14–15, in which Paul engages a similar problem, and concludes with a reference to Christ as prototype of what Christians should be to each other (Rom. 15:1-2). The reason lies in the Corinthian situation itself, or in what Paul had heard and deduced from it, a situation he could not assume was matched at Rome, though the problem itself may have been universal in all his churches. We have no clue to the situation among the Christians at Corinth except

Commentary *Chapter 9*

through the letters of its apostle. But the irony, even the sarcasm threading all through this section ("we know," v. 1: "we know," v. 4; "this liberty of yours," v. 9; "you, a man of knowledge," v. 10; "your knowledge," v. 11) suggests a stimulus sufficient to Paul's response. It is not the first, and will not be the last time Paul will take off the gloves with his Corinthians.

Chapter 9

In his preface to 1 Corinthians of 1530, Luther writes of chaps. 8–12 that Paul "everywhere . . . forbids the strong to despise the weak, since he himself, even though he is an apostle, has refrained from many things to which he really had a right."[59] The tensions between "weak" and "strong" clearly furnished Paul an occasion for citing his own example. But the sudden alteration of mood, the heat and passion steaming up from this chapter, the questions full of defense (cf. also the ubiquitous "don't you knows" at the commencement of the sections, vv. 13ff. and vv. 24ff.), the heaping up of the pronouns in the first person (18 times), the use of verbs in the first person (31 times), all this concentration on the self—equalled only by the second epistle— makes clear that Paul had more in mind than setting an example for the strong toward the weak. There was more afoot in Corinth than dismemberment of the congregation through party spirit, more than a laying claim to a superior knowledge which spurns the corporeal alignment, more than libertinism. Whether because of it, or whether Paul may have appeared to occasion it, hand in hand with the tension and division at Corinth went a challenge to his apostleship, thus to his authority.

In this chapter, Paul passionately replies to the apparent charge that by maintaining himself financially he gave evidence of his own insecurity respecting his apostolic authority. A true apostle would have accepted a salary, would have regarded remuneration for his activity as his sacred right, and not have punctured his week with tanning hides for tents. Not out of any upper-class Greek or Roman disdain for manual labor, not from Levitical precedent (Num. 18:31), nor from that of the Jewish mission in the Diaspora, but because Jesus himself had instructed his comissioners and disciples to take salary for their preaching (Matt. 10:5-10; Luke 10:1-8). In Thessalonica, Paul's behavior furnished no pretext for calling his apostleship into question. On the contrary, it served as an example to the "idlers." In writing to the Thessalonians, Paul's reference to his waiver of rights (1 Thess. 3:9; the same term, "authority," occurs five times in our chapter, in vv. 4, 5, 6, 12, 18) is not a defense, but an aside. The situation at Corinth was vastly different. No one there had sold the farm to wait for Jesus on the nearest hill.

Opening Salvo—The Claim to Apostleship (9:1-2)

Am I not free? Am I not an apostle? Have I not seen Jesus our Lord? Are you not my workmanship in the Lord? (v. 1). In the Greek, the particle translated **not** is a heightened negative, and in the interrogative awaits an affirmation: **Am I not free?** Certainly! **Am I not an apostle?** Absolutely! **Have I not seen Jesus our Lord?** No doubt of it! **Are you not my workmanship in the Lord?** Obviously! Each assertion in the sentence is in tandem with the next, so that each stands or falls with the other. If free, then an apostle; if an apostle, then having seen the Lord; if having seen the Lord then you are my work in the Lord. But for Paul's detractors the connection between his freedom and his apostleship was not at all obvious. Indeed, it was Paul's peculiar notion of freedom which called his apostleship into question, which rendered problematic what he regarded as its basis (**have I not seen Jesus our Lord?**), as well as the concomitant of that apostleship in the foundation of the Corinthian community (**are you not my workmanship in the Lord?**). If a wedge could be driven between those first two assertions, the rest would fall like a house of cards—if not free, then not an apostle, then not, etc. . . .

If to others I am not an apostle, at least I am to you. For you are the seal of my apostleship in the Lord (v. 2). The statement compresses what precedes into what the occasion rendered most vulnerable—Paul's apostleship, and, as a result, the authenticity of the community founded by him. Further, the statement does not express what is, but what should be (then **at least . . . to you**). If the community at Corinth had clearly recognized its own existence as the validation (**seal**) of Paul's apostleship, there would have been little need for the defense which follows.

The Rights of an Apostle (9:3-7)

The two legal terms translated **defense** and **examine** in v. 3 conjure up a courtroom scene in which Paul appears as defendant, and his detractors or opponents as judges and examiners. In 4:3, Paul had already written that it was a "very small thing" to be "judged" (the same verb translated **examine** here) by the Corinthians or by any other "diet," adding, "I do not even judge myself." Has the apostle changed his tune? The statement made in connection with the first section requires qualification: It is not merely Paul's apostleship which is at stake here. Actually, where he himself is concerned, the title "servant" or "steward" would suffice (4:1), or even "apostle last of all" (4:9; cf. 15:9). All this heat and passion, all this wearying use of the first person, and in first position—it all has to do, finally, with his kerygma, with his proclamation of the Christ crucified, and on which the life of the community depends. What is so intriguing regarding Paul's self-assertions in this epistle is that they lie at the heights as well as the depths (cf. 15:8). But it is important to note within what contexts those "highs" or "lows" are reached. Conceding, for the purposes of debate, Paul's vulnerability to personal pique (he could have said with Shylock, "If you prick us, do we not bleed?"), those contexts in which Paul's "egoism" is most evident and least attractive always have to do with what he preaches—in ecclesiastical terms, with his "office" (cf. e.g., Gal. 1:1, "Not from men nor through man, but through Jesus Christ"). It is when what Paul preaches is challenged, attacked, or doubted that his self-assertions go beyond the bounds of propriety, precisely because the man and his office have become indivisible. And when what Paul preaches is challenged, what has resulted from that preaching is under suspicion: "Am I not an apostle? . . . are you not my workmanship in the Lord?" It is not merely that the apostle and

Chapter 9   *1 Corinthians*

his kerygma have become indivisible; the apostle and the Corinthians are one flesh.

To return to the defense: Rather than beginning with the explanation as to why he has waived his apostolic right to financial support (the very action which had thrust his apostleship in doubt), Paul opens with citing what it is to which an apostle is entitled, and in a barrage of questions which likewise demand the affirmative: **Do we not have the right to our food and drink?** Of course we do! (v. 4). **Do we not have the right to be accompanied by a** Christian **wife** (in the Greek, "a sister wife"), **as the other apostles and the brothers of the Lord and Cephas?** Absolutely! (v. 5). Our statement regarding Paul's "defensiveness" requires further qualification in light of his move from "I" to "we." There is another defendant in the case: Barnabas, Saul's entree to the Jerusalem community (cf. Acts 9:26-27) and to the church at Antioch (cf. Acts 11:25-26), his companion on the "first" missionary journey (Acts 13–14), and his co-referent at the Jerusalem conclave (Acts 15). Whatever "sharp contention" had arisen between them earlier (Acts 15:37-39) did not deter Paul from including him as one more "apostle" who did not teach for pay. The reference to **the other apostles and the brothers of the Lord and Cephas**—each group or person distinguished by the conjunction, and no doubt cited according to advance in rank—indicates that the term *apostle* had not yet hardened into a designation of Jesus' disciples to whom he had appeared and whom he had commissioned following his resurrection (cf. Acts 1:2, 25, 26; but not even Luke adheres to such a distinction; cf., e.g., Acts 14:14, in which both Paul and Barnabas are referred to as "apostles," neither of whom had been disciples of Jesus). Paul, of course, links apostleship to having seen the resurrected Jesus ("Am I not an apostle? Have I not seen Jesus our Lord?"), though he later distinguishes between "the Twelve," "the brethren," and "apostles" among those to whom the risen Christ appeared (15:5-7). To be an apostle, then, required having seen the risen Christ, though not all who saw him were apostles.

Commentary *Chapter 9*

Paul's question in v. 5 reflects a practice in clear contrast to that of Jesus' disciples during his earthly ministry (with the possible exception of Cephas [Peter], who was married prior to Jesus' call, cf. Mark 1:30-31). Others, apparently, did not share Paul's conviction that the "present distress" and the imminent return of Christ urged undivided attention to "the affairs of the Lord" in the celibate state. In view of the financial conditions prevailing in earliest Christianity, enjoyment of the companionship of wives while on their travels (the Greek reads, "to lead about a wife," with the accent on the prefix "about"; the verb is not used pejoratively, as though "the other apostles" had their partners by a noose) spelled an imposition for their hosts, yet, curiously enough, an imposition from which, in Corinth at least, they inferred the integrity of their guests. For Paul, this new practice represented the extreme of apostolic authority in such matters. Paul could claim title to the same extreme, but against the background of chap. 7, could hardly have regarded his celibacy as a waiver of rights. For this reason in what follows he returns purely to the matter of working with his hands to earn his own keep: **Or is it only Barnabas and I who have no right to refrain from working for a living?** (v. 6). Then follow references to military and agricultural custom, by analogy reinforcing Paul's right. (It would be almost 2000 years, in a part of the globe of which Paul will never hear, when officers and enlisted men in grey will go to war at their own expense and take their own arms and horses home after Appomattox.)

Torah Support (9:8-11[12])

Paul's "scriptural" support in vv. 9-10 consists of an exposition of Deut. 25:4 (v. 9), and a quotation (v. 10) whose source is unknown, though assumed to be Sirach (cf. 6:19), a book which the Jewish community did not include in its canon of Scripture. What is significant is that Paul could call his own peculiar interpretation of a passage in Deuteronomy **the law of Moses,** and support it from an apocryphal writing. Yet even in this respect Paul was not unlike his Jewish contemporaries. For years, if not centuries, the rabbis had proceeded according to the rule that whatever in "Scripture" referred to purely mundane matters was not merely capable of being interpreted in terms of the higher, spiritual life, but that it actually urged, required such interpretation. The support for such a procedure did not lie in a notion of Torah as something entirely at one's disposal, of the "Bible" as a book to be treated as one pleased. However vulnerable the theory, and however capricious its application may finally have turned out, the support for such exposition lay in the concept of Torah as divine, transcendent, as God's, and thus as too lofty to be confined to a single reading, much less to a single reader or interpreter. One Hassidic author writes:

> Until the wise [i.e., the scribes] research it, the Torah is not complete, but forms only one half, and only through their researches does the Torah become a complete book. For the Torah is interpreted in each generation according to the needs of just this generation, and God illumines the eyes of the wise, so that they perceive in his Torah what corresponds to this generation.[60]

If the Jews were a "people of the Book," they were also a community of interpreters. No scripture was a matter of private interpretation (cf. 2 Peter 1:20, an eminently Jewish concept). For this reason also, precedent, appeal to the community of readers in the past as reinforcing contemporary exposition, played such a great role among Jewish interpreters. And for this reason also, not merely the content but also the form of Jesus' preaching devastated the exegetes of his day: "You have heard that it was said. . . . But I say to you . . ." (cf. Matt. 5:21ff.). He made no appeal to precedent.

The seven rules of Torah-interpretation which Judaism assigned to Hillel included "from the easy to the hard," and of which Paul again makes use here: **Is it for oxen that God is concerned? Does he not speak entirely for our sake?** (vv. 9b-10). And, in harmony with another principle of interpretation (no word of Scripture is to be read in isolation but always in relation to another), Paul cites the Scripture of doubtful origin to reinforce the contention that the word about oxen is actually about human beings: **Because the plowman should plow in hope** . . . more, that it actually applies to himself and Barnabas. But, as if his readers were unable to take in at one gulp the interpretation of Deut. 25:4 as ultimately referring to Paul and his coworker (an interpretation which to his opponents could only appear as labored) he leaves the "scriptural" evidence behind, and in another move from the "hard to the easy" appeals to his activity among the Corinthians as establishing his apostolic right: **If we have sown spiritual good among you, is it too much if we reap your material benefits?** (v. 11). And in the same move he ends with a comparison unfavorable to his allies or his enemies: **If others share this rightful claim . . . do not we still more?** (v. 12).

In v. 12b, Paul turns to the matter of his behavior which had occasioned the challenge to his apostleship, thus, for him at least, to his kerygma and to the community's integrity, as well as to the reason for it: **Nevertheless, we have not made use of this right, but we endure anything rather than put an obstacle in the way of the gospel of Christ.** Simple logic would require Paul's continuing this line of argument, his pressing toward reasons for waiving his rights and thus throwing his status in doubt. But his fire will not out, the passion will not down. He interrupts his thought and again takes up the topic of apostolic rights, this time by reference to Levitical practice, and to a divine command which should settle the matter for good and all.

Levitical Practice and the Word of the Lord (9:13-14)

Verse 13 comprises a parallelism. **Those who are employed in the temple service** (in the Greek an over-conciseness, "those who work the temples") is equivalent to **those who serve at the altar** (the expression in the original is more cultic in flavor— "those who wait upon the altar"). The phrase **get their food from the temple** (literally, "eat the things from the temple") is equivalent to the phrase **share in the sacrificial offerings** (in the Greek, "share in the altar"). "Thus also the Lord commanded those preaching the gospel to live from the gospel" is still another overconcise expression for **should get their living by the gospel.**

Do you not know? The inference to be drawn from the question is that Paul not only expects his readers to recall matters essential to faith and life, but also such historical-liturgical details (relating to a single, discrete religious community) which to any modern reader would appear arcane. Who remembers Num. 18:8,31; or Deut. 18:1-3? Were Paul's Gentile congregations aware of, or expected to be aware of, Old Testament law? And would the Corinthians be able to see the analogy between the privileges of priests and Levites and that of Paul or Barnabas? The argument appears to limp. At first sight, it could better have preceded the interpretation of Deuteronomy, and thus taken its place in an entire sequence of arguments moving from the "easy to the hard." But if the adverb in v. 14 (RSV, **in the same way**) counts for anything, the opposite is true, despite the digression in v. 12. The "lesser" of Levitical practice was notches above the "lesser" of animal husbandry. It related specifically to human beings in the service of what lay at Israel's heart and core, its worship of God. If "Moses" could be interpreted to read that preachers had a right to their keep, then when he did so state explicitly, he furnished an analogy to one greater than himself who commanded that "those who preach the gospel should live from the gospel" (cf. Matt. 10:10; Luke 10:7—a word in which Jesus commanded his disciples not to mix the message of the kingdom of God with money matters; cf. also Gal. 6:16). So the arguments move on an ascending scale, after all. Paul's passion was controlled, and the Jesus-tradition settled the matter. There was no higher authority to which to appeal. So much for rights!

Paul's Waiver of Rights and its Purpose (9:15-18)

There is an anacolouthon in v. 15b. Paul does not complete his sentence. He begins, **I would rather die than,** breaks off, then begins again, "no one shall empty my boast." The RSV leaps over the gap (**I would rather die than have any one deprive me of my ground for boasting**), but the words to be supplied should read, "I would rather die than make use of these things." Now, after heaping up all the evidence securing the right of an apostle to his keep (evidence from military custom, from agriculture, from the Torah, from Christ himself), Paul states that he has waived that right, made no use of it. But it was crucial that his right be established, entirely apart from the use of it, since his apostleship stood or fell with it, at least for those who had concluded from his waiver that he had none. The words "I have not written these things that it should be so with me" in v. 15b pertain to his use of that right, not to that right itself, as the initial sentence in v. 15a makes clear. (The little conjunction translated **nor** in the RSV would thus be better translated, "so, so then . . ."). But with all the suspicion which his waiver of rights occasioned, with all the doubt it cast on his apostleship, and as a result, on the integrity of the congregation he had established, with all the personal injury it appears to have brought him, it could not tip the scales against what Paul would never let go: "No one shall rob me of my boast!" Obviously, that "boast" could not lie in anything perceptible to the Corinthians. How could it, when Paul had offered up to it everything to which they could point and say, "there, there is the true mark of an apostle!" Whatever the boast, it rendered him a poor second to "the other apostles and the brothers of the Lord and Cephas," a poor trade for Moses and the command of Christ. And, whatever that boast, it had nothing to do with what Paul himself did, with something to which he himself could point and say, "There, there is the true mark of an apostle, no matter what others suppose!" Verses 16 and 17 make that clear. Paul's preaching, his activity, gave him nothing of which to boast. It was all a necessity, an inevitability (cf. the remarks on 7:26) "laid" on him, a requirement apart from his own volition, his own choosing, and to neglect which could only mean his ruin: **Woe to me if I do not preach the gospel!** (v. 16b). So if there is no choice—"preach or be damned"—where is the **reward**, where is the **boast**? (The two terms **reward** and **boast** are all but synonymous here; to suggest that the reward is distinguished from the boast as supplying the reason for the boast—

the RSV translation of "boast" as **ground for boasting** in vv. 15 and 16 leans toward such a distinction—this gives the term **reward** a nuance Paul would never have conceded.) **Just this,** writes Paul, "that I preach the gospel free of charge, and thus make no use of my rights given me in the gospel" (the use of the preposition together with the definite article and the infinitive, translated **that** in the RSV, need not denote a result or purpose clause).[61] If to preach was a necessity, an inevitability, if Paul had no choice but to preach, he still had a choice. He could affirm the necessity of it, could concur in the inevitability of it, could say yes to it with all his heart, could reckon it as a "necessity of immutability." Or, he could refuse to concur in it or affirm it, could submit to it as against his will, reckon it as a "necessity of compulsion." But if he could say yes to it, then he could act to make that yes concrete, could make his destiny the object of his love, in contrast, say, to the Stoic, who comforted himself with his inner freedom in face of cosmic fate or accident. And how would Paul's yes appear, once it took on hands and feet? It would assume the shape of a waiver of rights, a sacrifice, a thanksgiving. This is what Paul will never let go, and which he was convinced the use of his rights could only endanger—his concurring in, his yes to, his choice of, his deciding for the inevitable, his thanks! "No one shall rob me of my thanks!" Whatever shape others' thanks would take—he would not legislate for them—this was Paul's. But if, as this apostle believed, the risen Christ made his way in the world in those who were his in the shape of suffering and cross (Paul's curious notion of "reward" or "boast") his thanks was suited, fitted; it comported with that persuasion.

> But because the sacrifice consists in what God gave us and has about it the crystalline necessity of the divine will, it becomes a business of joy. . . . The sacrifice itself is not carried out with groaning but crowned with joy, and is part of our blessedness. For it is thanksgiving.[62]

All Things to All Men (9:19-23)

Now, after establishing his rights, and his right to waive his rights, Paul returns to the theme of freedom struck in v. 1 (cf.

Commentary   *Chapter 9*

8:9-13): **For though I am free from all** . . . (v. 19a). The Corinthians had supposed that the freedom derived from their "knowledge" was the freedom to live as nonaligned, to regulate their existence as independent and self-contained. There was nothing new or surprising in that notion. The Stoic's call to "endure" assumed there were things beyond one's control—fate, the ineluctable and inevitable. But if it was a call to endure, it was also a call to "renounce," to deny whatever of thought, willing or action sprang from unbridled impulse or passion. So if one could not control or dispose of what lay outside or beyond the self, beyond existence, one could nevertheless control or dispose of existence itself. That "could" spelled freedom, a freedom rooted in nature, and made concrete in action. In the Corinthians' terms, though perhaps not in the Stoic's (still, the early founders of Stoicism were an acidic, exclusivistic, even cynical lot) it meant despising, regulating, legislating for the weak, putting them through their hoops. Paul's understanding of freedom was as much athwart the common, popular definition as his idea of reward or boasting. The dialectical sentence of v. 19, **though I am free from all men, I have made myself a slave to all,** forms the thesis of this little section; it is echoed in the opening lines of Luther's *Freedom of the Christian* ("a Christian is a free lord over all things and subject to no one. A Christian is a servant of all things and subject to everyone"). The verses which follow make clear precisely in what Paul's freedom and slavery consist, and what purpose they serve. **To the Jews I became as a Jew.** The words reflect nothing of race or pedigree, not because Paul could not "become" what he already was—a Jew. The parallel in v. 20b, **to those under the law . . . as one under the law,** makes that eminently clear. For Paul, what distinguished Jews from all others was an orientation of existence about codified law, believed to be given from the Creator himself through the hand of his instrument, Moses, interpreted and applied to contemporary existence by the prophets which followed him, and in obedience to which lay salvation. For Paul, Judaism was not a racial, but rather a historical or religious community, gathered about the Law in temple or synagogue.

Chapter 9   *1 Corinthians*

Paul could hardly have referred to his having "lost" what he had in Judaism had he thought otherwise (cf. Phil. 3:1-8). His later references to Judaism seem to contradict that contention, until we note that such references are most often attended by a qualifier (e.g., "my kinsmen according to the flesh," i.e., according to definitions which exclude the divine initiative; cf. Rom. 9:3, in the RSV incorrectly translated **by race**). And the reference to the Jews as "God's people" is not intended to conjure up the idea of bodily descent, but quite the opposite—the idea of God as holding together a spiritual community established by him, despite its rejection of the Messiah, thus despite having lost every *earthly* reason for existence (cf. Rom. 2:29; 9:8 against Rom. 11:1ff.). In the face of Gentile and Jewish definition of Jewishness as denoting race, Paul adheres to his definition of the Jew as one "under the law." To the one under the law, then, he "became" as one "under the law." Among Jews he observed the rules, rites, and ceremonies prescribed by the Torah which constituted them Jews. But he did so with one proviso—**though not being myself under the law,** that is, without acknowledging such observance as guaranteeing status before God. Thus, what for the people gathered about the Torah in temple or synagogue represented an end was for Paul only a means. It is no accident, of course, that Paul first mentions what he became to the Jews, and then only what he became to those on the other side of the Torah. In the divine economy, Judaism had the advantage, though that advantage accruing to it derived from the sovereignty of God who chose it to be a "light," and not from pedigree. In v. 21, Paul continues: **To those outside the law I became as one outside the law,** that is, among Gentiles he behaved as though Moses had not existed, as though there were no codified law with centuries of its exposition or application. But again with the proviso: **Not being without law toward God but under the law of Christ.** It would be fatal to interpret this clause as identical to the phrase **under the law** in v. 20, as though Paul had merely exchanged one external authority for another. Rhetorical considerations aside (the formulation **under the law of Christ** is occasioned by the parallelism), by use of the phrase "under the law of Christ" Paul refers to his relation to God through Christ as to a sphere or power within which he has been caught up, and which exercises as much if not more compulsion upon him (cf. v. 16) as did the Law of Moses. (Weiss translates the phrase, "rather bound to Christ in law," stating that the genitive "of Christ" accents relation to the person; cf. Weiss on 9:20.) To *this* compulsion he was able to give consent, to give thanks through his waiver of rights. To the other he could not— not "would not," but *could not*—give consent. Not because the Law did not demand such consent; it did so. And not because the Law was something that did not deserve such consent; it did so. If Freud saw in the Law only curse and not blessing; if the moral requirement appeared to him only as prohibition, as a feeling of guilt, as punishment,[63] Paul was not one for whom the term *Law* was pejorative. "Law," "Torah," "commandment," "requirement," were good words. Paul could not give to the Law what it required or deserved, because the Law had been forced into an alliance with the "flesh," with historical existence in which the self was bound, fated, doomed to be for itself, intent, bent, enslaved to nonalignment—either apart from God, hostile to God, at enmity with God, or with God, using God as a means of establishing itself, its right, its safety. For the apostle, the inevitable consequence of such alliance was sin and death (Gal. 2:16; 3:10-12, 19, 22; 5:4; Rom. 3:9-20; 7:5-23, etc.). Christ had appeared in order that the one whom the Law desired, for whom the Law had waited, could appear—one who could love God with heart, strength, and mind. So it was God who had rendered life by judicial decree provisional, had rendered temporary an existence in which the Law could only summon up an external compliance, until faith should appear by which the Law could be established. Paul was neither a nomist nor an antinomian. What drew his fire from the one quarter was the assumption that doing the works of the Law availed with the God who had sent Christ to call to faith those who should do his will, thus nullifying the very Law it struggled to observe. The nomists were in reality antinomians. And what drew Paul's fire from the other quarter was the assumption that faith gave it carte blanche, diplomatic immunity, and thus refused God the obedience which faith should yield, in the end nullifying the very faith it claimed to uphold. The antinomians were in reality nomists, bound to the tyranny of the self as criterion for thought, willing, and acting:

> Doing the works of the law and fulfilling the law are two very different things. . . . To fulfill the law . . . is to do its works with pleasure and love, to live a godly and good life of one's own accord, without the compulsion of the law. This pleasure and love for the law is put into the heart by the Holy Spirit. . . . So it happens that faith alone makes a person righteous and fulfills the law. . . . Oh it is a living, busy, active, mighty thing, this faith. It is impossible for it not to be doing good works incessantly. It does not ask whether good works are to be done, but before the question is asked, it has already done them, and is constantly doing them. Whoever does not do such works, however, is an unbeliever. He gropes and looks around for faith and good works, but knows neither what faith is nor what good works are. Yet he talks and talks, with many words, about faith and good works.[64]

To the weak I became weak. The verb **became,** introducing the single sentence in vv. 20-21, is now repeated at the head of the sentence in v. 22, embracing the "weak" on either side of the Torah, those **under the law** and those **outside the law.** To what extent Paul had accommodated himself to those of "tender" conscience, at least in the matter of eating, he had already demonstrated in chap. 8, and will again, in chap. 10. The purpose for this activity is given in the repeated **that I might win . . . in order to win** (vv. 19, 20a and b, 21, 22), intensified in the **that I might . . . save some** in v. 22. Win whom, save whom? **The more,** the majority (v. 19); **some** (v. 22)—not all. There were limits set to Paul's activity, not merely by his own humanity. The summing up of his activity and his purpose in v. 23 ("I do it all for the sake of the gospel, that I may share in its blessings") makes clear that Paul's winning and saving were tied to his obedience to his fate, his own necessity, which meant to the one who had commenced, circumscribed and fixed the limit to his ministry (cf. 4:19; 16:7). It was God, after all, who had determined the "more." It was left to Paul to be a Jew to the Jew, as outside the Law to those outside, and to the weak—in or outside the Law—as weak.

But if Paul's freedom could not be construed in terms of Polonius's advice to Laertes ("to thine own self be true, And it must follow, as the night the day, Thou canst not then be false to any man"), then, clearly, it had to be a self, a freedom for the other. Then freedom lay in alignment—with the Jew, the Greek, and the weak. And if Paul's slavery could not be construed as mere accommodation, then clearly that waiver of rights, that consent, that surrender of the self for the other had to derive from a prior bondage—**I do it all for the sake of the gospel**. . . . Both that freedom and that slavery would be misunderstood, misinterpreted. Both would be construed as issuing from historical accident or circumstance, even from preoccupation with the self—not merely once, but 100 times over. When in the 1930s the church prepared to apply to itself a paragraph of German law prohibiting non-Aryans from occupying positions of responsibility in the Third Reich, more than one Christian appealed to 1 Cor. 9:19 as encouraging accommodation to historical circumstance, in this case, to a "separate but equal" position for Jewish Christians. The slavery and freedom would be misconstrued, since both took their character from what to the world could only appear as folly, "the word of the cross." But it was that word which enabled a Jewish preacher to abandon all considerations of race and pedigree and preach to Aryans, enabled him to stand beyond Judaism and Hellenism and unveil the position of both Jew and Greek before God—there, where there was no longer Jew or Greek.

> When Paul became a Jew to the Jews and a Greek to the Greeks, that really does not mean that he preached to the Jews what the Jews wanted to hear, and to the Greeks what sounded agreeable to them. He preached the crucified, to the Jews a scandal and to the Greeks foolishness.[65]

The Apostolic Discipline (9:24-27)

With yet one more "don't you know," Paul concludes the argument which began with asserting his rights and continued with the reason for waiving those rights, and moves toward the de-

Chapter 9   *1 Corinthians*

scription of his activity—all of it warped, bent, oriented to, and rooted in his service to the gospel (note the refrain at the close of each main section: "the Lord commanded that those who preach the gospel should get their living by the gospel," v. 14; "that in my preaching I may make the gospel free of charge, not making full use of my right in the gospel," v. 18; "I do it all for the sake of the gospel," v. 23. The refrain reappears by implication in v. 27: **lest after preaching to others I myself should be disqualified**).

The Greek of vv. 24-27 may be translated thus: "Don't you know that those who race in the stadium all run, but one obtains the prize? So run that you obtain [v. 24]. And everyone who competes abstains in everything; these, then, so that they obtain a perishable wreath, but we an imperishable [v. 25]. So, here is how I run, not uncertainly (as though no one knew what I was after), and this is how I box, not punching the air [v. 26]; but I give my body a black eye [RSV: **I pommel my body**] and make it my slave, lest somehow, after I have preached to others, I myself should be worthless" (v. 27). The Corinthians were no strangers to figures drawn from the games. The Isthmian contests of Corinth were second only to those at Olympus. All that reference to abstinence (v. 25; RSV: **every athlete exercises self-control,** a pale second to a word which implied 10 months of forgoing the "hair of the dog" and wenching till the wee hours), to boxing, punching the air, giving the body "a black eye" (v. 27)—it was all the argot of a town which had invented the gladiatorial combat.

If any had the notion that everything Paul had written thus far applied to him alone (**only one receives the prize**), v. 24 dispelled it: **So run that *you* may obtain!** With all its heat, apology, defense, and rationale, with all its personal reference and use of the first person singular, the argument had kept one eye on the reader, on the Corinthians with their rights, their freedom. In the end, it was all one long, loud call to "be imitators of me!" to do it "all for the sake of the gospel," the word of the crucified who had died to end all division between Jew and Greek, weak and strong.

Any other way than this (Paul will return to this "way" again in chapter 13) spelled worthlessness, being a "castaway," as the old KJV reads (this time the figure is taken from commerce and banking, from the minting of coins and disposing of bad pennies). "Run, train, aim the punch, hit the body where it hurts—under the eye—make it your slave. That body has a future—the prize, the wreath! [6:13b-14]. By the gospel, in the gospel, for the sake of the gospel, fall clean and bright from the mold!"

Chapter 10

The chapter is composed of three similar sections. In each a specific question or assumption is addressed. The first section deals with the question of the sacrament as guaranteeing immunity (vv. 1-13), and is introduced by Paul's reference to information which both he and his readers share—in this instance, knowledge of Israel's history: **I want you to know, brethren** . . . (v. 1). The second section treats the question of participation in the heathen cultus (vv. 14-22), and is met with an imperative construction: **Therefore, my beloved, shun the worship of idols** (v. 14). The third deals with the question of eating meats sacrificed to idols (10:23—11:1), and is introduced by Paul's recitation of the slogan: "I can do everything" (RSV: **all things are lawful,** v. 23).

In each of the three sections, the introduction is followed by reference to the paradosis (tradition). In vv. 1-13 the reference is to Israel's history, summarized in the quotation from Numbers 14 and Exodus 32. In 10:23—11:1, the reference is to Psalm 24 (which perhaps belonged to the liturgy of the ancient autumnal festival, its mid-point the celebration of Yahweh as king). In the second section (vv. 14-22), Paul appeals to the paradosis of the Lord's Supper. The references to **cup** and **blood, bread** and **body** in v. 16, as well as to **drink the cup of the Lord** in v. 21 are the Pauline "logarithms" for the Supper. They were not the apostle's invention, but derived from what he had received, and which he describes in 11:23 as "from the Lord." This "shorthand" is reflected in all three synoptic accounts of the Supper, which draw

Chapter 10 *1 Corinthians*

on a tradition antecedent to Paul. And the logarithms have their trajectory in the postapostolic period, for example, in the Dialogues of Justin Martyr.[66] The point is worth noting, since 1 Corinthians 10 is an instance in the New Testament in which what is "from the Lord" is raised to the level of Scripture. For this reason, section two (vv. 14-22) lacks any reference to the Old Testament.

In each section, imperatives occurring with varying frequency follow the citing of the tradition, and in each instance a final reference is made to God or Christ. In v. 13, the reference is to the faithfulness of God who will not allow temptation beyond one's strength to endure; in v. 27 it is to the God who is jealous for his honor; and in 11:1 appears the injunction to imitate Paul just as he is an imitator of Christ. The latter is not an appeal to an imitation according to which one retains some measure of autonomy over against God, but has its context in what Paul elsewhere writes of Christ as the subject of existence and activity. What is significant here is that in analogy to his raising the Christian paradosis to the level of Old Testament Scripture, Paul gives to the risen and exalted Lord the place reserved for the Father in sections one and two.

The organizing principle in each of the three sections is the paradosis or tradition—the Old Testament, or that which is "from the Lord." That principle does more than furnish a focus or perspective for Paul's discussion of the problem—it is something he hurls into the debate which is calculated to end the matter. Paul thus uses the same remedy in chap. 10 as he had applied in chap. 4 to the Corinthians' sitting in judgment on each other ("not beyond what is written," v. 6). And, in chap. 11, Paul will set the paradosis against the confusion created by the Corinthians' refusal to distinguish their own feasts from the Supper.

The Sacrament Does Not Guarantee Immunity (10:1-13)

The Story of Israel (10:1-5)   For what purpose precisely, this narrative from Israel's history? Again Paul leaps to a discussion whose occasion we can only infer (cf. 6:1ff.; 9:1ff.), but which appears to have gone beyond the eating of meat sacrificed to idols or reclining at table in pagan temples (8:10). Such actions led Paul to champion the cause of the weak, though he left open the possibility of such behavior in the absence of the weak ("if anyone sees you, . . . if his conscience is weak"—conditional clauses, 8:10), though perhaps not for himself ("if food is a cause of my brother's stumbling"—the reality of the premise assumed, 8:13). Such a possibility is not left open here. Paul neither champions the weak nor espouses the tenet of the strong, but simply commands: "Flee idol worship!" (v. 14). To modern readers, such a command to a Christian congregation may appear absurd. But in Graeco-Roman cities and towns idol worship, the veneration of the gods, was not confined to temples. Every municipal event— the games, the festivals, the celebration of victory in war, remembrance of the fallen in battle, holidays commemorating the founding of a city, the hailing of local heroes, pledges of allegiance—to say nothing of affairs taking place in the ordinary household—births, marriages, deaths, succumbing to or recuperating from sickness, employment, or joblessness—it was all attended by invocations and sacrifices to local and state deities. Mere presence at such events spelled participation—there is hardly anything to suggest the Corinthians were actually performing priestly duties!

I want you to know, Paul begins, and proceeds to interpret Israel's wilderness wandering in correspondence with the Christian sacraments: **Our fathers were all under the cloud, and all passed through the sea.** The reader could scarcely miss the correspondence, but if so, v. 2 made it all too clear: **And all were baptized into Moses in the cloud and in the sea.** The cloud, then, was a kind of baptistry. And the reader could scarcely miss the correspondence between the manna and water in the desert and the bread and wine of the Supper: **And all ate the same supernatural food and all drank the same supernatural drink.** It is more or less customary to assume that Paul conceived these events in Israel's past as having sacramental effects, and that from that point drew analogies with Christian practice. Exactly the

Chapter 10   *1 Corinthians*

opposite is true. For Paul, what tied such phenomena in Israel's history to Christian existence was not what those phenomena possessed in themselves independently of anything else, needing only to be recognized or interpreted by midrash. If that were true, then we might expect some hint, some faint clue in Jewish, rabbinic interpretation of Israel's desert sojourn toward such analogies as Paul draws here. If Paul had any precedent for speaking of **our fathers** as **baptized into Moses** (!) we are not aware of it (in a Talmudic legend, God built huts from the cloud for the wilderness wanderers). Where then does the reading, the move, the interpretation, begin—for Paul? It begins with Christ, with Baptism and the Supper. Events now taking place give to Israel's history its sacramental character. Paul's way of reading the Old Testament here, the hermeneutic underlying his interpretation, and preceded by a remark clearly indicating that it is the only one possible ("I do not want you to be ignorant, brethren, that . . . ;" RSV, **I want you to know**) is as daring as anything he writes. Further, it is customary to describe Paul's exegesis here as "typological." Paul himself uses this term in vv. 6 and 11 (in the RSV translated, **as a warning**). But if by "typological" is meant only that occurrences in the life of Israel are allowed their historical integrity, that the persons, places, and events in Jewish history are not allegorized or made to represent something other than themselves, but nevertheless prefigure persons, places, and events yet to come, Paul is not engaging in typological exegesis here. Beyond their historical significance, the cloud and the sea, the desert manna and water from the rock not merely prefigure but actually possess sacramental character—because, Paul writes, "they drank from the supernatural Rock which followed them, and the Rock was Christ." For the expression itself, Paul may be drawing on an old Jewish legend according to which the rock which Moses struck at Horeb or Meribah (Exod. 17:6; Num. 20:7-11) accompanied Israel through its wanderings,[67] but his point is that because Christ was present in Israel's experience, the cloud, the sea, the manna, and water from the rock were to Israel what the water, bread, and wine are now to Corinth—signs of a humanity the Christ would later assume. Because Christ was the rock, because, with all its historical contingency (**baptized into Moses**) he was the true subject of Israel's history—**the Rock was Christ**—whatever occurred in that history told of him. However odd or alien to linear thought which commences with the Old Testament and searches for its fulfillment in the New, as though the New required establishing by the Old and not the reverse, Paul's interpretative "move" is from Christ, from Baptism, from the Supper, from the New back to the cloud, the sea, the manna, and the rock, back to Israel's history, to Moses, to Abraham and the patriarchs, to the Old Testament.

On occasion, Paul will use every tool of the interpreter's trade—midrash, "rabbinic exegesis," typology, allegory, analogy—but in the end always warped to that "move," that presupposition that since Christ is the end of Israel's history, he is also its beginning. It was a "move" which paralleled his own history: "Paul, called by the will of God to be an apostle of Christ Jesus." That "call" required that everything which had occurred to that point—history, genealogy, religion, "Jewishness," experience—be stood on its head, interpreted from the one who had called.

Nevertheless, Paul continues, **with most of them God was not pleased; for they were overthrown in the wilderness** (v. 5). The presence of Christ, the "sacraments" did not guarantee Israel immunity. Had the Corinthians supposed that the sacrament of Baptism, say, by the deed's merely having been done (*ex opere operato*) conferred immortality? Did this notion also belong to Corinth's "wisdom"? Other cults, with their rites of baptism by water or blood promised the initiate rebirth to all eternity, and in Paul's world it was thought the better part of valor to join more than one religious society, since if this deity or that stumbled at death's portal, another might negotiate it, leading his devotees across. (Apparently, initiation into the mysteries of Eleusis unconditionally guaranteed a blessed lot after death. Diogenes sneered that since the thief, Patakaion, had been initiated at Eleusis, he would have a better fate after his death than Agesilaus and Epaminondas, heroes of the war between Sparta and

Thebes.) For such reasons, might it have been of some importance to the Corinthians by whom that rite of initiation was performed, so that parties, factions could develop, each laying claim to a greater security than the other: "I belong to Paul, . . . to Apollos, . . . to Cephas," the one "puffed up" in favor of the one against the other (1:12; 3:4; 4:6)? Whatever the influences upon Corinth from the outside; whatever false conclusions it may have drawn from the preaching of the apostle himself; whatever shape or congeries of shapes its religions may have taken; and whether or not Paul accurately read the situation of this congregation bursting at the seams (1:4-5 was not spoken only in irony)—problems whose solutions are equal to the number of interpreters who attempt them—Paul believed the Corinthians needed to hear that the Christian faith was not a mystery religion which through rites and ceremonies could secure its members against death and the judgment of the gods; that magic had been displaced by faith which required being seized ever anew; that in Jesus Christ they had gained not only a Redeemer God but a Lord and Master whose final appearing charged the present with its urgency.

Warnings for Us (10:6-13)

These things, writes Paul in v. 6, "were types for us." Not the cloud, the sea, the manna, and water from the rock—they were, Paul had said, precisely what they typified ("and the Rock was Christ")—but rather the desert disaster, for which reason the RSV translates: **These things are warnings for us.** Then follows Paul's four-part dirge over Israel's immorality, each part preceded by a warning to Corinth: **Do not be idolaters as some of them were; as it is written, "The people sat down to eat and drink and rose up to dance"** (v. 7). **We must not indulge in immorality as some of them did, and twenty-three thousand fell in a single day** (v. 8). **We must not put** Christ (RSV, **the Lord**) **to the test, as some of them did and were destroyed by serpents; nor grumble, as some of them did and were destroyed by the Destroyer** (v. 10).

Each sentence begins with the conjunctive particle (lit., "and not"). In each, the particle is followed by a verb in the imperative

(vv. 7 and 10) or the hortatory subjunctive (vv. 8 and 9). In each but one (v. 7) the same verb is used twice, first in summons, then in a description of what actually occurred: **We must not indulge in immorality . . . not put to the test . . . nor grumble. . . .** In each but one (v. 7) the judgment follows the action: **And twenty-three thousand fell in a single day** . . . were being **destroyed by serpents** . . . **were destroyed by the Destroyer**. In each the subject of the sentence is **some of them**—"some of them committed immorality," etc. The references in these verses are all to events occurring during Israel's wanderings recorded in Exodus and Numbers, and which flesh out the line in v. 5: "For they were overthrown in the wilderness." The first is to Israel's revelry following its worship of the golden calf (the quotation from the LXX of Exodus 32); the second to the plague following its worship of the Moabite Baal (Num. 25:1,9); the third to the sending of serpents to the Israelites following their complaint against Moses and God (Num. 21:5f.), and the last to the sudden deaths of the spies who brought back discouraging reports from Canaan and set the people to murmuring (Num. 14:2,36-37), or to the earthquake and fire which destroyed Korah, Dathan and Abiram, and the 250 who rebelled against Moses (Num. 16:11-35). Though Paul's sequence does not correspond to that of the chroniclers, it is not from memory at random (in one instance, Paul's memory does not serve: Numbers 25 records that 24,000 were destroyed by the plague, whereas the number of Levites mustered following the exodus totaled 23,000, cf. Num. 26:62). The first two references are to banqueting in honor of the gods—the subject at hand—the last two to murmurings which evoke God's wrath, a theme repeated in v. 22. In Numbers, the second and third references are to punishments meted out indirectly (plague, serpents), the fourth to punishments "before" or "from the Lord" (Num. 14:37; 16:35). In his last reference, however, Paul interposes Satan as agent of punishment. The title **the Destroyer** rooted in a tradition which identified Satan with the angel of death in Egypt (Exod. 12:23 LXX; Wis. 18:25; Jub. 48:2-9; cf. Heb. 11:28). Paul had already made the identification in 5:5 ("deliver

Chapter 10   *1 Corinthians*

this man to Satan for the destruction of the flesh"). From the verb used of the serpents and **the Destroyer** in vv. 9 and 10 (*apollymi*), Aeschylus had derived the name of Apollos, "the Strangler," god of the plague, his symbol the grasshopper—and, since the reign of Augustus, the symbol of imperial Rome.[68] Did Paul make that identification here as well (cf. Rev. 9:11)?

In v. 11, the requiem closes with a repetition of the thought in v. 6, the two verses forming an inclusio or frame. The rhetoric, the repetition, the rhythm, arouse the suspicion Paul may have had occasion to use these words before. But the Corinthians could scarcely have missed the application to themselves, signaled in that **some of them . . . some of them . . . some of them . . . some of them.** At any rate, Israel's sacraments, the presence of Christ, were the very means of its disaster.

At the conclusion of v. 11, the RSV translates: **these things happened to them as a warning, but they were written down for our instruction**. . . . Retaining the moral or paraenetic sense of the term translated **warning** (again, **these things** are not the cloud, the sea, etc. but the disaster), we should translate, "These things happened to them as a warning [sc. 'to us'], and were written down for our instruction" (construing the little postpositive as a conjunction, not as an adversative). This translation preserves for v. 11 its character as inclusio with v. 6. The conclusion of v. 11, **for our instruction, upon whom the end of the ages has come,** is not simply an assertion that since Christ is both the end and beginning of Israel's history, whatever occurred to Israel was spoken of him, and thus of whomever belongs to him—a thought already reflected in 9:9-10 ("is it for oxen that God is concerned? Does he not speak entirely for our sake?"). The accent does not lie on "us," but on what has "come" upon us. The Corinthians are situated at "the end of the ages" (the Greek reads "ends," but the term simply marks the end of a unit, and, as for "ages," Paul was not one for dividing history into periods or epochs). They are already facing the "present distress," the "footsteps of Messiah," and the time for his appearing has been pushed ahead (7:26, 28-29). Their judgment is as near to them as Israel's—

nearer because more certain. The eschatological context in which v. 11 sets Paul's argument gives to it the character of a "how much more," of a move from the lesser to the greater, the "easy" to the "hard": "If such occurred with Israel, how much more with Corinth at the 'end of the age'!" The worshipers of Baal, the murmurers and rebels in Israel were able to entertain some possibility of escape—the rebellion of Korah, Dathan, and Abiram was, after all, in the name of God ("And they assembled themselves against Moses and Aaron and said to them: 'You go too far! For the whole congregation, they are all holy, and the Lord is among them. Why do you exalt yourselves above the congregation of the Lord?'" Num. 16:3). The Corinthians, however, were not: **Therefore let any one who thinks that he stands take heed lest he fall!** Then, as if relenting his harshness, or as if to avoid the interpretation of his warning as calculated to frighten them into appropriate action, Paul adds a promise in v. 13: "This test you face, this possibility of idolatry, of conceiving God in your own image, as a projection of your own willing, thinking and feeling on some grand, cosmic scale; this chance for 'wisdom,' for an understanding of God as designed to actualize your potential; this option to define faith, hope, and love from below, as natural, human qualities, differing from the Christian perhaps, but only in degree; this opportunity for 'religion' is as common to human existence as breathing in and out. And to resist it, is not beyond your strength, because this trial [not 'temptation'] lies within the will and permission of God who is 'faithful,' keeps his promises—Israel made it out of the desert, inherited the land!—and will see to it that the test is matched by an escape, by your ability to endure!" For years, theologians have argued the question as to whether or not Christ's sinlessness derived from an inability to sin (*non posse peccare*), or from his ability not to sin (*posse non peccare*). If Paul had been prone to such artful distinction in regard to Christian existence, he might have chosen the latter alternative. According to Paul, sin was no longer fate. The Christian had been set free. This much the party of the strong understood. The subject for debate was *in what* that freedom should consist, *how* it should be given legs, made concrete. Everything hung on the answer, and, since the Corinthians were at the "end of the ages," there was precious little time in which to give it. If freedom were to be defined from below, as freedom for the self, and even in the name of God, it was an illusion courting disaster. No such freedom exists. This was the "test" which God had allowed—the possibility of idolatry, of living by what did not exist. And this was the promise which God had made—that this "test" could be stood, this possibility could be averted, "escaped."

The Cup of the Lord and the Cup of Demons (10:14-22)

Therefore, that is, seeing that Israel's sacraments did not guarantee immunity; that "it is not the water indeed which does such great things"; seeing that destiny hangs on how one stands the test, **therefore, my beloved, shun the worship of idols.** After joining in this simple sentence a declaration of love and a stiff command, Paul proceeds to demonstrate the illogic of the Corinthians' bizarre behavior: **I speak as to sensible men; judge for yourselves what I say.** What calls for judgment is not whether or not the cup is a participation in Christ's blood or the bread a participation in Christ's body. Paul is neither reflecting upon the tradition of the Supper nor upon a practice in which the sharing of the cup preceded that of the bread (cf. Luke 22:17-20). In Paul's argument the bread appears last for the sake of the idea of the **many** as **one body** in v. 17. (The traditional terminology of the Supper allowed Paul to speak of the community as the body of Christ only by way of the word concerning the bread.) Nor is Paul offering an interpretation of the Supper to which persons of sense would agree. The questions in vv. 16 and 17 assume consent, prior agreement ("it is so, is it not . . .?"). What requires sensible judgment is whether or not that participation in pagan sacrifice involves the "strong" in a radical inconsistency, at least for anyone with eyes to see.

In form, Paul's argument in this section is similar to that in 6:15-17. The nature of the relation between Christ and the believer is of such a kind as to allow no other. But whereas in chap.

6 the apostle stops short of identifying that relation in terms of the "one body," since the primary accent lay on corporeality and its destiny ("for the Lord"), and only secondarily on unity, here the accent on the unity of the believer with Christ and its implications for Corinthian practice moves Paul to the concept of the two as comprising a single organism. By virtue of their eating and drinking, the Corinthians share the blood and body of Christ—not the blood and body of Golgotha. Paul would scarcely have recognized his teaching in a literal reading of the old hymn:

> *There is a fountain filled with blood*
> *Drawn from Immanuel's veins;*
> *And sinners, plunged beneath that flood,*
> *Lose all their guilty stains.*

His references to Christ's body and blood are to the life of the risen one who entered historical existence ending in his death. It is the existence of this one which the Corinthians share. Still, if it is the existence of the risen one who was crucified with whom the Corinthians comprise "one body," it is of equal significance to Paul that that unity not be understood as derived from nature, from an identity of substance which the believers enjoy with Christ. If in Paul's time, the Gnostic notion of the "redeemed Redeemer" had not yet emerged full blown (i.e., the notion that Christ passed through the aeons to waken souls whose body had robbed them of awareness of their true origin and destiny, salvation occurring by the Redeemer's assuming flesh to call souls to consciousness of their identity with God, thus redeeming both himself and his "brethren"), the germ for that idea had long existed. Everywhere there lay the assumption that somehow, in some fashion humanity shared the identity of substance with deity. And it is of equal significance to Paul that the unity between Christ and the believer not be understood as derived from mere rites or ceremonies, as, for example, with the "mystery religions," for which those rites, purely by their having been performed, effected a union with the god.

Chapter 10 *1 Corinthians*

Corinth had just been warned against construing its faith as a mystery religion (vv. 1-13). The words concerning participation **in the blood** or **in the body** signal a discrete, concrete event totally apart from nature, even alien to nature, for which reason nature would always oppose it as "folly," as a "stumbling block" (1:18, 21, 23), a "thought" of God which none but his own Spirit could comprehend (2:11)—the Christ crucified. The true character of this event could not be perceived or corroborated through demonstration, miracle, or sign; neither could it be deduced from observation of the world or human existence ("for Jews demand signs and Greeks seek wisdom," 1:22). It lay entirely outside, apart from human thought or action—the folly was God's (1:25). Therefore the sharing, the participation, and thus the **body,** the organism, the oneness of the many, could not occur on the initiative of the many, but on that of the one who gave his life to share. This is the meaning of v. 17: **Because there is one bread, we who are many are one body, for we all partake of the one bread.** There is one Lord who gives participation in his life in the common loaf. To all this the Corinthians had given their consent, with it they all agreed. But what they ignored was the force of that word "participation," and which led to such inconsistency as could be recognized by the "sensible." Let the Jew then spell "participation": **Consider the people of Israel.** The Jew had earlier served to bolster an apostle's right to support (9:13): "Are not those who eat the sacrifices partners in the altar?" ("Altar" is a substitute for the name of God required by the parallelism.) Is that partnership in the altar capable of division, of extension, of being shared with any other? Is it conceivable that a priest would confuse Yom Kippur with offering a bull to Zeus? Participation means exclusivity—this one altar and no other, this one bread and no other. Then, as if to fend off misunderstanding, Paul repeats in question form the slogan which he had earlier agreed he shared with the strong ("we know . . .," 8:4), a question requiring an answer in the negative: **What do I imply then? That food offered to idols is anything, or that an idol is anything?** As for the ox to Zeus, to paraphrase the words of those profane medieval monks, "ox you are and ox you will remain," and as for Zeus or anyone else in the pantheon, he is a nothing. This time, however, there will be no apology for the weak who cannot shrug off their superstition—"But some, because of custom till now of the idol, eat food as really offered to an idol" (8:7). This time there is no relegating of the matter to the sphere of the indifferent ("We are no worse off if we do not eat, and no better off if we do," 8:8); this time no conditional clauses ("if anyone sees you," 8:10). This time there will be no appeal from the summons ("shun the worship of idols") for either strong or weak in the proposition that "an idol has no real existence," and "there is no God but one" (8:4). This time the issue is participation, or a division of participation which the nonexistence of gods does not render harmless. For "what they sacrifice" (the oldest manuscript witness to 1 Corinthians reads, "what the Gentiles sacrifice") **they offer to demons and not to God** (or, as the Greek allows, "and not to a god"). **I do not want you to be partners,** sharers, **with demons** (v. 20). For Paul, then, beneath the nothing, beneath those nonexistent gods lay something for which the nothing could serve as stand-in, surrogate, for which those gods could be a means by which the nothing could effect a sacramental union—dark and hostile powers, unidentifiable with the sum total of human wickedness, intent on enthralling, destroying. Both the Jew and the Greek had been in their grip, and for both the attempt at dividing what could not be divided, the attempt at *koinōnia,* participation, partnership in this one body, this one bread and at the same time in another, whether Law or pagan practice, spelled a radical inconsistency whose consequence could only be a slavery to the "elemental spirits of the universe" which that Law or practice served as means (cf. Gal. 4:3-5, 8-9). However much the talk of demons, "goblins and ghosties and things that go bump in the night," may appeal to a generation whose childhood was robbed of fantasy, few in the modern world regard it as having anything to do with reality. Of all the aspects of New Testament teaching, references to an invisible world of spirits engaged in cosmic conflict with God over his creatures has been

Chapter 10   *1 Corinthians*

the most subject to demythologization, to the point where they now appear laughable and absurd. Since the Enlightenment, it has become a cliché to speak of human existence as autonomous, answerable only to itself, dependent only upon itself, as neutral, of the causes of good or evil as lying in existence itself, and not in perforations or invasions of the human sphere on the part of celestial or chthonic powers. Of a century more than any other marked by brutality, heaped with the bones and ashes of 6 million Jews, 10 million Ukranians, and 27 million Chinese (the count from Uganda and Kampuchea still awaiting tally), and toying with the extinction of the race, Paul might have inquired whether or not such *autonomy* required demythologizing. The truth for Paul is that humans are not thrown back upon themselves to create their own heaven or hell; that the question of existence is not of masters but which shall be served, and that such service entails a total, undivided allegiance without remainder: **You cannot drink the cup of the Lord and the cup of demons. You cannot partake of the table of the Lord and the table of demons!** Would the "sensible" sense the inconsistency, would they "judge" that the boast of freedom, reflected in all that Corinthian sloganeering screened a penchant, a "hang" for its opposite, engined perhaps by an anxiety, a fear of the freedom which such service to the one Master, the one Lord guaranteed; that when all was said and done the "strong" were as weak as the "weak"? Or, Paul asks, **shall we provoke the Lord to jealousy?** The question hides an allusion to the synopsis of Israel's idolatry in the Song of Moses: "And [the Lord said] they have stirred me to jealousy with what is no god; they have provoked me with their idols" (Deut. 32:21), and with the sound of it still in his ears he asks again: **Are we stronger than he?** The question is framed so as to demand denial—"we are not stronger than he, are we?" Strong, stronger, strongest in face of this one: "See now, that I, even I, am he, and there is no god beside me. I kill and I make alive; I wound and I heal; and there is none that can deliver out of my hand. For I lift up my hand to heaven, and swear, As I live for ever, if I whet my glittering sword, and my hand takes hold on judgment, I will take revenge on my adversaries, and will requite those who hate me" (cf. Deut. 32:39-41).

Meats Sacrificed to Idols (10:23-30)

With the repetition of the slogan in 6:12 (in 6:13 that slogan had ramified to the analogy of sexuality with eating: "Meats for the belly and the belly for meats"; in one way or another, food was a principal preoccupation at Corinth!), Paul leaves the issue of participation in pagan sacrifice and returns to the question of eating meat derived from it, first raised in chapter 8. This section, however, does not simply mirror the earlier argument, but sets it against a broader definition of that "anyone" kept in view in chap. 8. It does not contain an apology for the "weak." More significant, because this section does not address the intramural conflict of weak and strong, it makes far more explicit than the preceding the character of Christian conscience and the role of the "other" in the question, "What shall I do?" Repeating his proviso to the Corinthian slogan, signaled in the adversative (**not all things are helpful . . . not all things build up** [cf. again 6:12; 8:1]), in v. 24 Paul draws a wider circle for action on behalf of the common good by moving from "the brother" (8:11) to "the other" (RSV, **the neighbor**). The verses following give a directive and its support from Scripture: **Eat whatever is sold in the meat market** . . . "for the earth is the Lord's and the fulness thereof" (Ps. 24:1; cf. Ps. 50:12; 89:11). The argument moves from *a* to *c*, the syllogism lacking its minor premise. But that premise had already been furnished: "All things are yours, whether Paul or Apollos or Cephas or the world . . ." (3:21-22). So the argument reads: "The earth is the Lord's; what is the Lord's is yours; the earth is yours." The reference to conscience in v. 25 ("without conducting any examination for the sake of conscience"; the term is drawn from the legal sphere, as in 4:3-4) is obviously to that of the eater, and not of the observer, as in 8:7, 10, 12. "Eat what you please, without a care for conscience." Customarily, interpreters read these verses as reflecting Paul's allegiance to the party of the strong, allowing the matter to rest there. But such

Chapter 10   *1 Corinthians*

reading hardly exhausts the import of Paul's statement. What induces Paul to take his stand with the strong has nothing whatever to do with the strong, but with an understanding of conscience which the behavior of the strong—accidentally!—reflects, that is, that the conscience of the Christian is in principle free. For this reason "I can do everything" (no thought, no action outside the realm of possibility), again, a tenet with which the slogan of the strong (accidentally!) agreed. If Paul's agreement with the strong were something more than coincidence, how explain all those provisos, those qualifications, corrections, emendations, revisions of the thesis "I can do everything" in chaps. 6 and 8? We can only infer the occasion for Paul's accidental, coincidental agreement with the strong. Was it a notion of freedom as freedom for the self, from which then derived a notion of conscience as "knowing together with" the self, as calling the self to be for itself and only for itself ("let your conscience be your guide," "to thine own self be true")? Or was it a word from Paul himself ("all things are yours," "the earth is the Lord's"), a word which one could "know together with," be riotously happy to judge right or wrong "together with," and from which that "Corinthian" notion of freedom as nonalignment, nonengagement, as immaterial and irrelevant to the "brother" or the "other" derived? Or had the Corinthians merely heard Paul's first word, and not the word respecting conscience, right and wrong? He had already been misunderstood, or deliberately interpreted to err on the side of obligation: "I wrote to you in my letter not to associate with immoral men, not at all meaning the immoral of this world . . . since then you would need to go out of the world" (5:9-10). Why not then on the side of freedom? Standing alone— "eat what you please, the earth is the Lord's"—Paul's first word simply reads: "Enjoy! Enjoy! The highest aim of life is to enjoy!" It does not stand alone. But if conscience is in principle free, what other word could be added to Paul's first word, to rescue it from hedonism? If there is nothing in the self, no "divine voice," no "dictate" from within to approve the good or reprove the evil now, then how is one to know the one or the other? Or, if one is no longer obliged to observe a law which summons from the outside: "Thou shalt . . . thou shalt not," then "together with" whom or what judge right from wrong? If the Christian's knowledge of good and evil is neither autonomous, of the self, by the self, and for the self; nor heteronomous, imposed by a lawgiver, to what other consequence could "eat, enjoy, eat without a care for conscience" lead than to behavior "of a kind that is not found even among pagans" (5:17)? Never in all his life would Paul have surcease from that question. In one fashion or another it would pursue him, a persistent angry mongrel snapping at his heels from Jerusalem to Achaia to Jerusalem again. Whether snarling at him from Corinth, forcing him to break off speech in midsentence, to edit, simplify, condense what needed time to say and hear ("among the perfect we do impart wisdom . . . but I, brethren, could not address you as spiritual. . . . I fed you with milk, not solid food; for you were not ready for it; and even yet you are not ready," 2:6; 3:1-2), or growling at him through some fictive opponent at Rome ("are we to continue in sin that grace may abound?" Rom. 6:1), from Jew and Greek the charge that his proclamation of justification by faith in the Christ crucified inevitably leads to moral laxity would never leave him. That charge, in Churchill's phrase, was Paul's "black dog." And it had a litter of pups against which 2000 years of Christendom would buy insurance—in a *lex natura*, in a "third use of the law," or the "spirit of Jesus"—to say nothing of moralists who had moved out of the neighborhood.

Paul's next word follows in vv. 27-29a. The answer to the question "What shall I do?" is served up by the "other," whether host or guest is of no importance to Paul. The other's conscience, the other's "voice," the other's "dictate" from within or without, autonomous or not, the other's need, the other's lack, the other's weakness, the other's strength shapes, yields, and gives the answer to the ethical question—**if some one says to you, "This has been offered in sacrifice," then out of consideration for the man who informed you, and for conscience' sake—I mean his conscience, not yours—do not eat it.** What to do? See the other, hear the other! Paul did not intend that his "brief" against the Gentiles as "holding down" or banning the truth, as refusing to glorify God or give him thanks, and in consequence as "given up" to ruin (Rom. 1:18ff.) should be applied to every non-Jew who drew breath. There was goodness and honor in the world outside the church and synagogue, and that goodness and honor were no mere "shining vice," because God was in the world, had written "what the law" requires on its heart (Rom. 2:14-15). For this reason Paul could plunder, purloin, expropriate "whatever" was true, honorable, just, pure, lovely, and gracious from that world (Phil. 4:8; "the lines of communication to what is natural and humane in Hellenism remain completely intact").[69] To deny goodness to the Gentile meant to deny God's presence in the world. So, Paul's "exclusivity" did not occur at the point of division between Jew and Gentile. Nor, where questions of conscience were concerned, did it occur at the point of division between believers and unbelievers. Paul's definition of the "other" who should answer the question "What shall I do?" was as broad as humanity itself: **If one of the unbelievers invites you. . . .**

> But he, desiring to justify himself, said to Jesus, "And who is my neighbor?" Jesus replied, "A man was going down from Jerusalem to Jericho, and he fell among robbers. . . . Now by chance a priest was going down that road. . . . So likewise a Levite. . . . But a Samaritan. . . . Which of these three, do you think, proved neighbor to the man who fell among the robbers?" (Luke 10:29ff.).

There is no question from whom Paul learned to stand things on their head. Not, "*Where* is my neighbor?" but "*Which* of these . . . proved neighbor?" And "not *your* conscience but that of the *other*" (the RSV reverses the order)—the conscience of the "weak" (6:19); the "brother" (6:11); the "other" (10:24), "one of the unbelievers" (10:22), any one, any one at all.

Verses 29b-30 seem strangely out of harmony with everything said till now. In fact, they read like a rebuttal of Paul's argument: **For why should my liberty be determined by another man's scruples? If I partake with thankfulness, why am I denounced**

because of that for which I give thanks? If the "other" gives the answer to the question "What shall I do?" then is not freedom of conscience only a freedom "in principle," in theory, in a vacuum, and no freedom at all? For where is there the possibility of freedom when I can never escape the other, some other, any other who regulates my behavior? Before the manuscript tradition began to congeal, did some hyper-Paulinist, believing his hero had gone too far, had conceded too much, "sold the farm," register his objection in the margin of his exemplar? Short of this solution, some commentators suggest that Paul is merely adding force to the thought in 29a ("and as for conscience I do not mean yours, but the other's"), that, despite all, the Christian is really free— "within."

> Stone walls do not a prison make,
> Nor iron bars a cage.
> . . . If I have freedom in my love,
> And in my soul am free,
> Angels above that soar alone
> Enjoy such liberty.

The suggestion will not wash. Paul never construes freedom subjectively. Whether added later or quoted by Paul in unmediated fashion, when matched against their context vv. 29b-30 cannot be interpreted as expressing Paul's own thought. They assume a notion of freedom in total contrast to Paul's, a notion oriented to the "I," the self, as getting one's self "in hand" and gaining mastery over whatever is alien to it, threatens it. For the apostle, it was precisely by getting one's self in hand, not the inability to do so, that spelled the absence of freedom. Freedom, liberty, came by way of renouncing all orientation to the self in a historical, concrete, and radical surrender of the self to the other. "Eat whatever is sold . . . 'the earth is the Lord's' . . . conscience is free." This word meant most to the Corinthians. But the word which meant most to Paul, his last word, is that the neighbor, **another man's scruples,** if they do not yield the criterion for the approval or disapproval of conscience, they do nevertheless give content to the ethical question. **So, Paul concludes, whether you eat or drink, or whatever you do, do all to the glory of God.**

All to the Glory of God (10:31-33 [11:1])

Years ago, a little book entitled *The Borderland of Right and Wrong* was published for the purpose of monitoring Christian behavior. It contained the story of a London preacher who had invited the noted expositor and pulpiteer, Charles E. Spurgeon, to share the pulpit with him on a given Sunday. The one should take the interpretation of the text and the other its application. The London preacher proceeded to digress on the topic of his deliverance by the Lord from the evils of smoking. During his turn at the pulpit, Spurgeon announced that that very afternoon he intended to smoke a cigar "to the glory of God." The inevitable occurred—Spurgeon's face began to appear on cigar bands, and the London preacher resumed his habit. Paul would have cringed at such crude interpretation of his summons. It was not the eating nor not eating which should glorify God, but the waiver of all rights to self in the eating or not eating. And the purpose of such a waiver did not lie in giving the other title to eating or not eating, but in the other's surrender of rights for still another, for Christ and thus the neighbor (not the converse—Paul did not identify humanitarian action as such with "anonymous Christianity," did not regard the "event of God" as somehow occurring in service to the neighbor). It was this waiver of rights and its purpose—**to the glory of God,** that is, **that they may be saved**—which lay behind his summons to **give no offense to Jews or to Greeks or to the church of God.** It was this which furnished the spring for his activity, summarized in the words **I try to please all men in everything I do,** an echo of his "job description" in 9:19-23. Therefore Paul could call the Corinthians to be imitators: "I am nothing; the other, Christ and the neighbor, are everything—imitate me!"

■ Worship at Corinth (11:2—14:40)

Chapter 11

In chap. 11 Paul deals with two quite distinct and separate issues, the one in vv. 2-16, the other in vv. 17-33. In the case of the first, it is impossible to determine whether or not the issue had surfaced by way of oral report or written communication. Paul makes no reference to what he has heard (as, e.g., in 1:11; 5:1), or to what he has read (7:1, 25; 8:1). In the case of the second, Paul makes specific reference to what he has heard (v. 18; from "Chloe's people"?). In addition, the use of the present tense (e.g., "you come together, not for the better, but for the worse," v. 17; cf. vv. 18, 20-21, 29-30) reflects Paul's confidence that he has the facts in hand. The conditional clauses appearing in the first part of the verse (vv. 6 [twice] and 16) suggest a wobblier basis in fact. The differences between the two sections, however, exceed such matters. The argument in vv. 2-16 makes no reference to a word of the Lord calculated to settle the matter, unlike vv. 23ff. (cf. 7:10; 8:14). The "traditions" to which Paul refers in v. 2, and for the retention of which he commends the Corinthians, are not immediately identifiable with what he "received from the Lord" in vv. 23ff. They could refer to Paul's own counsels as distinct from (cf. 7:12, 25) or together with a "command of the Lord." The qualification which Paul appends to his argument in vv. 11-12 argues for the first possibility. Or, again, the curious position of v. 2 at this point in the epistle—in the usual Greek letter it would have appeared at the beginning, not in the body of the letter—suggests that Paul may have intended it to serve as introduction, not merely to vv. 3-16, but to the entire discussion of the worship at Corinth, concluded at 14:40.

The first section in this chapter, therefore, does not rank as equal in weight to the second, though Paul would scarcely have taken kindly to the suggestion that for this reason it may be set down as "one man's opinion," conditioned merely by custom and the times. To this section, as to any other in which Paul explicitly or by implication differentiates his counsel from a "command of the Lord," the word "I think that I have the Spirit of God" applies (7:40). And that Paul's "I think" reflects more than a modest challenge to anyone of a different opinion is indicated by the substitution of his own word for a word of the Lord wherever the latter is lacking. The apostle's audacity cannot be subtracted from that "I think."

Women's Deportment at the Worship (11:2-16)

Commendation (11:2) Whether or not we construe v. 1 as introductory merely to what immediately follows (vv. 3-16), or to everything stated till chap. 15, in light of the critique, the attack, the passion, heat, and irony aimed at the Corinthians thus far, the verse seems singularly inappropriate: **I commend you** (the word in the Greek means "praise") **because you remember me in everything and maintain the traditions even as I have delivered them to you.** In face of his repeated summons to recall what they have forgotten or ignored ("don't you know?"), how can Paul praise the Corinthians for remembering and holding fast? Is the statement simply a *captatio benevolentiae*, an attempt at ingratiating himself with his readers in preparation for charging them with further obligation? It would be convenient to assign the verse and what follows, together with all such curious inconsistencies in our epistle, to another or even several other letters of Paul to Corinth. Psychological, to say nothing of structuralist, exposition of the Corinthian correspondence may establish that Paul did not compose his letters to Corinth in their present form, but, to date, agreement has been so minimal as to allow us one of two unsatisfactory conclusions respecting this verse: Either Paul is softening up his readers for renewed attack, or addressing himself to the community as a whole, without thought for any party and its disturbance.

Women without Head Covering (11:3-6) The reference to the male in v. 4 (and v. 7) seems only for the purpose of furnishing a counterfoil to the remarks applied to the female in vv. 5-6 (the same may be said of the references to the male in vv. 7 and 14).

The behavior described, that is, the women's praying and prophesying with uncovered heads (or even unbound hair? not **unveiled,** as in the RSV), can only pertain to the gathering of the community. To restrict Paul's injunction to women's behavior in their own homes would be absurd. The activities described are clearly of a public character. In 14:26, the reference to the community's "coming together" for a psalm, a teaching, a revelation, for speaking in tongues and their interpretation, includes the activity described here. Apparently, then, some (several, a few, a handful?) of the Corinthian women appeared and participated in the community's worship with heads uncovered or with hair loose. Contemporary Orthodox as well as some conservative practice still calls for head coverings for women. In Reform synagogues it remains an option, though most women worship with heads uncovered. The space which Paul gives to his prohibitions against the habit, to say nothing of the principle or doctrine from which he derives his prohibitions, suggests that the custom was not a mere reflex, without rationale, sprung from mere accident, but rather a deliberate act rooted in an understanding of the altered relation between the sexes as reflected in the gospel. For the women at Corinth, their appearance and participation at public worship with heads uncovered was apparently meant to signal that equality of male and female in Christ which Paul himself had preached (cf. Gal. 3:28), to which he had already alluded in our epistle (7:4), and which he would reiterate in the "qualification" to his argument in vv. 11-12. The observation is not insignificant, since it is not the fact of the women's appearance, but the *mode* or manner of that appearance which draws Paul's fire. Jewish women, but not only Jewish women of proven morals and good character, covered their heads or bound up their hair in public; others did not. (According to the still valid halakah [cf. Joseph Caro, *Shulchan Arukh*, section *Even ha-Ezer* 21:2], the Jewish married woman must appear at worship, but also elsewhere in public, with head covered.) Lascivious persons often wore their hair cut short or shaved their heads. Paul's words in vv. 5-6 could be interpreted to read: "Without a cap or kerchief a woman might as well be bobbed. If she will not cover her head, let her take a razor to it and play the male!"

Paul proceeds first to his argument by stating that the woman's head must be covered to symbolize her subordinate position in the chain of command: **The head of every man is Christ, and the head of a woman is** the man (RSV: **her husband**), **and the head of Christ is God.** The verse is curious, and from several points of view. Christ is named first as the head of every man, and God as the head of Christ is named last. One would expect the sentence to read: God is the head of Christ, Christ is the head of the man, and the man is the head of the woman, for which reason the woman's subordinate status must be made explicit. Further, the reference to Christ, to the man, and to God as the "head" of the other, is in singular contrast to what Paul has written thus far of the relation between God or Christ and the believer, or between man and woman (cf. e.g., 1:30; 2:16; 3:9, 16, 23; 4:1; 5:7; 6:17, 19; 8:3, 6, 11; 10:4; 11:1). Where the believer's relation to Christ is concerned, such language is not at all Paul's preference, as his frequent reference to the "body of Christ" indicates (6:15; 10:16-17; 12:12-17). Next, the verse suggests an ontological reflection on the relation between each pair in the chain of command, that is, on the relation of the one to the other with respect to substance or essence. If Paul abandoned the concept of the "people" or "Israel of God" used in his earlier letters (cf., e.g., Gal. 6:16) for that of the "body," since the latter better suited his conviction regarding the believer's oneness with Christ, nowhere does he state or imply that that oneness is a oneness of essence. The incorporation of the believer into Christ does not denote a transfer from humanity to deity. Baptized into Christ, sharing his life, suffering or reigning with him, the believer is not Christ, but remains his creature, human, finite. And as for the relation of Christ to God, while the apostle elsewhere refers to or implies their unity of essence (cf. Phil. 2:5-11 or Rom. 1:4, where the accent does not lie on Christ's designation as Son of God, but as Son of God "in power"), he nowhere else refers to any ontological or substantial subordination of Christ to God, as the phrase "and the head of Christ is God" implies. Elsewhere in Paul that subordination is conceived as functional (15:28). The point, however, is not that Paul *could not* speak of a subordination of Christ in essence to the Father—he obviously implies it here—but that he *does not* to this point, nor ever again. Finally, when the phrase "and the head of the woman is the man" is excised from the verse, it bears striking similarity to what any Hellenist or Stoic of Paul's time could have written: "The head of every man is Christ [or, the Logos, that 'principle' by which everything in the cosmos holds together], and the head of Christ [or, the Logos] is God." That is, man "mirrors" or "images" (note how Paul moves from "head" to "image" in v. 7) the Logos, and the Logos "mirrors" or "images" God. In later speculation, "mirrors" or "images" is made to read "is of the same stuff as [the Logos] God." The reference to man's "dishonoring his head" by covering it (note the punning on the word **head** in v. 4, the second reference equivalent to "Christ"), or to the woman's "shaming her head" by uncovering it in v. 5, implies that in each case the relation to the archetype, to the one mirrored or imaged (in the man's case, Christ; in the woman's, the man) is obscured. There was nothing in Paul's Bible even faintly resembling this verse, though Paul's contemporary, Philo of Alexandria, is proof enough that any number of Old Testament passages could be interpreted to read as this verse does. Did Paul expropriate a piece of Jewish speculation, with the metaphysics of which he did not agree or did not even bother, and for the purpose of establishing his point that Christians are not lofted to a sphere where they can ignore nature or custom, simply because they do not effect salvation?

"Image," "Glory," and the Qualification (11:7-12)   With the exception of v. 10, Paul's argument here is easier to grasp. The woman's mirroring her archetype, her subordination to the man (the RSV translates **husband** in v. 3, and **man** in the verses to follow; the Greek in each instance denotes the male), symbolized by wearing the kerchief or headpiece, is rooted in the status given her at creation: The **woman** was created **from** the **man,** not the

Chapter 11 *1 Corinthians*

man from the woman; and the **woman** was created **for** the sake of the **man,** not man for the sake of the woman (vv. 8-9; cf. Gen. 2:22f. and 2:18). Thus, the man is God's **image and glory,** but the woman merely the **glory** (not "image") **of** the **man.** The argument is Jewish, echoed in the morning prayer best known to Gentiles by virtue of its quaintness. The head of the house prays: "Blessed art Thou, O Lord our God, King of the universe, who hast not made me a woman," and the woman: "Blessed art Thou, O Lord our God, King of the universe, who hast made me according to Thy will." **That is why** [for the reasons just cited], **a woman ought to have a**—what?—**on her head, because of** (for the sake of?) **the angels.** The verse is an interpreter's "cross." The term used in the Greek, and which the RSV translates **veil** (though neither in this verse nor in v. 6 is the reference to a veil, but to something over the head) is usually translated "authority." "The woman should have an authority on her head," which could be interpreted to mean, "should have on her head the means for exercising power." In that case, the conclusion to the verse should read: "Because of the angels," that is, because of inflaming the lustful glances of the ("fallen," according to Tertullian)[70] angels when she comes near the heavenly sphere in prayer. The verse would then contain an allusion to Gen. 6:1ff., which records the seduction of the "daughters of men" by the "sons of God" attracted by the women's beauty. Or, the term "authority" could simply be translated "covering," and the conclusion of the verse read to mean "for the sake of the angels," that is, lest the woman give the angels occasion for grief at her impropriety. Of the two, the latter reading is the more far-fetched, particularly since evidence for the translation "covering" (or "veil") is virtually nonexistent, and the notion of the angels as somehow aghast at human behavior is given no strong support in the literature between the Testaments from which Paul may have derived it. On the assumption the first reading is the least incorrect, it would harmonize with what Paul writes earlier of the presence of demonic spirits or powers (cf. 10:20-21). At the same time, the terseness of Paul's reference here or elsewhere indicates that he shares with the gospel tradition a disinterest in setting forth any full-blown doctrine regarding the demonic sphere. That earlier or later preoccupation with demonology touching the origin of the world of spirits, their names, hierarchical rank, or function, was of no concern to Paul beyond the belief that such a world existed, that it was intent on thwarting the purposes of God, was already in defeat and would ultimately be destroyed (cf. 15:24-25).

The term "qualification" as applied to vv. 11-12 is too imprecise. It implies a concession, of the type encountered, e.g., in 7:6, in light of which Paul's argument would read: "Let the woman cover her head as signal of her subordination, though of course, Christianly speaking ('in the Lord'), neither male nor female is independent of (or, different from?) the other." The little word which introduces v. 11, and which the RSV translates **nevertheless**, could with greater right be translated, "now, to come to the point. . . ." The two verses are not a qualification, but a fundamental principle of Paul's faith: "There is neither Jew nor Greek, there is neither slave nor free, there is neither male nor female, for you are all one in Christ Jesus" (Gal. 3:28). The natural order is not an order of salvation.

The Appeal to Propriety, Nature, and Custom in the Churches (11:13-16)

Following vv. 11-12, Paul resumes his argument against the woman's appearing and prophesying with her head uncovered, and in support appeals first to his readers' sense of propriety: **Judge for yourselves; is it proper for a woman to pray to God with her head uncovered?** (v. 13). Again, Paul expects an answer in the negative. Next, he appeals to **nature** (vv. 14-15), and in a last effort to the custom prevailing in **the churches of God** (v. 16). On the face of it, Paul's argument would have suffered little had he omitted these appeals. Having begun loftily enough, with reference to the "chain of command" ("the head of every man is Christ . . .," v. 3), to the biblical narrative of the creation (vv. 7-9), and to the presence of an invisible world of spirits (v. 10), he descends to a call for judgment on the basis of precedent, in seemingly clear contradiction of the principle enunciated in vv. 11-12. In imitation of a Cicero, Stoiclike he infers obligation from what "nature teaches"—which in the end helps little, since Paul did not regard long hair as a substitute for a covering ("if a woman will not cover her head, then let her take a scissors or a razor to it," vv. 5-6)—and finally to his own practice and to ecclesiastical convention (**we recognize no other practice, nor do the churches of God**). And all this, not about praying or prophesying, but about caps and kerchiefs! The commentators in chorus refer to the vulnerability of the entire discussion in which Paul, bereft of any specific tradition or command of the Lord, makes hobbling, limping appeal to anything within reach in support of his injunction.

In reaction to the usual reading, note first that in our chapter Paul is not calling for change. It was custom at Corinth (included among those "churches of God" in v. 16) for the women to appear and participate in the worship with heads covered. Paul affirms the custom, addressing himself to its violation. His entire argument is thus directed toward preserving the status quo, and not toward superimposing a custom, Jewish or otherwise, upon his readers. And again, that status quo had only to do with the "how," not the "that" of the women's participation—in itself a revolutionary phenomenon, at least within a community which included Jews, and not merely Gentiles. Further, far from yielding material for romanticizing on the theme of the apostle's humanity, a man concerned with everyday things in an everyday world, however mundane, Paul's argument, together with its "qualification" in vv. 11-12, is only a variation on the theme struck earlier in chaps. 6 through 10. For the sake of the situation addressed (i.e., women's deportment at the worship) the original "I can do everything" (6:12 and 10:23) is now altered to read "neither the woman is without the man nor the man without the woman in the Lord; for as the woman is from the man, so also the man is through (born of) the woman; and all is of God" (vv. 11-12). The Christian is free, answerable to nothing which may serve others as a norm or criterion, whatever its source, heaven or earth, and however established—within or outside the self. Hence, any conceivable thought or action falls within the range of possibilities: "Everything is permitted to me," according to the original usage of the phrase, "nothing stands in my way," nothing in terms of a law beyond my willing it, whether legal or psychic. (In Jewish circles, where the term "permitted" served to describe what was prescribed by the Torah, thus by God, the phrase would have been particularly offensive; cf. 3 Macc. 1:11; 4 Macc. 5:18; 17:7 LXX.) All of this means that the Christian is free from self-preservation, from whatever the self must live by in order to justify itself to itself and thus retain itself, from whatever gauge or measure the self requires in order to establish itself before God or another, and for this reason free for the other; for whom no rules obtain—only life for the other. And that life is not formless, without shape, an abstraction. How can it be when the other's existence is an existence in this world, temporal, historical, bounded by tradition and law ("to those under the law I became as one under the law," 9:20), or by "nature" and the order of the cosmos ("to those outside the law I became as one outside the law," 9:21)? To the existence of the other, such things as precedent, custom, habit, and convention belong, so that life for the other may assume the other's "scruples," but without itself requiring them for self-preservation. It is not merely because Christian existence does not spell distance from the world that it cannot ignore tradition, law, or nature. If this were all, if Paul were merely calling the Corinthians to a "Christian naturalness," to an acknowledgment of their historicity, to an existence within space and time, in which such things as tradition, law, custom, and convention prevail, they would have been justified in claiming their "authority" over convention, for what else could such acknowledgment imply than a return, in Paul's own words, to slavery to "the elemental spirits of the universe," to the self, which all that tradition and custom were calculated to preserve? Or, if Paul's summons to women to wear their heads covered at worship is merely a summons not to anticipate the "then" in the "now," to preserve the imperceptibility of the truth that "woman is not independent of (different from?) man nor man of woman," till it should somehow, some day

Chapter 11 *1 Corinthians*

be disclosed to all—and where in this epistle is it ever assumed that the preservation of imperceptibility is a human affair?—if Paul's summons is to allow what is "in the Lord" to lack concreteness in the here and now, then the thousands who have dismissed such quaint and antique statements as he makes in this chapter by appeal to their "historical conditioning" have greater right than those who hold to them simply because they appear in the Bible. On the other hand, if, with all its curious appeal to the "chain of command," to nature and to the custom of the "churches of God," the essence of Paul's argument here is the very same as that of the arguments preceding or following ("give no offense to Jews or to Greeks or to the church of God," 10:32; "so then, my brethren, when you come together to eat, wait for one another," 11:33), then it is finally not to "nature," temporality, preservation of imperceptibility, to avoidance of anticipation of the "then" in the "now"; then it is not to acknowledgment of their historical existence to which Paul is summoning his Corinthians, but to life for the other. That life for the other will take historical shape, but it is the life for the other which is the constant. Its historical shape is the variable; it requires "translation." **Judge for yourselves!** Paul says, or, as he writes later, "in your thought be mature!" (14:20). Reason, reflection, observation determine the historical shape which life for the other assumes. And as for the observation of "nature" and what it "teaches" as determining that shape, for Paul, unlike the Stoic, "nature" itself was a variable, not a constant—"for the shape of this world is passing away" (7:31). The apostle had called the Corinthians to concretize their surrender to the other in a manner touching the times. The manner is odd, curious, antique, but to treat it as the constant and thus dismiss it can screen a rejection of life for the other, as well as a rejection of reason needed to determine its shape—"judge for yourselves!" For faith, for Christ, as Luther wrote, "is not like wine in the cask." The natural order is not an order of salvation, but cannot on that account be ignored without plunging existence into fantasy and thus giving nature a power it does not deserve.

The Supper at Corinth (11:17-34)

Life for the other had been inhibited in the Corinthians' participation in the Supper. Paul's reference to the one as hungry, to the other as drunken, or at least euphoric (v. 21), to despising those who have nothing (v. 22), suggests a context for the Supper prevailing only in isolated sectors of present-day Christianity, that is, the agape or "love feast." The purpose of the agape was not primarily socioeconomic, aimed at alleviating the hunger of the poor who came to share it, though it might well have done so. Paul's assumption that members of the community had houses in which to eat and drink (v. 22), or his injunction to the hungry to eat at home (v. 34) is evidence of that. Frequently, in antiquity, the sharing of a meal marked an intimacy which only death could rupture, or it created between persons who previously were only strangers a bond which transcended loyalty to nation, tribe, or class. The despair or horror attaching to struggles between *xenoi* or "guest friends" who once had shared the same table is attested in the literature (cf. Ps. 40:9, "Even my bosom friend in whom I trusted, who ate of my bread, has lifted his heel against me," reflected in the Johannine footwashing scene, John 13:18). Within the setting of this love feast, some Corinthians had turned the Supper into a carousal. In vv. 17-22, Paul describes the situation as he has heard it; in vv. 23-26 delivers the paradosis (tradition) intended to bring order out of the chaos, and in vv. 27-32 interprets his "text" in respect to the Corinthian situation, concluding with an appeal and promise in vv. 33-34.

Chaos (11:17-22) Verse 17 appears to serve as a transition, facing backward and not merely forward as in the RSV (**but in the following instructions I do not commend you**). The verse may thus be read: "Now, setting this to rights [i.e., the problem of the women's deportment at worship treated in vv. 2-16], I do not praise you that you come together rather for the worse and not the better." The phrase "I do not praise you," set in contrast to that *captatio benevolentiae* in v. 2, is repeated in v. 22, and furnishes an inclusio (frame) for Paul's sketch of the chaos at Corinth. The terms translated **when you assemble as a church** and which

Chapter 11   *1 Corinthians*

recur in v. 20 (**when you meet together**), assume the same public context as did the terms "praying" and "prophesying" in vv. 4-5. The meaning of that little comparative "better" is disclosed not merely in vv. 31-33, but includes everything which Paul till now had subsumed under the rubric of the "common good," or of "building up" (6:12; 7:35; 10:23)—of life for the other. As to the "worse," Paul first writes, **when you assemble . . . I hear that there are divisions among you; and I partly believe it.** It is not necessary to interpret the "schisms" in this context as applying to the splitting of the congregation reported by "Chloe's people" (1:10-11; 3:3-4). The same informants may simply have added a eucharistic bedlam to the tally of aberrations in the congregation. At this point, the Corinthians themselves may have been unconscious of any ideological component to their behavior, and simply taken a bacchanalian relish in celebrating their new God. It is impossible to state with any certainty whether or not the indignities at Corinth sprang from conscious appropriation of an architectonic in which thought, intent, and action were all fitted together, and which could be denominated "libertinistic pneumaticism," "Judaism in reverse," "Jewish-Christian" or "Hellenistic-Christian Gnosticism" or "perfectionism." The scholars' lack of consensus as to precisely what worldview or synthesis of worldviews underlay existence at Corinth may derive from the same rage for order or coherence as moved Titus to hunt for the raison d'être of Jewish religion in one great, single symbol or image in Jerusalem's temple. Sloth may lie behind giving up the search, but does not rule out the probability of a "theology" developed ex post facto. What Paul sees at Corinth, whether or not the Corinthians see it (and what, really do they see?—"Don't you know?" 3:16; "Don't you know?" 5:6; "Don't you know?" 6:2; "Don't you know?" 6:3; "Don't you know?" 6:15; "Don't you know?" 6:16; "Don't you know?" 6:19; "Don't you know?" 9:13; "Don't you know?" 9:24!), or what Paul sees despite what the Corinthians do not, is an entirely different matter—an existence struggling to get free of engagement, alignment, of relation, of corporeality, of humanity, of life with earth and flesh and the other, struggling to assert itself over, beyond, or despite the other, and all in the name of Jesus. Whether reflected in party spirit, in factions, in benediction on the status quo by concession to immorality, in legal disputes, in demanding celibacy or marriage, in hazing the weak, in sacramentalist hocus-pocus, in defying custom, and in midst of all pulling the rug out under its own feet, denying its own right to exist by construing Paul's waiver of rights as historical accident, and thus denying his apostleship—all of it trumpeted in those astigmatic, myopic, one-eyed slogans ("I belong to Paul . . . to Apollos . . . to Cephas . . . to Christ"; "everything is permitted to me"; "meats for the belly and the belly for meats"; "we all have knowledge"; "there is no idol in the world . . . no God but one"; "why is my freedom judged by another's conscience?")—for the apostle it all coalesced, cohered, interlaced. It all belonged together, hung together. For some, for a few (!) but enough to make a difference ("do not be deceived; bad company ruins good morals!" 15:33), or for many at Corinth, existence—Christian existence—threatened to harden into dogmatic positions. It tended to degenerate into persuasions, "schools" (the term translated "faction" is father to our modern word "heresy") rivaling the church, a phenomenon together with the "present distress," the shortening of the "time," the wearing away of the shape of the cosmos (6:26f.) as signaling the end, the "Day" to be revealed with fire. "There must be siege and capture, choices, schools among you, so that those among you who are approved may be manifest" (v. 19). That word translated **genuine** in the RSV, and taken from the ancient business of coinage, is never free of associations with temperature, heat and melting point; cf. 3:12-13. Paul's note at the conclusion of v. 18 does not give qualified credence to what he has heard—"**I partly believe** there are divisions among you"—but rather to the divisions at Corinth as omens of the end. (If the words **I believe** were used in neutral fashion here, it would be the only instance of such usage in the New Testament). The language belongs to the apocalyptic genre, literature in the service of revelations which envision a final salvation and another world. To that genre belongs the description of rivals to the truth emerging at the end of time, a description lodged in the tradition of the sayings of Jesus (Mark 13:21-23; Matt. 24:23-26; cf. 2 Peter 2:1-3). Nowhere in the New Testament, however, is it stated that the appearance of those "false Christs" is for the purpose of facilitating judgment at the last day. The RSV translation, **that those who are genuine among you may be recognized** could be interpreted to read "that God or the angels may have an easier time distinguishing the good from the bad." The syntax rather suggests the reading, "that those who are genuine, who have fallen true from the mold, may be manifest among you, clear to you," a thought echoed, for example, in 1 John 2:19: "They went out from us . . . that they might make clear that they all are not of us." In vv. 20-22, Paul describes the consequence for the Supper arising from the Corinthians' schisms: "For this reason [or, 'next,' in any case, linking what follows as effect to what precedes as cause; the RSV omits the conjunction] when you gather at the same place it is not to eat the Lord's Supper." The accent lies on the phrase **the Lord's Supper** (by far the earliest designation of the sacramental meal in primitive Christianity). The Corinthians have ignored their Host, to whom *both* the sacrament (from which one might come away hungry, but scarcely drunk) *and* the agape or (the love feast) belong. Some appear with full hampers, as though the event were for the purpose of ingestion, satiation, even stupor, while others play the role of hungry onlookers. The Supper is the Lord's, but **each one goes ahead with his own meal,** to treat it as if he were host, and as if it were not **for you** (v. 24). "Eat at home!" Paul writes, "leave off the agape and the Supper or come to it with your stomachs full, or do you intend to demonstrate that you despise the churches of God by shaming the poor?" The Host, his Supper, and the agape, that context in which the Lord should bind all to himself and each to the other—they had all been ignored in elbowing a way for the self: **Each one goes ahead with his own.** Self had crashed the line. The inclusio rounds off Paul's description: "**What shall I say to you?** Shall I praise you? I will not praise you for this!"

The Paradosis (11:23-26) Into the chaos Paul sets the teaching. **I**, he writes, **I received**—and with that use of the pronoun, which could have been omitted (the verb contains its subject), as much as says, "You and I are at opposite poles!" **I received from the Lord what I also delivered to you.** What is at stake here requires more than another "Don't you know?" more than an appeal to the "name" (1:10), to a command of the Lord in indirect speech (7:10; 9:14), or to his status as apostle. The thing to catch the conscience at Corinth had been reached from hand to hand—**from the Lord . . . to you.** Only once more will the likes of such a statement appear: "and last of all . . . he was shown also to me" (15:8). Paul is not merely abbreviating here, omitting the transmitters of the tradition which he received for the sake of the first in line. There is more than one alternative to reading the verse as though Paul had read "catechism" for the risen Christ. What he received and transmitted was not something which "for all practical purposes" came "from the Lord." What he was given and gave in turn, whatever its mediation, had only one subject, actor, or principal, and who stood as its guarantor.

We owe to the disorder at Corinth the earliest known tradition of the Lord's Supper, beginning with **the Lord Jesus** in v. 23b and concluding with v. 25. The scene is tersely set: **On the night when he was betrayed** (v. 23b). Later, that brief historical reference will explode into a tradition about which narrative, parable, passion prediction, conflict, and school speech would congeal and consume almost a third of synoptic record. In the case of at least one Evangelist, the simple verb **betrayed** would draw to itself an entire cast of characters and events surrounding the Jesus-tradition at its commencement, its high-water mark and its end, casting the shadow of Jesus' death over his entire career (cf. Mark 1:14; 3:19; 9:31; 10:33; 14:11, 42; 15:1, 15), and leading one 19th-century scholar to set a precedent (not altogether healthy) in the description of the Gospel accounts as "passion narratives with rather lengthy introductions" (Martin Kähler). The action of Jesus himself is as briefly narrated: He **took bread, and when he had given thanks, he broke it, and said, "This is my body**

which is for you. Do this in remembrance of me." In the same way also the cup, after supper, saying, **"This cup is the new covenant in my blood. Do this, as often as you drink it, in remembrance of me"** (vv. 23b-25). There is no reference to date, from which one might infer the Passover (cf. Mark 14:12, 16; Matt. 26:2, 17-18; Luke 22:1, 7-8, 11, 13, 15; John 18:39), or some lesser cultic feast as the context for the Supper (cf. Mark 14:1-2; Matt. 26:5; John 13:1; 19:31, 42). There is no concern for place such as preoccupied the first three Evangelists (Mark 14:13-16; Matt. 26:17-19; Luke 22:8-13; but cf. John 13ff.). If for Paul the words **the Lord Jesus . . . took bread** were intended to identify the Supper's Host, then that Host was sovereign over time and place. There is no reference to the content of Jesus' thanksgiving which could shed light on the Supper's occasion, much less to which the words **do this** could be applied principally or exclusively, as if the validity of the Supper stood or fell with its repetition. If the command did not apply to the whole of the action—taking, blessing, breaking, speaking—only the words which make clear what occurs in the action could enjoy such distinction, since they are the nearest antecedent to the pronoun **this: This is my body which is for you. Do this.** . . . Finally, there is no reference to the frequency with which the Lord's Supper should be celebrated, only that temporal adverb **as often as** in v. 25, repeated in Paul's "commentary" in v. 26.

A comparison of Paul's tradition with that of the first three Gospels yields differences and similarities (Mark 14:22-25; Matt. 26:26-29; Luke 22:14-20). Mark and Matthew add, and Luke prefixes to Jesus' words concerning the bread and cup, the announcement that he will never eat Passover or drink "from the fruit of the vine" until he drinks it "new" in the kingdom of God (Mark 14:25; Matt. 26:29; Luke 22:16, 18). In midst of these words, Luke records Jesus' taking a cup, an action later repeated following the distribution of the bread (Luke 22:17). All four accounts agree regarding the action immediately preceding the words concerning the bread: He took; he gave thanks (in Paul and Luke a verb is used from which our term "Eucharist" derives, but which is synonymous with the term for "blessing" in Mark and Matthew; cf. Luke 14:19 and vv. 23-24 in our chapter, together with 10:16, "The cup of blessing which we bless"); he broke, and he spoke (Mark 14:22; Matt. 26:26; Luke 22:19). In all four accounts, Jesus says of the bread, **this is my body.** Mark and Matthew, however, prefix to these words the command to take (Mark 14:22), or to take and eat (Matt. 26:26), a command which Luke attaches to the first cup (Luke 22:17: "Take this, and divide it among yourselves"). Mark and Matthew repeat the action concerning the cup which Paul (and Luke 22:20) implies in the simple "likewise" or "in the same way" of v. 25. In Matthew, following Jesus' taking the cup, he summons the disciples to drink (Matt. 26:27), and in both Mark and Matthew the words surrounding the cup read: "This is my blood of the covenant which is poured out for many," or "for you" (a phrase which Paul appends to the words concerning the bread, v. 24), Matthew then adding, "for the forgiveness of sins" (Mark 14:24; Matt. 26:28). On the other hand, Paul and Luke read "this cup is the new testament (**covenant**) in my blood" (Luke 22:20). More significantly, perhaps, Luke adds to the words concerning the bread, "Do this in remembrance of me" (Luke 22:19), a summons which Paul attaches not only to the words concerning the bread, but also to those surrounding the cup, adding "as often as you drink it" (vv. 24-25). Aside from what he shares in common with all the Evangelists, as well as from what he adds, and apart from his omission of Jesus' refusal to eat or drink, Paul's account is all but identical to Luke's.

From this comparison, several conclusions may be drawn. The most obvious is that the tradition concerning the Supper had not hardened to the point of total agreement among its transmitters. In this tradition also the same similarities and differences prevailed as are reflected in the remainder of the Gospel record of Jesus' sayings and doings. From Luke's references to the two cups, to say nothing of the references of all three Evangelists to the Supper's date, it may be inferred that the Gospel narrative was made to reflect the liturgical practices of the community from

Chapter 11   *1 Corinthians*

and for which it was written (in Luke, e.g., the celebration of the sacrament in the context of the Passover). The narrators exercise the same sovereignty over this portion of the tradition as over the tradition as a whole. The question is whether or not the same may be said of Paul, who describes his tradition as "from the Lord," that is, whether or not that phrase applies not only to the content of the tradition but also to its form. The consensus of scholarship is that it does not. But that consensus derives largely from drawing an analogy between Paul's use of the Jesus-tradition elsewhere (cf., e.g., 9:14—a clear reference to the tradition as reflected in Luke 10:7, but scarcely a literal quotation), and his transmission of the words of Jesus here. If Paul's introduction to Jesus' words with the verb **saying** in vv. 24-25—which do not precede any other reference to the Jesus-tradition in this epistle—does not reflect a more literal recitation than the same term used in the Gospel accounts, the situation at Corinth was serious enough to require it. Were the action of the breaking of the bread and the "words of institution" absorbed, overheard, or only mechanically performed at Corinth? We can only speculate. At any rate, because of his greater proximity to the event of Christ, and thus his proximity to a tradition which had already threatened to scatter before the Gospel writers could check it, and because, as he believed, Christ stood as the tradition's guarantor, for the historian Paul's recitation of Jesus' sayings and doings at his Supper assumes first place.

Paul's recitation of the Supper narrative is for the purpose of rectifying the situation at Corinth. He gives no "doctrine" of the Supper here. The question concerning the relation between the earthly element and the body and blood of the Lord lies outside his discussion. But he might have warmed to those later debates concerning the meaning of the words **this is my body . . . this cup is the new covenant in my blood.** Such language was not merely metaphor; by the word of Jesus an actual metaphor, a "transference" had occurred—from "my body is like this" to "this is my body." The Supper marked a creation, this time not from nothing, but from something, from "like this," like the old covenant to "is this," to the new covenant. There was continuity between the old and the new; the new had its antecedent in the old, for there had already been a covenant, an arrangement, a "disposal" (the meaning of **covenant**) of God concerning what was his. The metaphor was actually a transference, but that transference from old to new also involved radical change. Those historical conditions to which the old covenant tied a single, discrete people were to be altered with the death of Christ. The conditions to which "seeing is believing" belonged, to which the key to living well disclosed to a reason which assumed the identity of humanity and deity belonged, would be radically altered to an existence which neither sense nor perception could sustain—"for Jews demand signs and Greeks seek wisdom, but we preach Christ crucified" (1:22-23). And with that change in historical conditions whatever tied existence to it—covenant, law, nationhood, religion—would be torn to tatters: "To those who are called, both Jews and Greeks" (1:24). The new was discontinuous with the old, but not because the old had worn away with misuse—God had remained faithful to his covenant—rather because God would draw closer to his creatures in a disposal which the old had promised but itself could never give. The metaphor was a transference:

> Behold, the days are coming, says the Lord, when I will make a new covenant with the house of Israel and the house of Judah, not like the covenant which I made with their fathers when I took them by the hand to bring them out of the land of Egypt, my covenant which they broke, though I was their husband, says the Lord. But this is the covenant which I will make with the house of Israel after those days, says the Lord: I will put my law within them, and I will write it upon their hearts; and I will be their God, and they shall be my people. And no longer shall each man teach his neighbor and each his brother, saying, "Know the Lord," for they shall all know me, from the least of them to the greatest, says the Lord; for I will forgive their iniquity, and I will remember their sin no more (Jer. 31:31-34).

The prophet could not see beyond an existence constituted or regulated by law, could only see that, however new the new would be, its only aspect would be continuity with the old. For

Chapter 11 *1 Corinthians*

this reason he could see no other reason for the coming of the new than the breaking of the old—"I will make a new covenant . . . for they have broken my covenant." But he involved himself in a happy inconsistency when he promised that when the new appeared the law would no longer encounter one from without—"I will put my law within them." But if so, then it was all over with whatever existence had been tied to, the external, the outward, the perceptible, the visible, the legal—or the invisible derived from perception of the visible. And with that change in historical conditions existence itself would change: "For I will forgive their iniquity, and I will remember their sin no more." The only question remaining was how—how would life change, how would God draw so close, or how would life change because God would draw so close? **This is my body which is for you. . . . This cup is the new covenant in my blood**—a "participation" in the body, in the death of Jesus, and a participation in the one whom God made "wisdom . . . righteousness . . . sanctification and redemption" (1:31), and these two without contradiction, since the crucified and the exalted one are inseparable, the exalted one continually giving what the dying one gave once for all. Paul would have warmed to the debate. In their own fashion the Corinthians had reversed the order of the transference, had moved from "is this" to "like this," had succumbed to the urge for life free of participation, rendered life with Christ and each other symbolic in a rage for existence as individual and self-contained, for the perceptible, the visible—"meats for the belly and the belly for meats."

For as often as you eat this bread and drink this cup, you proclaim the Lord's death until he comes (v. 21). The words are Paul's, and they are his interpretation of Jesus' word, **Do this in remembrance of me.** The "anamnesis" or remembrance of Jesus was not to consist in merely pondering the circumstances surrounding his death. Not even the Gospel's passion narratives were composed for the purpose of insuring recollection of the Good Friday events. Their readers were to see in Christ's death the shape which their own discipleship should take ("if any man would come after me, let him deny himself and take up his cross and follow me," Mark 8:34 and parallels), should see their own destiny mirrored there. There was a certain clumsy propriety in the Württemberg government's deletion from the hymnbook of 150 years ago the old, familiar "O Haupt voll Blut und Wunden" ("O Sacred Head, Now Wounded")—a hymn dear to the heart of the Swabian pietist—if it was merely meant to call the bloody afternoon to recollection. If the new covenant marked participation in the death of Christ, then to "remember" him by eating and drinking at his summons meant to announce that the one who gave a share in his death had been made the "power of God and the wisdom of God" (1:24), had been raised to the status of Lord, so that whatever occurred since that death, whatever happened next, had him as its subject and goal. It meant to announce that if that goal was still hidden from sight, appearing only under the sign of its opposite in defeat and humiliation, requiring faith to penetrate the sign, that faith would finally be dissolved in sight— **you proclaim the Lord's death until he comes.** Paul's interpretation belongs to the same genre as was reflected in his references to the "revelation of our Lord Jesus Christ" (1:7-8); to "the rulers of this age being destroyed" (2:6); to "the Day" (3:12-15); to the "coming" or "Day of the Lord" (4:5; 5:5); to the saints about to "judge the world" (6:2); to "the present distress," the "shortening" of the time, the "shape" of the world as passing away (7:26, 29, 31); to the "imperishable wreath" (9:25), and to the arrival of the "end of the age" (10:11). It belongs in the same context as the first three Evangelists give to their passion narratives when they add or prefix to them the words: "Truly, I say to you, I shall not drink again of the fruit of the vine until that day when I drink it new in the kingdom of God" (Mark 14:25).

Commentary on the Paradosis (11:27-32)   Following the paradosis, Paul draws conclusions from it which pertain to the crisis at Corinth. **Therefore,** he begins (or "so that"), **whoever eats the bread or drinks the cup of the Lord in an unworthy manner.** . . . Christians have torn at each other for years over the meaning of that term **unworthy,** principally because Paul's warning has been loosed from its context. If the apostle was intent on reminding the Corinthians of the Supper's Host, of the eating and drinking as giving a share in the death of the one whom God had made Lord, and thus a share in the life of any other who belonged to him, then the meaning of that word **unworthy** could scarcely be restricted to a lack of intellectual or dogmatic appreciation for what was occurring "in, with, and under" the eating and the drinking. Paul was breaking a lance with those who could not, but might yet still, see (hope is driving the apostle to write, to hurl the paradosis into all this chaos) that participation in the body and blood of Christ denoted a life for which the "I" and its separateness from all other "I's" was only a myth invented for the sake of that deep, primal urge in us all to get free of the other. For this, whatever dogmatic or ideological differences might arise would merely be a symptom, but only a symptom, and Paul was after getting at the disease. **In an unworthy manner** meant succumbing to the rage for distance, disassociation, narcissism, marked in Corinth by going ahead with one's own meal and despising the hungry, the church of God, the body and its Host. **Whoever** eats and drinks in such manner, Paul writes, **will be guilty of . . . the body and blood of the Lord.** The RSV translates, **will be guilty of profaning,** presumably of confusing the Supper with any other meal or carousal—which the Corinthians had already done, for to what else could that **in an unworthy manner** refer if not to profaning? Paul's warning here is more ominous: Whoever eats or drinks in such fashion will have the body and blood of Christ, the death of Christ, on his head—again, not the body and blood, not the death, of Golgotha. Those references to participation in Christ's body and blood in 10:16 and in our chapter, or to culpability for the body and blood of the Lord in this passage here are not to a magical turning back of the clock effected by the sacrament. (In that ancient superstition conjured up by the dogma of transubstantiation, the communicant thought he could pick the flesh of Jesus from his teeth.) On the other hand, to construe the participation or culpability "as if," as if a participation in or a culpability for the body and blood of the Lord, is not the only alternative. If, as Paul preached, God had made himself known in the death of Jesus, then that meant that the nature of God, the life of God consisted in setting himself, his Godhead, his power and possession as God in question, in planning life for his creature and death for himself, in saying no to himself and yes to his creature. It meant a wedding of Godhead to ruin so intimate that God's death could never be called a "departure" from himself—could never be called "God" without also being called the "crucified," could never be called the "crucified" without also being called "God," a "negation" which the resurrection did not put an end to, but rather established, fixed, and sealed. So much for traditional metaphysical concepts of God according to which he cannot suffer without coming into "contradiction" with himself, and so much for notions of God as simply a God "in relation"! But if the life of God consisted in this negation, then that meant that God was victor over death; death could not put an end to him, since there was no end to his suffering. Then that meant that to those whom he gave a share in his life he gave a share in his death.

> We have penetrated to the center of Christian faith. It can be expressed in many ways. But no attempt to speak of the center of Christian faith—or better, to speak *from out of* the center of Christian faith—may be abstracted from the fact that the death of Jesus Christ has something to do with us only because it has to do with God. Every attempt to hold God aloof from the suffering of this death in ideas, dogmas, and liturgies, ignores the essence of Christian faith.[71]

But, as the apostle warns, this also means that one might try to give God a reason for his death in a rage for an alienation which only God could suffer, that his creatures might never be alone—when God needed no reason, when he had his own reason. And as to good eventually coming of evil, as to things somehow coming right in the end, as to culpability lodged in that urge to get free of the other as furnishing at least an occasion for God's being-for-us, as to doing evil "that good may come," "that grace may abound," Paul will have much to say later on: "How can we who died to sin still live in it?" (Rom. 6:2).

Let a man examine himself, and so eat . . . (v. 28); let him test to see how he falls from the mold (that term from minting and banking again) before he shares the death. If the test is failed, if the "body" is not discerned; if the Host is not acknowledged, if the "corporate" nature of our existence with him and thus with each other which that eating and drinking, that sharing of his death gives is not recognized, a judgment will be fitted to the guilt (v. 29). In one way or another the Host will make clear the Supper is his. Corinth had already tasted judgment: **That is why many of you are weak and ill and some have** "fallen asleep" (Paul's word for the Christians' death, cf. 15:6, 20). The statement is daring, risky. It cannot be applied wholesale, as though to every sin some visible, palpable calamity belonged, a mathematics which Jesus flatly rejected (Luke 13:2-5; John 9:1-3), and which Paul denied, at least as applying to himself. For when the Corinthians drew suspicions concerning the genuineness of his apostleship from the outward circumstances of his life, Paul roundly opposed such calculation, and insisted there were other reasons (chap. 9). And Paul did not regard his case as exceptional. If the shape of the Corinthians' own existence mirrored God's choice of what was "low and despised in the world, even things that are not, to bring to nothing things that are" (1:28); if their life for the other could assume the shape of deprivation, or suffering ("were you a slave when called? Do not let it weigh on your mind," 7:21), such arithmetic applied neither to them nor to Paul. It is false, then, to state that Paul derives the sickness or death of the Corinthian Christians from their participation in the Supper. They derive from the judgment of the Lord which has its basis in the manner in which they sinned against him at the Supper. This puzzling verse thus needs chap. 10 for its interpretation—the sacrament does not guarantee immunity! But it also needs v. 32: The consequence of not **discerning the body** is a judgment from the Lord whose rule extends to corporeality ("many of you are weak and sickly, and some have fallen asleep"), a judgment which does not wait for the "Day," but reaches to the here and now, **that we may not be condemned along with the world.** Lexicographically, there is virtually no difference between the terms for judging and condemning. The one may accent the decision of the judge, and the other its execution, but the conclusion drawn from v. 29 in v. 30 (**eats and drinks judgment upon himself . . . that is why many of you are weak . . .**) and the parallel drawn between being **judged by the Lord** and being **chastened** in v. 32 indicates that Paul has used the terms to denote two quite distinct events. There is a difference between being "judged," being "educated" even with death, and being "condemned with the world," a difference between coming to the end of life for not having judged or "examined" oneself, and coming to an end with God. For Paul, one death was not as good as any other.

The Appeal (11:33-34) In vv. 33-34, Paul makes his appeal: **My brethren.** . . . The apostle and this kaleidoscope of humanity, these Corinthians who had "invented" everything that could go awry in future but without yet developing a nomenclature for it, were for all their striking differences still kin, belonged to the same tree. The "blood," the death they shared was thicker than division. **When you come together to eat, wait for one another.** The travesty made of the Supper; the lunging ahead with one's own meal, the despising, the humiliating, the eating and drinking "unworthily," the guilt and the judgment—it all turned on neglect of that one truth that they were there for each other because another had made them his own. Verse 34a repeats in imperative form what had appeared in the interrogative in v. 22, and v. 34b abbreviates the argument in vv. 31-32. If for Paul one death was not as good as another, neither death was to his taste: **If any one is hungry, let him eat at home** (literally, "in the house"), **lest you come together** "for judgment" (the RSV incorrectly translates, **to be condemned;** the distinction made between "judged" and "condemned" should be retained). The chapter concludes with Paul's promise to set in order whatever else might pertain to the Supper at Corinth (**the other things**). What else could?

Chapter 12
Speaking in Tongues and the Test (12:1-3)

The healings of Jesus had elicited from his opponents the charge that he cast out demons by the power of Beelzebul (Mark 3:22). Paul, the equal of any "Pentecostal" at Corinth (cf. 14:18), on one occasion being lofted to the third heaven and hearing things a person may not utter (2 Cor. 12:2ff.), soon suffered the fate of an outsider in a church preoccupied with structure and organization. Or, was the structure imposed so as to contain that original fire which seized the earliest apostles, but which appeared unseemly to a hierarchy struggling to maintain good order in a world where such things occurred outside as well as within the church? "Give heed to the bishop, and to the presbytery and deacons," summoned Ignatius in a moment of rapture. Goethe, commenting on that primitive, Pentecostal wave, once wrote:

> If you seek for this brook you will not find it. It has gone astray into the swamps, avoided by all well-dressed folk. Here and there it waters some heather in secret, and for this, one may thank God in quietness. But our theological cameralists embrace the principle that one should dike in all its traces, pave streets, and lay sidewalks on it.[72]

Origen (d. ca. A.D. 254) suggested that the Corinthians had been invaded by Ophites, the "snake-people," and Chrysostom (ca. 347–407) could not manage chaps. 12–14: The entire affair had been too long unused and forgotten. Whether by institutional or other, "critical" means, the fire, the wave, the movement had been tamed. Glossolalia, speaking in tongues, comes and goes, and there are leagues from the heretic Montanus (late 2nd c.) to the French Camisards (ca. A.D. 1700), from the Camisards to the Irvingites of England (18th c.), from the Irvingites to the Apostolic Faith Mission at 312 Azuza Street in Los Angeles. The speaker in tongues, however, is only the more colorful representative of people for whom the tradition can never be a yoke, who not merely challenges churchly opinion or worldview, but heralds the coming of the new. Still, the danger lurking in charismatic movements is that of enthusiasm, of "ultrasupernaturalism," for which spirit and corporeality or human nature are at odds, a corporeality supernaturalized in the experience of faith. The enthusiast is not content with encountering God in the world, but must construct another world where God and the soul may meet free of the limits of historical existence. The enthusiast has seized the "then" in the "now," a seizure parent to the individualism, imperialism, and antisacramentalism which mark the danger of a "charismatic movement." For if I have already achieved the next world, "why should my liberty be determined by another man's scruples" (10:29), and not rather the other's scruples determined by my liberty? Or perhaps, why give such strict attention to the business of eating and drinking when God is mine without mediation? But the obverse side of enthusiasm, and which could furnish the impulse or prepare the ground for a charismatic experience, or at least show itself once the initial rapture has cooled, is that the world it has invented must somehow become visible, provable, demonstrable in the world it has abandoned. The obverse side is the desire to have done with the trembling and the questioning and to fix something or other as proof for faith.

In Corinth, where tongue-speaking had created sufficient stir to force the apostle to devote three entire chapters to it, one motive for the conflict lay in ignoring the pan-human character of the phenomenon. **Now concerning spiritual gifts, brethren,** writes Paul (again, no doubt a direct reference to the letter from Corinth—cf. again 7:1, 25; 8:1), or, "concerning spiritual persons" (the substantive may be either masculine or neuter), **I do not want you to be uninformed.** The phrase is all but identical with that ever-recurring "Don't you know?" since the Corinthians already knew what Paul said they did not know (v. 2, **you know** . . .). It was a matter of not wanting to know, of refusing to know, at least of hesitating to come to grips with what they knew. **You know** and what follows is as clumsy in its syntax as its sense is clear. **You know that when you were heathen, you were led astray to dumb idols, however you may have been moved** (RSV) is as helpful a translation of 12:2 as its alternatives, though it requires

Chapter 12   *1 Corinthians*

connecting in periphrastic construction words which appear at the beginning and at the end of the sentence (**you were** and **led astray**).

For the Corinthians, apparently, glossolalia constituted the principal sign of the presence and power of the Spirit of God. For Paul it was equivocal, ambiguous. If he had not regarded it as such, he would not have later used the analogy of the flute, harp, and bugle ("if even lifeless instruments . . . do not give distinct notes, how will anyone know what is played?" 14:7), or have asked, "if, therefore, the whole church assembles and all speak in tongues, and outsiders or unbelievers enter, will they not say that you are mad?" (14:23). The word "mad" translates a more or less technical term for the ravings of pagan religious devotees who experienced such vehement ecstasy while in the possession of their gods that they "blew a fuse." "You know," writes Paul, "you see with your mind's eye what occurred at such events." But however equivocal (there is ample evidence to suggest that the phrase "speaking in tongues" was a technical term already in use, developed in Judaism),[73] Paul did not doubt that it could be a genuine activity of God. Verse 2 does not intend to distinguish the phenomenon in paganism from that in Christianity, but rather to draw an analogy—speaking in tongues exists within and outside the church. But if the Corinthians had assigned priority to that phenomenon, then it had been made the criterion of Christian existence, had been made to stand alone, without reference to origin, norm, or goal, without connection to anyone or anything other than itself. Then it had been loosed from what gave it meaning. Hence, after reminding his readers of the equivocal nature of speaking in tongues, Paul applies a test to it, brings it under a control. Verse 3 states the test in general terms: **No one speaking by the Spirit of God ever says "Jesus be cursed!" and no one can say "Jesus is Lord" except by the Holy Spirit.** The phrase **Jesus be cursed** appears only for the sake of contrast with the acclamation as Lord (*kyrios*). The suggestion that some Corinthians cursed Jesus in ecstasy, or that Gnostics among them cursed the earthly, historical Jesus, may be attractive, but lacks evidence. The meaning is not that, however lofty his readers' moments of rapture, a true and authentic speaking in tongues could never contradict their Christian confession. If that were so, Paul would scarcely have insisted later that the gift should be used in rational and orderly fashion. Paul is here attempting one more time what he deserves to be celebrated for as pioneer—to bend, warp the notion of Spirit, his nature, power, and manifestations into the service of what God has done in Christ.

Varieties of Gifts; the Test Particularized (12:4-11)

To the Corinthians' accenting the one, Paul now opposes a variety of "manifestations of the Spirit," wrests the initiative for those manifestations from the Corinthians' choice, lodging it in the divine willing, and in midst of his enumerations gives the test stated in v. 3 specific application. **Now there are varieties of gifts.** . . . The term **gifts** in v. 4 (*charismata*) is synonymous with the term translated "spiritual gifts" in v. 1 (*pneumatikōn*), but the latter in Greek does not contain the notion of "gift." Whether or not the term in v. 1 was a Corinthian invention, Paul's term for the Spirit's manifestations was "gifts" (*charismata*), a word deriving from the same stem as the term "grace" (*charis*). Paul's choice of language here is deliberate, critical. The "pneumatic," the "spiritual person" is such, not by natural endowment or by training, but by grace, by the divine favor. Then follows the triadic formula, which prepares the way for Paul's test stated in the particular: **Varieties of gifts . . . the same Spirit . . . varieties of service . . . the same Lord . . . varieties of working . . . the same God who inspires them all in every one.** "Trinitarian" teaching, the stimulus for which lay in the doxological portions of Paul's correspondence (cf. the "binitarian" formulas but also the alternation of persons in the formulas of Rom. 1:7; 14:13, 30; 16:27; 1 Cor. 1:3; 2 Cor. 1:2; Gal. 1:3; Phil. 1:2; 1 Thess. 1:1; Philemon 1:3, and finally the full-blown trinitarian formula in 2 Cor. 13:14), has its "germ" here as well—God is the origin, the Lord and the Spirit are the origin, of the gifts. And if Paul conceives the persons in that triad as enjoying an equality (wheth-

Chapter 12   *1 Corinthians*

er or not he could be pressed to regard that equality in terms of substance, as did the later church, is another matter), he uses the terms **gifts, service,** and **working** synonymously to denote the genus of manifestation to which the various species in vv. 8-10 belong. All three constitute the "manifestation of the Spirit" (v. 7). Neither person in the triad is identified with a particular species of charisma. Again, in assigning to **service** (the Greek is plural) a status equal to that of **gifts** or **working** (in Greek, "workings of powers," v. 10, that is, of "miracles," cf. 2:4), Paul hides a critical, polemical note: Mundane, unostentatious, everyday deeds of service are ranged among the supernatural phenomena of the Spirit. In v. 7, Paul particularizes the test: **To each is given the manifestation of the Spirit for the common good** (cf. 6:12; 7:35; 10:23). The test of a genuine gift is thus its goal, its "whither." To say "Jesus is Lord" is an acclamation whose result is life for the other, since the Spirit by which that confession is made has his goal in the **common good.** Paul's test is none other than the one applied till now. The confession of Jesus and turning from self to the other are twin: "Christ, our passover, has been sacrificed. Let us, therefore, keep the feast . . . with the unleavened bread of sincerity and truth" (5:7-8); "God raised the Lord and will also raise us up by his power . . . shun immorality" (6:14, 18); "you were bought with a price; do not become slaves of men" (7:23); "for us there is one God . . . and one Lord . . . take care lest this liberty of yours somehow become a stumbling block to the weak" (8:6,9); "have I not seen Jesus our Lord? . . . I have become all things to all men" (9:1,22); " 'the earth is the Lord's' . . . give no offense to Jews or to Greeks or to the church of God" (10:26,32); " 'this is my body' . . . when you come together to eat, wait for one another" (11:24,33).

The enumeration of the species of gifts in vv. 8-10 does not reflect a hierarchy. As to form and content, the **utterance** (Greek, "word") **of wisdom** and the **utterance of knowledge** in v. 8 are the same—an understanding expressed in speech (cf. 1:5 and 2 Cor. 8:7) of how God will act and what he will require, derived from knowledge of how he has already acted and what he has already required. In v. 9, "faith" follows the **utterance of wisdom**—from which many have inferred that the term denotes a particular type of faith, and in support of the inference appeal to 13:2 ("if I have all faith, so as to remove mountains"), or to Mark 11:22-24 and Matt. 17:20. If the inference is correct, then such faith is directed to the "workings of powers" or "miracles" in v. 10. If it is not, if there is no reason but to construe faith according to its usual meaning (the result clause in 13:2, and the conditional clause in Mark 11:23 and Matt. 17:20 are far more suggestive of a quantity than a type of faith), then Paul's intention is merely to indicate that all members of the community are pneumatics. In either case, the position of **faith** in the list does not reflect a hierarchy. Further, in v. 10, **prophecy** appears sixth on the list, whereas in 13:2 it appears second, and in 14:1 first among the spiritual gifts (cf. Rom. 12:6). Finally, **kinds of tongues,** together with their interpretation, take up the rear at the conclusion of v. 10, but in 13:1 and 14:2 assume first and second place in the enumeration. More important is the fact that these verses expand the thought in vv. 4-7. Between the frame (inclusio) of vv. 6 and 11 (**the same God who inspires them all in every one . . . all these are inspired by one and the same Spirit**—yet another "binitarian" formula), the Spirit appears as agency (**through the Spirit,** v. 8), criterion or norm (**according to the same Spirit,** v. 8), the means (**by the same Spirit,** v. 9), the sphere ("**in the Spirit**" v. 9), and finally the initiator of the gifts (**as he wills**). And this Spirit has determined upon variety for the **common good** (**to one . . . to another,** v. 8; **to another . . . to another,** v. 9; **to another . . . to another, . . . to another, . . . to another, . . . to another,** v. 10; **all these . . . to each one individually,** v. 11).

The Analogy of the Body and the Necessity for Variety (12:12-31a)

If one result of the Corinthians' accent upon tongues as the preeminent mark of Christian existence is that they made it the *criterion* par excellence of Christian existence, another was that they ignored or spurned the truth of the church as Christ's body.

Chapter 12   *1 Corinthians*

In language reminiscent of Stoic philosophy which conceived the entire world as an organism, Paul proceeds to outline the existence and necessity of diversity within the body. Verse 12 begins with the word translated "as" or **just as.** The organism-concept furnishes Paul an illustration, an analogy. It is auxiliary to his underlying idea of the church. Evidence for this is in the fracture of the Stoic notion at strategic points. First, the organism-concept is pressed into the service of Christology: **For just as the body is one and has many members, and all the members of the body, though many, are one body, so it is with Christ** (v. 12). That the name **Christ** is not merely a surrogate for what the Stoic might call the "law of nature," "God," or the self, is made clear at the second point of fracture: **For by one Spirit we were all baptized into one body . . . and all were made to drink of one Spirit** (v. 13). The Stoic notion has been historicized. Not only was the body of Christ in existence before anyone could belong to it. (The Gnostic too could assign a certain priority in time, if not in essence to his "Christ," to that "archetypal man" who descended to "redeem" his brethren, to call them to recollection of their true origin and goal which had been forgotten with the "soul's" imprisonment in the flesh.) That body of Christ was also alien to human existence. It was not given with existence, was not something that merely needed to be called to mind as given with it. Belonging to the body, becoming a member of this body required a historical event, an act outside the self, in which the self played no role—**we were all baptized into one body**—an event which Paul would later describe as doing violence to the self, putting it to death ("we were buried therefore with him by baptism into death," Rom. 6:4). And as for the priority of that body, it could not be described as analogous to the world's being there before ever we were, or as analogous to a "Christ-Adam" whose only change occurred when he took on vile flesh to make his descent to redeem. There was a time when this body was not, when it required the death of the one who assumed flesh before it could be.

In vv. 14-26, Paul employs the analogy of the organism to demonstrate the absurdity of denying diversity within the unity of the body, as well as the absurdity of denying the unity within the diversity. The argument has about it the character of a fable, and the humor ought not be slighted for the "moral." The best known of its type, the fable of Menenius Agrippa, is related by the first-century Roman historian, Livy:

> In the days when man's members did not all agree amongst themselves, as is now the case, but had each its own ideas and a voice of its own, the other parts thought it unfair that they should have the worry and the trouble and the labour of providing everything for the belly, while the belly remained quietly in their midst with nothing to do but to enjoy the good things which they bestowed upon it; they therefore conspired together that the hands should carry no food to the mouth, nor the mouth accept anything that was given it, nor the teeth grind up what they received. While they sought in this angry spirit to starve the belly into submission, the members themselves and the whole body were reduced to the utmost weakness. Hence it had become clear that even the belly had no idle task to perform, and was no more nourished than it nourished the rest, by giving out to all parts of the body that by which we live and thrive, when it has been divided equally amongst the veins and is enriched with digested food—that is, the blood.[74]

If the foot should say, "Because I am not a hand, I do not belong to the body". . . . **If the ear should say, "Because I am not an eye, I do not belong to the body"** (vv. 15-16), which, being interpreted, means: "If the one with the gift of faith should say, 'Because I do not have the gift of healing, I do not belong to Christ's body'. . . . If the one who distinguishes the spirits should say, 'Because I do not have the gift of prophecy, I do not belong to Christ's body. . . .'" To this absurdity Paul responds: **If the whole body were an eye, where would be the hearing? If the whole body were an ear, where would be the sense of smell?** which could as well be read: "If all the members of Christ's body were prophets, where would be the distinguishing of spirits . . . ?" That Paul does not regard these gifts as in the permanent possession of their recipients, somehow to be used at will (thus viewing the variety or diversity as labile, volatile), and that he does not regard the diversity itself as a law to be observed without exception, is suggested by his remarks in 12:31; 14:1 and 5: "Earnestly desire the greater gifts, . . . earnestly desire the spiritual gifts, especially that you may prophesy. . . . I want you all to speak in tongues, but even more to prophesy." Conceivably, there could be occasions on which the entire body could be an ear or an eye—the other side of that coin which Paul turns up here. At any rate, as with the analogy of the organism, what the body is and how it is constituted—in this instance its diversity—is a divine arrangement: **God arranged the organs in the body, each one of them, as he chose** (v. 18). (The "but now," RSV, **but as it is,** at the beginning of v. 18, a tiny conjunction linked to a temporal adverb, will, in Paul's letters, often be an alert to an essential point in his argument, cf. 5:11; 7:14; 13:13; 14:6, or even to an activity of God which has sliced "then" and "now," "this" and "that" into two irreconcilable halves, cf. 15:20—a role those little words will play to the point of exhaustion in Romans.) In vv. 14-17 Paul had contended for the many in the one, for the diversity in the unity. The diversity exists (v. 14); it does not deny the unity (vv. 15-17), and it exists by God's design (v. 18). No body without the members! Now, in vv. 19-26, Paul contends for the one in the many, for the unity in the diversity. No members without the body! (**If all were a single organ, where would the body be?** v. 19.) Then, humor aside, Paul responds to the absurdity of denying the unity in the variety (**the eye cannot say to the hand, "I have no need of you," nor again the head to the feet, "I have no need of you,"** v. 21), with a reference to the care for the one which the many guarantee. But with that, a new, alien note has been introduced into the analogy. The "weaker" parts of the body may be indispensable (v. 22), but the care of the remainder for those parts is not inherent. It is assigned. We **invest with the greater honor** and respectability what is "more without honor" or "without respectability" (v. 23). The suggestion that the first term refers to the rump and the second to the sexual organs, or that the verb translated **invest** is intended to echo the rite of circumcision may be a mite strained, but hardly inappropriate. Or again, it is God who gives greater honor to the disadvantaged or inferior part, **that there may be no discord in the body, but that the members may have the same care for one another,** with the result (or purpose) that **if one member suffers or is honored,** the others suffer or rejoice (vv. 24-26). That alien note, that use of the pronoun **we** (and can Paul be missing from that **we**?), or the word that God assigns **greater honor** to what "we suppose" (v. 23) to be dishonorable and lacking in respectability—an honor which the "respectable" do not require (v. 24)—for which reason the many guarantee care for the one (v. 25); that fracture of the analogy is the clue to the fact that all this while the subject under discussion has never been the organism, the body, but Corinth, with its healers, miracle workers, prophets, speakers in tongues and interpreters, the body of Christ. Christ's Spirit "apportions to each one individually as he wills" to prevent schism, factionalism, party spirit—"I belong to Paul," or "I belong to Apollos . . .," or "I have no need of you"—and to cause each to care for the other, for the "common good."

If the Corinthians had not yet tumbled to the subject Paul's analogy was calculated to serve, v. 27 puts it squarely: **Now you are the body of Christ and individually members of it.** Then follows a new enumeration, this time not of gifts (nor of office) but of their recipients, and, due to the use of ordinal numbers in the listing, according to their importance for the body. Glossolalia, ecstatic speech, lofted to the status of a (or the) principal test of faith, robbed of its independence, and checked against its modality or use, its relation to the "common good" and not against its mere appearance, is demoted to last place. One last time, in vv. 29-30, Paul reduces to the absurd the denial of diversity in the unity: **Are all apostles?** The little negative prefixed in the Greek to each of the seven interrogatives requires an answer in the negative—"no!" "indeed not!" "surely not!" By signaling their use, Paul has checkmated pneumatic individualism, that bedfellow of enthusiasm, desacralized the gifts and once more proved himself pioneer. For, if use for the body, if the "common good" furnishes the criterion, then whatever "serves" (v. 5) that good is a charisma and every Christian a charismatic. In Romans 12, Paul will write, "so we, though many, are one body in Christ, and individually members one of another. Having gifts that differ according to the grace given to us [the RSV then inserts a clause entirely appropriate to Paul's rule of modality] let us use them: if prophecy, in proportion to our faith [or, 'in correspondence with our faith'] . . ." (Rom. 12:5-6). "All for one and one for all"— life for the other, and thus use for the other. But if the other gives the content and goal to action, then nothing in itself is virtuous, nothing in itself is sacred, and applause is nothing to desire.

The chapter ends with Paul's summons **earnestly** to **desire the higher** (or "greater") **gifts,** and his promise to show the Corinthians **a still more excellent way** (v. 31). The verse should not begin with an adversative, as though Paul were calling the Corinthians to be zealous for gifts he had not already described. More than one meaning attaches to that little postpositive conjunction which the RSV translates **but** (**but earnestly desire the higher gifts;** cf. 14:1, where the same conjunction is used, and hardly for the purposes of contrast). And as for the term translated **higher,** it must take its meaning from everything which preceded. Those gifts which are **higher** (the original reads "greater") receive their rank according to the criterion of their use for the body. In chap. 14, Paul will no longer leave to inference what he regards as "greater" or more useful when judged by that norm. Verse 31a thus faces backward, and v. 31b forward to what follows in chap. 13. As more than one interpreter has noted, the transition from 12:31b to 13:1 is not at all smooth. But this verse makes one thing clear: What Paul is about to describe to his Corinthians is not one more gift, a gift "higher" or greater but no different from the others in kind. Only as object of pursuit can it be described as enjoying commonality with the gifts ("make love your aim, and earnestly desire the spiritual gifts," 14:1). To the extent the phrase **more excellent** suggests only a difference in degree between the gifts and this **way,** it is false. And this **way** is not a way to the gifts, a route leading to the gifts, as though there could be no gifts apart from this way. Paul had already called attention to the panhuman, thus equivocal nature of speaking in tongues. If such a phenomenon could exist outside as well as inside the church, it could also exist apart from this **way**. It is precisely this possibility which Paul addresses in chap. 14. This **way** is not a way conceived as a path to something else, to some end or goal other than itself. It is not a prerequisite or a supplement (cf. Lietzmann on 12:31). This **way** is its own end and goal, for which reason it is called a **way**, since it never leads to anything other than itself. Paul's promise deserves better treatment than a translation which construes everything which precedes **way** as its modifier: **I will show you a still more excellent way.** Perhaps "still, I will show you a way beyond all this" does it better justice.

Chapter 13

A Norwegian who taught in Sweden and sometimes wrote in French expressed earlier contemporary opinion when he denied Pauline authorship to 1 Corinthians 13, stating that 12:31a and 14:1b neatly connect, whereas 12:31b and 14:1a do not, and that the concept of love throughout chap. 13 is un-Pauline, and thus an ad hoc insertion against Gnosticism by a later hand. Later, the scholar confessed to having erred, revised his opinion, charged the awkwardness of language to Paul's account, described the chapter as a digression, and concluded:

> One of the most impressive traits of Paul's character is his energetic defense of pedagogical needs and the experiences of practical life against religious enthusiasm and speculation. In unparalleled fashion he combines incorruptible moral sobriety with a lofty flight of the spirit.[75]

The chapter has been torn to tatters. At a thousand and one nuptials it has been held up as a model for conjugal bliss, or been otherwise touted as an ideal toward which to strive, all on the assumption that the knowledge of its content is somehow self-evident, given with existence, the only requirement that of opting for it. It has been made the tool of feeling and irrationality, used

Chapter 13 *1 Corinthians*

to flay the hide from truth, as though truth and love were mortal enemies, or at least rivals needing reconciling:

> What you think belongs to all,
> your own is only what you feel;
> should He be your very own,
> feel the God of whom you think.[76]

Or, the chapter has been pirated and indentured to a system based on Greek notions of virtue, according to which love, the highest Christian virtue, justifies and gives to faith its shape. In the words of the old medieval slogan, "the greatest virtue chiefly justifies; love is the greatest virtue; therefore love chiefly justifies."

To all this Paul's great hymn to love gives the lie. The hymn has nothing to do with "moral sobriety," if by "moral sobriety" is meant something within the sphere of human possibility. It has to do with something beyond the range of human possibility, and to the point where not even the knowledge or awareness of it can be assumed. For this reason it cannot serve as an ideal, but that does not mean that it has nothing to do with reality, with becoming concrete, with action. The subject of this hymn cannot be made a cloak for unreason or an enemy of truth, because it is truth's other side—but that does not mean the other side of a truth construed as a human possibility. It cannot be impressed into the service of a system which identifies it with other "virtues," though "higher" or "greater," so that it could somehow give "form or comeliness" to what is lower or smaller than itself. Paul's hymn to love is as radical a statement as any he has made thus far. It is as polemic, as critical a statement against Corinthian religion as any made thus far. And it is not a "digression" or an "excursus." Everything Paul has written thus far has led up to it. All that impatience with the myth of the self as somehow enjoying identity with the divine and thus as needing nothing but itself; all that preoccupation with engagement, alignment, with corporeality; all that hammering away at the other as furnishing the question and the answer to action and intention; all that concentration on the "body"; all that accenting of use for the "common good" or modality as furnishing the criterion for judgment—all this has prepared for it.

Years ago, one interpreter wrote that Paul could not have written 1 Corinthians 13 had he not known the historical Jesus.[77] As a historical judgment, that statement is false, but it needs only the removal of the adjective *historical* to render it true, and in a sense deeper than that interpreter may have seen: If, for Paul, love is to the spiritual gifts what Christ is to the members of his body, and if love is the presence of Christ in his body, then "love," that "way beyond all this" spells "Christ," and the hymn has not only one occasion or stimulus, as that old interpreter wrote, but finally only one subject:

> Nowhere, I think, does Paul come so near to Jesus as in the 13th chapter of Corinthians, though the name Jesus is not named, and no word from him appears. But it is spirit of the spirit of Jesus which has deepened (not canceled) the law through love, whose faith springs from love and whose hope is borne by love. Here they are near to each other, the unrivaled master and his pupil, this so unequal pair: Jesus and Paul.[78]

From the standpoint of structure and style, the hymn is as remarkable a piece as any in the Bible. Easily divided into three sections, the first deals with the uselessness, the nothingness of the gifts apart from love (vv. 1-3), the second with love's nature and activity (vv. 4-7), and the last with its imperishability (vv. 8-13).

The Gifts as Nothing without Love (12:31b—13:3)

> The form and content of these animated sentences agrees exactly: Five times the initial conditional clauses begin in the same way; they roll on like waves, in the second verse swelling to a three-part sentence, and smash on the threefold "but have not love," and the concluding clauses express the vanity of the effort with a penetrating sameness: "I am nothing . . . I gain nothing."[79]

If I speak in the tongues of men and of angels—if I speak that strange language of the Spirit that can be heard at worship; if I join in the angels' praise, in that "new song," that hymn from a world no one can learn. . . . **If I have prophetic powers, and understand all mysteries and all knowledge, and if I have all faith, so as to remove mountains**—if I can tell the future, if I know the hidden counsels of God, can penetrate to the depths of deity, and have a faith great enough to move the earth. . . . **If I give away all I have, and if I deliver my body to be burned**—if I turn all my possessions to alms, if I plunge into martyrdom (the later reading is preferable to the earlier, "if I deliver my body that I may glory"). . . . The verses scale the heights of human possibility. Each act or function is heroic, exceptional, and all together represent what any contemporary of Paul, religious or not, would have regarded as the highest and best in humanity. And all of it, writes Paul, is for nothing, useless, and even if such an incredible thing were possible that all these gifts should somehow come into the possession of one single individual, if there were at least one human being about whom it could be said that he incorporated in himself all these powers, any one of which is denied the ordinary mortal, he would be nothing; none of it would be of any use to him—if **I have not love.** Three times, as noted in the quotation above, that refrain "if I have not love" appears. Three times the "I" is separated from "love." Three times the "I" is subject of the verb, but only of the verb "to have," never of the verb "to love." The RSV, harking back to a long tradition, retains that careful distinction.

There are parallels to these verses in ancient Greek and Jewish literature. In the Greek, the most striking, perhaps, is the elegy of the poet-general Tyrtaeus, whom legend has it roused the Spartans to battle with his song 800 years before Christ. Part of that ancient dystich reads:

> I would neither remember nor write of a man,
>   whether greatest on foot or in the wrestler's art,
> if he had the stature and strength of the Cyclopes,
>   and could conquer Thracias' north wind,
> if he were comelier in shape than Tothonas,
>   and richer by far than Midas and Cinyras,
> if he were more kingly than Pelops, Tantalus' son,
>   and had a sweeter tongue than Adrastus,

> if he had all fame—but had no courage to rush to the fight;
> for a man is not good in battle,
> if he does not dare to look on bloody death,
> and standing toe to toe reach to make attack:
> This is virtue, the highest prize among men,
> and the loveliest for a youth to win.[80]

Whether or not Paul had ever heard that hymn—and some believe he had—together with its author he hides under those conditional clauses ("if . . . if . . . if . . . if") the assumption that the impossible could be possible. But the parallel ends there. For while Tyrtaeus leaves behind every excellence or activity calculated to set one on a par with the gods for the sake of that one virtue—stomach for combat—Paul plunges love back into the arena of the ordinary and everyday.

The Nature and Activity of Love (13:4-7)

> Here too the style and rhythm of the sentences are more than merely a mode of external form. The setting of the sentences in a long, continuous series, advancing uniformly from one to the other part without special transitions and connections—fifteen verbs in these three verses!—allows us to see the calmness and also the unflagging nature of love, till in the last verse its all-encompassing power finds expression through that simple and fourfold accented repetition of the "all," and the entire series of ideas is closed.[81]

The section is framed by two positive statements in vv. 4a and 7: **Love is patient and kind . . . bears all things, believes all things, hopes all things, endures all things.** In the eight clauses between, the nature and activity of love are disclosed by what it is not. Love does not submit to unbridled passion which tears at community (**is not jealous**); it does not boast or preen itself, make the other feel and suffer over the distance from it ("does not boast, is not puffed up," v. 4b; RSV 4b-5a). Love does not sneer at custom or propriety by a public display of its knowledge or liberty, setting itself off from the "weak" and rupturing the normal connections of human society—that finer, more "spiritual" manifestation of

Chapter 13   1 Corinthians

selfishness (**is not . . . rude, . . . does not insist on its own way**). It is stranger to bitterness, though unbelief and arrogant ignorance on the right or left could give it ample reason to "keep score." It clings to the other and lets the other's guilt go (**is not irritable or resentful, v. 5**). Love does not feel better by its contrast with injustice, does not gloat over its winnings in the match with unrighteousness, hiding it all with a sad face for the loser. It declares holiday whenever there is a truth which gives the other advantage (**it does not rejoice at wrong, but rejoices** *together* **in the** truth [RSV, **the right**], v. 6). The distance between the "I" and love in this section is as unbridgeable as in the one preceding. The hypostasizing, the anthropomorphizing of love, giving it arms and legs, treating it as the subject of thinking, intending, and acting is no mere poetic device, but intended to describe the great gulf fixed between it and everything human.

Melville's last novel but one opens with the appearance on April Fool's of a lamblike mute on a riverboat who happens on a placard near the captain's cabin offering reward for the capture of a mysterious imposter. Pausing at the spot, the stranger produces a slate, traces some words upon it, and holds it on a level with the placard—"Charity thinketh no evil." Jostled aside by the passengers, he writes again: "Charity suffereth long, and is kind." Thrust aside again, he writes "Charity endureth all things." Amid stares and jeers he moves slowly up and down, changing his inscription to read "Charity believeth all things," and then, "Charity never faileth." In contrast, the barber of the boat throws open his premises for the day, rattles down his shutters, sets out his ornamental pole, and hangs over his door the pasteboard sign: "No trust."[82]

There is an analogy to this section in Jewish wisdom-tradition:

> The genuine man . . .
> does not defraud his neighbor. . . .
> And the spirits of error have no power over him. . . .
> Envy will not penetrate his thinking;
> no malice dissipates his soul;
> no avarice intrudes upon his integrity.
> For he lives by the integrity of his soul,
> and perceives all things by the rectitude of his heart. . . .[83]

Here, however, the gap between "virtue" and human existence has been closed. "Man" is the subject, and when the author of this piece further describes that "genuine man" as "making no place for an outlook made evil by this world's error, in order that he might envision no turning aside from any of the Lord's commands," he is nautical miles from the impossibility Paul is hymning here, which, for all its "infinitively qualitative difference" from any human excellence or virtue, queues up not only with the good, but with the evil. How else would the possibility be open to it of keeping score, of clinging to the other's guilt and letting the other go, of self-aggrandizement over the presence of injustice— and in the end run the risk of identification with the evil: "This man receives sinners and eats with them" (Luke 15:1)? The closest analogy by far to our hymn is in an apocryphal book called "first," "third," or even "second Esdras," and it comes within a hair's breadth of Paul:

> Truth is great, and stronger than all things. The whole earth calls upon truth, and heaven blesses her. All God's works quake and tremble, and with him there is nothing unrighteous. Wine is unrighteous, the king is unrighteous, women are unrighteous, all the sons of men are unrighteous, all their works are unrighteous, and all such things. There is no truth in them and in their unrighteousness they will perish. But truth endures and is strong for ever, and lives and prevails for ever and ever. With her there is no partiality or preference, but she does what is righteous instead of anything that is unrighteous or wicked. All men approve her deeds, and there is nothing unrighteous in her judgment. To her belongs the strength and the kingship and the power and the majesty of all the ages. Blessed be the God of truth![84]

The sage's "truth" was as impossible of human achieving as Paul's "love." It had to do with God.

Bears all things, believes all things, hopes all things, endures all things. . . . These terse sentences hark back to the initial verse in the section ("love is patient and kind," v. 4a), and together with it comprise the "frame." The fact that believing and hoping are set between bearing and enduring makes clear that their object (**all things**) is not anything at all, nor something which could accrue to love's advantage. Love waits, does not keep the other on a leash, do the other's walking for it, or stand by ready with an indictment when the other falls. It believes the other can walk; it sets all its hope on the other's walking, but springs to catch the other before the other falls, then begins the process of believing, hoping, and bearing all over again. In this way, by holding its breath for the other, gauging its intention and action by the other, love "endures." But this does not mean that love, this love, the love of which Paul is speaking, would not exist if there were no other. The fact that if there were no other this love would create another, call the other out of nothing to be borne, believed, and hoped for, does not render the other a necessity for this love. For if this love needed the other to exist, if it were dependent upon the other for its life, then what it bore, believed, and hoped would only be the means to its enduring, would only be a means of self-preservation. It is not necessity that makes love take its nature and activity from the other. It is not dependence on the other that makes love endure. It is freedom. This love can decide, can decide to exist for the other, act for the other. It could have decided not to be what it is; could have decided to be something else than love. It has no reason, no stimulus, no occasion for being what it is other than its own willing, its own deciding. This love is free. Freedom is simply another name for love.

The Imperishability of Love (13:8-13)

Again, the form and content of the section exactly correspond; the division of the sentences matches the lively movement of ideas: The positive thesis which furnishes the theme of vv. 8-13 stands at the beginning (v. 8a), and is taken up again at the conclusion (v. 13). Three abbreviated, identically constructed sentences state the contrast (v. 8b-d), their basis given in vv. 9 and 10. This makes clear the contrast between what is partial, transitory and what is perfect, but also the contrast between "now" and "then". . . . The contrast is carried through by a double comparison: between the child and the man (v. 11: three times the phrase "like a child" appears, following "when I was a child"), and between a seeing which is mediated, through a mirror; and a seeing some day to be without mediation. While v. 11 of course keeps entirely to the limit set by the figure and illustrates the destruction of what is imperfect (the verb "to destroy" appears four times in vv. 8-11!), the second comparison immediately points beyond itself, for seeing "face to face" is also a description of perfect knowledge. So the idea in v. 12 is livelier and finds expression in the double antithesis "now . . . then." Then, in the last sentence, in which "love," the theme of the entire section, stands as the last word, the train of thought returns to the beginning (v. 8), and at the same time to its goal.[85]

"Love," the "way beyond all this" (12:31b) will carry the gifts to their disappearance—**prophecies . . . will pass away . . . tongues . . . will cease . . . knowledge . . . will pass away** (v. 8b-d). Or, it will carry them to their God-appointed goal—**for now we see in a mirror dimly, but then face to face** (v. 12). The words **in a mirror** denote the manner of seeing: We cannot see the thing itself, only its refraction, "in a mirror, dimly" (literally, "in an enigma, enigmatically"). Whether, then, the goal of my gift consists in its nonexistence or in an existence so radically different from its present life that it will appear to be abolished (**when the perfect comes, the imperfect will pass away,** v. 10), the point is that the pneumatic, charismatic, the spiritual, the gifts, the manifestations—and glossolalia above all—are not the clear, unequivocal and unambiguous sign of the presence of eternity in time, of God in the world, tomorrow in the today, but are captive to the same tension between the "then" and the "now" which characterizes all existence. But if the tension between then and now will someday be resolved, what shape will that resolution take? Surprisingly enough, Paul does not write: "Now I know in part, but then I shall know fully," but rather, **Now I know in part; then I shall understand fully, even as I have been fully understood** (v. 12). The verbs "to know" and "to understand fully" both spring from the same parent root, and in other instances are for all practical purposes synonymous. But here "to understand fully" set in tandem with being "fully understood," makes clear that

Chapter 13   *1 Corinthians*

Paul has in mind two separate activities. That **fully** in **then I shall understand fully** will not be a filling up of what **I know in part;** what I know in part will not be resuscitated in my fully understanding. The tension will not be resolved when I have moved from the partial to the complete or perfect, when I have stepped off from what I know into what I shall fully understand, and with which what I know in part has enjoyed some connection, perhaps as its copy or imitation. There is no hope, no promise for what I know in part! That **in part** has no prospect of becoming "in full." **Now I know in part . . . then I shall understand fully,** and between those two lies the death of what I know, however I know it. **Knowledge . . . will pass away. For our knowledge is imperfect . . . but when the perfect comes, the imperfect will pass away** (vv. 8-10). What I know in part can no more inherit the future than can flesh and blood (15:50). The tension will be resolved when what I know in part has died and been raised to an understanding matched to the way in which "I have been understood." That latter phrase is nothing but a circumlocution for an activity of God who knows his own before they know in part or even fully understand. Its closest parallel in our epistle appears in 8:3, "If one loves God, one is known by him." But Paul had already struck this theme earlier: "Now that you have come to know God, or rather to be known by God" (Gal. 4:9). If love, if this impossibility, having nothing in common with conceivable virtue, and for which no "spiritual gift" can be made a look-alike, is despite all this a possibility, then it is because of something which occurred earlier to make it so, something which happened before it could be and from which it takes its origin and its power—in a "having been known" by God, in a choice by God: "For those whom he foreknew he also predestined to be conformed to the image of his Son" (Rom. 8:29). If love, if this love cannot exist but through such a choice or election, neither will "fully understanding." But if both exist through God's knowing beforehand, then to "understand fully" may be another name for love.

"Now then," or "but now" (RSV, **so**)—in any case, on the

alert!—**faith, hope, love abide, these three; but the greatest of these is love.** In 2 Cor. 5:7, faith and sight, in Rom. 8:24, hope and sight are opposed, but here they "abide." Not merely the triad, but also the accenting of the triad—**these three**—raise the ante, for if faith and hope are to be dissolved in a seeing **face to face,** how can they be said to **abide**? The proposal that we interpret that word *abide* to mean "does not fail" tears the sentence from its context, for it is in the "then," when tongues, prophecies, and knowledge have been destroyed, "when the perfect comes," when we see "face to face," when "I shall understand fully, as I have been understood," that faith, hope, and love "abide." The answer to the question must lie elsewhere. First, this formula in v. 13 is not without its parallels in the ancient, Hellenistic world, parallels which tout three, four, or even five "gifts" or "virtues" as the highest conceivable. If elsewhere Paul did not balk at expropriating what was best from his environment—let the "house rules" in chap. 5, the catalog of vices in chap. 6, or the quotation from Menander in 15:33 stand in evidence—it is not impossible to suppose that he has done the same here. Nor, as we have seen, would it be out of character for him to cite a slogan in vogue among his Corinthians. But in either case—and this brings us to our second point—Paul did not allow the parallel or slogan to stand without alteration. In almost every one of those ancient parallels, "wisdom," "knowledge," or "enlightenment" appears—obviously, since, for a good portion of that world, knowledge denoted union, even identity, with deity. And it may as well have done so for the Corinthians. In Paul's triad, "wisdom," "knowledge" is absent. Does the absence hide a polemic, an attack on what God had made foolish—"the wisdom of this world" (1:20)? If so, then **faith** and **hope** do not take their character from something with which we usually, if not always, associate them—from knowledge. Then that faith or hope which are a kind of knowing, though without external proof, yet still a knowing, is not what Paul has in view. Then the faith which abides is the consciousness that one is never the actor but always the one acted upon, never the giver, the donor, but always the recipient, always thrown back upon God as the source and reason for existence—and to all eternity. Then the hope that abides is a clinging to God, an arching of self toward God, a persistence toward God—to all eternity. Then what abides is the truly human, purged of its rage for the self, for disengagement, rid of its hankering to be for itself, to be God, but a God which God would never be. **But the greatest of these is love.**

> If faith is grounded in what God has done, if hope is directed toward what God will do, then love—from God, to God, and thus at the same time love for the brother . . . is the imperishable presence of salvation, the "bond of perfection" (Col. 3:14). As such, it is the greatest.[86]

Chapter 14

Now, after his initial response to the Corinthians' inquiry concerning spiritual gifts, and having sung his hymn to the "way" those gifts should travel, Paul seizes on the one spiritual gift at Corinth which enthusiasm and individualism had used to tear at unity—speaking in tongues—and to it opposes the gift most able to walk that way, the gift of prophecy. In arguments scarcely suited to his own interests ("I thank God that I speak in tongues more than you all," v. 18), the greatest charismatic of them all struggles to indicate that, because the Christian community is still bound by the conditions of present historical existence, that which the Corinthians believed had sling-shotted them into eternity needed setting within those conditions, for the sake of the other, the other's understanding—for the sake of love. This chapter is not a "descent" from the heights of chap. 13. There were no heights there. The impossibility which Paul hymned in chap. 13 is a possibility within present, concrete, historical existence: "Love is patient, is kind . . ." (13:4ff.). Nor does chap. 14 mark a "return" to normalcy, rationality. It is one thing to describe our knowledge as "in part" (13:9), as destined for destruction (13:10), its relation to "the perfect" as analogous to the child's relation to the adult (13:11), or to the relation of seeing "in a mirror, dimly" to that of seeing "face to face" (13:12), and quite another to damn the knowing, give the partial, the destructible a bad name and hang it, to spurn the "now," leap ahead of it, anticipate the "then" in it. The absence of knowledge or wisdom or enlightenment in Paul's triad may hide a massive critique, but only of a "wisdom" according to which the perfect has already arrived, the tension already resolved, the "then" already appeared—not of that knowing "in part." The partial, the enigmatic, the ambiguous, the equivocal, that bondage to the historical conditions of this world, that embracing of the tension between "now" and "not yet"— they are the signs of the humanity of the crucified, the stigmata of those in whom he makes his way in the world and will regain the world for God. It was precisely this rage to annul the tension, the distance, to exchange the "now" for the "then," to exchange the knowing "in part" for "understanding fully" without suffering the death between which emptied the cross of Christ (1:17). Love is not the enemy of "knowing in part," but of "understanding fully" when life, existence, still spells knowing "in part." And as for speaking in tongues, they belong to knowing "in part." They have their context in thought, in communication, in disclosure. That much, at least, belongs to knowing "in part."

The chapter may be divided into seven sections. After stating the principle or thesis in v. 1, Paul contrasts glossolalia and prophecy according to their function and consequences in vv. 2-5. In vv. 6-12, he illustrates the contrast by way of examples. In vv. 13-19 he applies the principle stated in v. 12. In vv. 20-25 he treats the two charismata from the perspective of the "outsider"; in vv. 26-33 he draws practical conclusions for order in the worship. In vv. 34-36 the apostle interrupts the argument with yet another statement concerning women's behavior in the assembly, and concludes with one more vigorous word in vv. 37-40.

Tongues and Prophecy Contrasted (14:1-5)

Make love your aim, and earnestly desire the spiritual gifts, especially (the comparative adverb does duty for the superlative, just as in 13:13) **that you may prophesy.** An instructor in logic would have preferred to attach the second half of this sentence

Chapter 14   *1 Corinthians*

to 12:31, and the first half to 13:13. The verse takes its curious character from the fact that it functions as a transition, but also enunciates a theme or principle. More curious still is Paul's summons to "pursue" love (RSV, **make love your aim**)—that impossibility made possible only through the choice or election of God ("then I shall understand fully as also I have been understood," 13:12). "How can I pursue what is or is not already in the cards"? If the Corinthians cared to ask that question, they would not have needed to tumble to the Romans correspondence for an answer. Paul was strewing his epistle with sufficient clues to indicate that divine election and human responsibility were not alternatives but twins; that pursuit made sense precisely because one had already been pursued; that behind the summons to pursue lay the assumption, the hope of the summoner that the pursuer had indeed already been pursued. Behind it lay the call of the summoner to believe that one had already been pursued, and that back of this assumption, this hope, and this call to faith it was useless to go, since it only paralyzed the pursuer for pursuit. Of himself the apostle had already written: "Paul, called by the will of God to be an apostle of Christ Jesus. . . . I decided. . . . I planted. . . . I laid a foundation" (1:1; 2:2; 3:6, 10), and would soon write, "By the grace of God I am what I am, and his grace toward me was not in vain. On the contrary, I worked harder than any of them" (15:10). And as for the Corinthians, those imperatives which till now had studded every chapter of this epistle were enough to indicate the capability for action of those who had been "called to be saints" (1:2).

Between the thesis or summons in v. 1, repeated in v. 5 (**but even more to prophesy**), and together with which it comprises a kind of frame, Paul contrasts the gifts of glossolalia and prophecy, and in a threefold alternation (tongues . . . prophecy, vv. 2-3; tongues . . . prophecy, v. 4; tongues . . . prophecy, v. 5), punctuated by adversatives or the adversative use of the conjunction (**but** . . . **but,** v. 2; **but,** v. 3; **but,** v. 4—note the adversative use of the comparative adverb in vv. 1 and 5: **but even more** . . .).

Typically, Paul does not contrast the two gifts by way of definition, but only by function and result. Since he had already described glossolalia as a panhuman phenomenon, thus lacking any guarantee of uniqueness, the most obvious inference would be that Paul regarded it as ecstatic unintelligible speech. (Did the Corinthians construe glossolalia differently, as xenolalia, speaking in a language previously unknown to the speaker, a view reflected in the language miracle in Acts 2:5-11?)[87] But prophecy too takes its definition only according to function or effects. There is something at stake here for Paul. The Corinthians could have realized by now that for Paul the definition of a thing was exhausted in its use, use for the other—which only means that in light of the event of the "Christ crucified" everything under the sun had been relativized, been torn from its moorings to some absolute, whether "law" or "nature"; that self, existence, knowledge, wisdom, love had lost everything to which they once referred, and for which reason they could no longer stand as "self-evident," settled, agreed upon, something fixed in a lexicon or a textbook, but took their character, were what they were, only from what they did for the other. Paul could agree with that noxious slogan, "I can do everything" (6:12; 10:23), if it meant *that*, if it meant that the constraint of science or logic had been thrown to the winds for the sake of life for Christ and the other. But if so, then existence was rooted in the sensuous and concrete where the other stood, and nowhere else. Then the "called" were called to be visible, tangible, empirical, and to nothing else. Then, if such a thing as being "washed, sanctified and justified" occurred at all, it occurred on earth, where the other stood, or nowhere else. But if so, then life was marked by ambiguity and hiddenness, by a knowing "in part," by the imperfect and destructible which belong to human historical existence. The cross of the one who had appeared "under the sign of his opposite," who had become a stumbling block and foolishness to Jew and Gentile, had made it so. To the definition of a thing belonged its effects, its use for the other.

The speaker in tongues, writes Paul, has no one but God as addressee (v. 2). But **he who prophesies speaks to men** (v. 3). No one hears the glossolalist, but he speaks **mysteries in the spirit** (v. 2; I prefer to leave the noun "spirit" in lower case, not because Paul draws any distinction between the "I" or soul and the Spirit of God. The absence of coherence or system in Paul's anthropology derives from his conviction that through faith the Spirit of God takes possession of the entire person. For this reason, existence cannot be explained psychologically. Better, for this reason an at times frustrating variety can prevail in Paul's use of anthropological terms which modern theory or practice might rigorously distinguish, and in order to accent one or the other aspect of existence "in Christ" or "in the Spirit." Here, as in the remainder of chap. 14, "spirit" writ small denotes the "self-consciousness" of the one who no longer lives from himself, but from God). But the one who prophesies speaks **upbuilding and encouragement and consolation** (v. 3). The one who speaks in tongues **edifies himself** (v. 4). But the one who prophesies **edifies the church** (v. 4). In the final contrast, following the repetition of the summons in v. 1 (**Now I want you all to speak in tongues, but even more to prophesy**), Paul ranks prophecy above glossolalia in a curiousness of phrase, perhaps stemming from the competition at Corinth: For **he who prophesies is greater than he who speaks in tongues.** Then he adds a promise, calculated to turn one of the opposites in the contrast into the other's obverse side: **Unless some one interprets, so that the church may be edified** (v. 5). The contrast is between a phenomenon which functions for the self ("no one hears"), has its effect on the self (**he who speaks in a tongue edifies himself**) and a word of judgment or consolation addressed to the other, drawn from God's prior saving activity, and resulting in the other's admission of guilt or strengthening in faith—the constant meaning of "prophecy" in either Testament.[88] In view of the promises in v. 5, it is doubtful that Paul's encouragement to speak in tongues, or his later injunction against placing tongues under tabu (v. 39), is meant to support the interpretation of uninterpreted tongue-speaking as benefiting the private person, though not the group (**he who speaks in a tongue edifies himself**), or the extraction from v. 15 of two separate events, one for the closet and the other for the sanctuary ("I will pray with the spirit . . . and with the mind also," cf. Lietzmann on 14:19). Since vv. 6, 9, 16f., 19, 23, and 26ff. clearly assume a public context for ecstatic utterance, it is far more likely that Paul conceived the gathered assembly as the only appropriate setting for glossolalia, provided interpretation occurred, and on condition the speaker retained self-mastery (v. 27)—this in conceivable opposition to a practice which till now may have prevailed with the apostle himself ("I thank God that I speak in tongues more than you all," v. 18).

Illustrations (14:6-12)

Paul now proceeds to illustrate his contention that tongues must adhere to the criterion of intelligibility or use for the other. In a series of examples drawn from the world of art and war, from ordinary conversation, and salted with interrogatives (note the appearance of the conjunction **if** in vv. 7-8, followed by the correlative adverb or indefinite pronoun: **how . . . ? who . . . ? how?**), the apostle reduces uninterpreted glossolalia to the absurd. **If even lifeless instruments, such as the flute or the harp, do not give distinct notes, how will any one know what is played?** (v. 7). **And if the bugle gives an indistinct sound, who will get ready for battle?** (v. 8). **So with yourselves; if you in a tongue utter speech that is not intelligible, how will any one know what is said?** (v. 9). The last question is followed by a declarative statement: **For you will be speaking into the air.** But Paul had just written that the glossolalist "speaks to God" (v. 2). The example, the analogy must not be stretched, but, for all that, the analogy is still what it is, and suggests a tinge of irony for that "speaks to God." The three examples are framed by Paul's application of the criterion to himself, also in interrogative form: **Now, brethren, if I come to you speaking in tongues, how shall I benefit you unless I bring you some revelation or knowledge or prophecy or teaching?** (v. 6). **There are doubtless many different languages**

in the world, and none is without meaning (in the original, "soundless," "toneless"); **but if I do not know the meaning** (in the original, "the power") **of the language, I shall be a foreigner to the speaker and the speaker a foreigner to me** (vv. 10-11).

The term from which our word *barbarian* derives has no etymology. It is onomatopoeic, an adaptation in sound to a noise heard but not understood, such as the "buzzing" of a bee, or the "mooing" of a cow, and in this fashion used to characterize the languages of tribes beyond the political or cultural influence of Athens, Corinth, or Rome. It was not long before the term emerged as a noun for the outsider, the alien, the Celt, Teuton, or "Palestinian." In v. 21, Paul will refer to a passage in First Isaiah, in which the prophet sets an onomatopoeic, racist expression, used by the Jew in disparagement of Assyrian speech, in the mouth of Yahweh. The Corinthians, with a history and culture reaching back 700 years, and whose art was such a thing of beauty Greece had never seen, would perhaps not miss the barb in that word "barbarian," and from a Jew. Then, as in v. 9, Paul applies his illustrations to the Corinthians **so with yourselves**—they were, after all, the target concealed in those personal references—and concludes with summoning to a principle, the application of which comprises the section following: **since you are eager for** spirits, **strive to excel in building up the church** (v. 12). The language of the causal clause (**since you are eager for** spirits) is odd. It reflects a notion of Spirit as multiple, each individual in possession of his own personal "spirit." The alternate readings in the manuscript witnesses, and the translation in the RSV (**since you are eager for manifestations of the Spirit**) indicate the church's embarrassment over an idea out of all harmony with Paul's teaching concerning the Spirit. But the clause suits that Corinthian accenting of the self as in isolation, and in the one clause Paul simply accommodates himself to it in order in the other to lay the axe to it. "Since you are zealous for spirits"— how could a community, presumably infected by the notion that the "soul" was one with every other, and thus with God, and to the point where individuality was accidental, a mere "signature" attached to the person by virtue of its imprisonment in corporeality, in bodies—how could it lose sight of that one for the many? The reason may lie deeper than in Corinth's adherence to ideas which allowed for such contradictions. It is so often assumed that the basis for resistance to Paul at Corinth was formal in nature, that Paul's opponents had somehow been schooled to think in ways which contradicted their Christian confession, that they had encountered discrete traditions, schools of thought, spheres of influence which they more or less consciously appropriated, and all calculated to produce such unrest in the community. The assumption may be correct. Corinth, between the two seas, was awash with a flood of religious options, and reaction to Paul's gospel of the cross may well have derived from conscious adoption of one or more worldviews. The apostle's repeated reference to "wisdom" and the like in chaps. 1–4 have for years furnished interpreters justification for assuming formal influences and their conscious adoption at Corinth, whether of Gnosticism, enthusiasm, libertinism, etc. But it is just as legitimate to suppose that Corinth's receptivity to influences alien to the gospel it had heard from Paul was already prepared for in a religiosity native to the human race, at least to its western half, and which those influences only gave a greater concreteness, a religiosity which begins with the world it sees and from it derives the world it cannot see. And since what is first seen or perceived is the self, the unseen is merely the self's abstraction, the self writ large. However ideally that world may be imagined or described, it never loses its character as abstraction, as a projection of the self. But then God may be explained as an objectifying of human subjectivity, or as a raising to the nth power of what is lacking in the self. Not only Paul's critics at Corinth construed faith in such terms:

> If God is such, whatever it may be, as I believe him, what else is the nature of God than the nature of faith? Is it possible for thee to believe in a God who regards thee favourably, if thou dost not regard thyself favourably, if thou despairest of man, if he is nothing to thee? What else then is the being of God but the being of man, the absolute

self-love of man? If thou believest that God is for thee, thou believest that nothing is or can be against thee, that nothing contradicts thee. But if thou believest that nothing is or can be against thee, thou believest—What?—nothing else than that thou art God. That God is another being is only illusion, only imagination. In declaring that God is for thee, thou declarest that he is thy own being. What then is faith but the infinite self-certainty of man, the undoubting certainty that his own subjective being is the objective, absolute being, the being of beings?[89]

According to Paul, for whom all was from God (1:13), faith was not a universally human capacity, by which one created God or could make of God an object. The argument that God is the projection of the self on a cosmic scale is a vicious circle. It will not do for the atheist who intends to be alone in the world, since it merely demonstrates the human's need for God. For Paul, faith had come from God as encountered in his word. In the word of the cross faith had appeared to humankind from God, and by faith humankind had come to stand in the presence of God. Thus for Paul, God remained subject, actor, initiator. Even as the object of faith he remained the subject, remained God over against humankind, and even as the subject of faith, as knower, as believer, humankind remained the "object" over against God. For the apostle, faith did not spell the identity of subject and object, of the believer and the one to be believed, of the Spirit and the "spiritual," the charismatic.

Conceding their religiosity, whatever its origin, a religiosity which in the end could make God a creature of faith; allowing for it all, Paul summons his readers to abandon it all: "Build up the church!" But it was the church, the body, that needed building up, not the head.

Application of the Principle of Verse 12 (14:13-19)

The section describes the condition on which glossolalia serves the principle stated in v. 12: **He who speaks in a tongue should pray for the power to interpret.** Following the summons the section is again formed by personal reference (**if I pray in a tongue** . . ., vv. 14-15, and **I thank God** . . ., vv. 18-19). The phrase **in** the **church** (v. 19) yields the context. Praying and singing **with the spirit** or **with the mind** (vv. 14-15) assume the gathered assembly in which unbelievers are also present (v. 16). Verses 23 and 24a, in which the term **outsider** precedes and follows the term "unbeliever," together with the "conviction" described in vv. 24-25, indicates that the person referred to is not merely one who lacks the gift of speaking in tongues or their interpretation, but is an "outsider" to the faith. In what such speaking in tongues consists, Paul indicates by the phrase **my spirit prays** (v. 14a), or **I will pray with the spirit** (v. 15), but more specifically by his use of the terms **give thanks** or **thanksgiving** in vv. 16 and 17. Whatever else glossolalia may involve, its essential character is thanksgiving. Negatively defined, in such thanksgiving the mind is **unfruitful** (v. 14). This does not merely mean without profit to the other, though it surely means that (cf. vv. 16f.: **Any one in the position of an outsider . . . does not know what you are saying. . . . is not edified**). It also means that the intellect is not engaged, the charismatic is not master of himself. Paul could as well have written of the glossolalist what his contemporary Philo wrote of the prophet:

> Whoever is truly inspired and full of God cannot grasp what he says with his understanding—he only transmits what is given him. . . . The prophets speak for God who uses their organs for the revelation of His will. . . . When [the prophet] is inspired, he loses consciousness, since thought vanishes and has left the citadel of the soul, but the divine Spirit has entered and taken up His dwelling in it.[90]

It was said of the Pythia at Delphi that when Apollo spoke through her, she did not understand what she said, that her stammerings required the interpretation of her priests.

On the other hand, despite the loss of mental control, what the glossolalist utters is not ecstatic gibberish, "frenzied" words, "of which no rational person can find the meaning: for so dark are they, as to have no meaning at all; but they give occasion to every fool or impostor to apply them to suit his own purpose."[91] According to Paul, speaking in tongues may be unintelligible to the outsider, even to the glossolalist (the latter possibility allowed for in v. 28: "If there is no one to interpret"), but it is not on that account incapable of being understood. It is a thanksgiving, designed to "build up," and for this reason demands disclosure, interpretation, the use of reason. The capacity for such disclosure or interpretation is not automatic; the gift of tongues does not imply the gift of their interpretation. Hence Paul writes: **Pray for the power to interpret** (note the distinction between glossolalia and interpretation in 12:30, as two discrete gifts, as well as allowance for the absence of the latter in v. 28). In Paul himself, however, both capacities appear to have been combined (in v. 6, the first conditional clause, "if I come to you speaking in tongues" need not be read as at odds with the second, "unless I bring you some revelation or knowledge or prophecy or teaching").

Did Paul regard interpreted glossolalia on a par with prophecy—a conclusion commonly drawn by his interpreters? Verse 5 ("he who prophesies is greater than he who speaks in tongues, unless someone interprets") suggests that he does. But the ranking of prophecy ahead of glossolalia and its interpretation in 12:29-30; the restriction of "warning" (RSV, **encouragement**) and "consolation" to prophecy in v. 3, and the clear contrast between the two activities in vv. 22 and 24f., point in the opposite direction. If for practical purposes Paul regarded interpreted speaking in tongues as equivalent to prophecy, then not equivalent without remainder, but only to that aspect of prophecy which excluded "warning," "convicting," "calling to account," or "revelation" (vv. 24, 30—Paul conceivably furnishing the exception). There is a boldness bordering on arrogance in Paul's treatment of the subject in this section and the one preceding. First, the reader will not have missed the contrast between the apostle's reference to his speaking "in tongues" (plural, v. 6), and the Corinthians' "speaking in a tongue" (singular, vv. 2, 4, 9, 13), a contrast perhaps softened by the alteration in person and number in vv. 5 and 14, but then chillingly revived in v. 18: **I thank God that I speak in tongues more than you all** (together with 2 Cor. 12:1ff., one of the few references to the psyche of Paul). Second, by giving preference to praying or singing "with the mind" over praying or singing "with the spirit" (the degree of the preference stated in v. 19, **I would rather speak five words with my mind . . . than ten thousand words in a tongue**), Paul appears to repress the activity of the Spirit for the sake of reason and intelligibility. Suspicions of presumption aside, how could one who earlier wrote "do not quench the Spirit" (1 Thess. 5:19), and would soon write, "do not forbid speaking in tongues" (v. 39), suddenly set mind, reason, intelligence at odds with Spirit, and clearly against his own interest (**I speak in tongues more than you all;** cf. 2 Corinthians 10–13, especially 12:1ff.)? The answer lies in that verb "to edify" in v. 17. For the sake of the other, Christian or not, bound to the conditions of the world which render life ambiguous, what the Spirit speaks must appear as an intelligible alternative to all the other alternatives confronting human existence. And that obligation to intelligibility is not something forced on Spirit, constraining the Spirit, as though human intelligence were somehow needed to harness or reign in the Spirit. The same caution, the same discretion is required to understand what Paul means by **mind**—and the remainder of his anthropological terms. That "mind" with which Paul prefers to pray he had already referred to in 2:16, not a mind or faculty alien or antithetical to Spirit, but the rational activity of one who no longer thinks for himself, in relation to himself, a mind from God, for God and the other— the "mind of Christ." And it was precisely to this mind, to this faculty of disclosure that the Spirit himself gave impulse: "I did not come proclaiming to you the testimony of God in lofty words or wisdom. For I decided to know nothing among you except Jesus Christ and, indeed, this one crucified . . . and my speech and my message were . . . in demonstration of the Spirit and of power" (2:1-4). It was, after all, the Spirit who urged to clarity, understanding, disclosure, interpretation. For Paul and the writers of the New Testament, speech, language, words were not an obstruction around which detour needed to be made in order for God to speak, in order for revelation to occur. Nor were they mere symbols for something which they were too poor to signify.

Chapter 14 *1 Corinthians*

The biblical writers did not embrace the old Roman dictum that "the translator is a traitor" (*traductor traditor*), nor would they have despaired of speech in the line from the hymn: "What language shall I borrow to thank Thee, dearest friend?" The event of the revelation within time and space spelled an incredible gain for that medium by which the creatures of time and space acknowledge one another and live together. That revelation of God under the sign of its opposite in the Christ crucified gave "courage" to language, gave to language the audacity to utter what it could not have uttered before. On the other hand, there was nothing in speech, in human discourse itself which furnished it the capacity for such speaking, as though the revelation of God could be deduced from mere grammar, logic, and syntax. That would have spelled the conquest of the revelation on the part of speech, and God would have come to expression as a mere name, never a "Thou." That event marked a "conquest" of language, but not as a silent, dumb aggressor, but rather as the "handmaid of the Lord" in which the "mystery" could engage, make its home. The mystery itself had enabled its interpretation, its disclosure in the "word of the cross." "Spirit" and speech, intelligible speech, clarity, were together in the fight.

Tongues and Prophecy from the Perspective of the "Outsider" (14:20-25)

Corinth needed "demythologizing." What it thought about God, what it said of God, or in this instance what it said *to* God threatened to make conquest of the revelation. When Paul summons in chiasma: **Do not be children** in your minds (RSV, **in your thinking**); **be babes in evil,** and in your minds be perfect (RSV, **but in thinking be mature**) the point is not that the Corinthians have been behaving childishly, for which reason the apostle invokes the use of "sweet reason." To be a child is to be "of the flesh," to "walk according to what is human" (3:1-3), to regard the world and the one who entered it from a human point of view (2 Cor. 5:16). Against such, Paul invokes "perfection." That term had enjoyed long history, and within a variety of religious persuasions, before ever Paul appropriated it. It could denote simply maturity (hence the RSV, **in thinking be mature**), or it could mark totality, and in this sense Paul uses it in antithesis to the "partial" in 13:10. In the moral sphere, it could denote the possession of all virtues as gauged by some system of values. But here, as in 2:6, it characterizes a mind or judgment by which the message of the cross is grasped as the wisdom of God and thus gives to existence its orientation, and a mind which construes that message as one more innerworldly phenomenon, one more human possibility, capable of being observed, tested, chosen, and used as any other. (Note the nuance given the term "perfect" in Phil. 3:15, where it denotes single-minded, undivided movement toward the "prize of the upward call of God in Christ Jesus.")

Following this summons, Paul now turns to its application with respect to glossolalia and prophecy, but from a perspective quite different from that assumed till now, that is, from the perspective of the "outsider." He begins with assigning a radically different historical context to an Old Testament passage in which First Isaiah predicts Yahweh's encounter with Israel through **men of strange tongues** and **the lips of foreigners** (Isa. 28:11f.). Paul has either altered his Greek text of the original Hebrew to read in the first person (**will I speak . . . they will not listen to me**), and added the particle (**even then . . . thus**) plus the phrase **says the Lord**, or he follows an exemplar still unknown to us. In the Hebrew of Isa. 28:13 appear mere nonsense syllables—*tsaw latsaw tsaw latsaw, kaw lakaw kaw lakaw*—an onomatopoeic construction in imitation of the alien Assyrians' speech. The passage may have been called to mind through association—unintelligible speaking at Corinth conjured up Israel's encounter with **men of strange tongues**. At any rate, Paul's recontextualizing of the Old Testament passage suggests that he regards the phenomenon of glossolalia at Corinth as constituting a fulfillment of the ancient prophecy. Just as in Isaiah's day God would speak to Israel only to hide himself, and thus render Israel all the more obdurate, so now, at Corinth, through the glossolalist, God speaks so as to be disbelieved. But does Paul regard this as inevitable or desirable?

Chapter 14 *1 Corinthians*

A further problem emerges in this section. When Paul next turns to prophecy, he appears to contradict himself. In v. 22b, he writes that **prophecy is not for unbelievers but for believers,** and in vv. 24-25 describes prophecy as convicting and calling the unbeliever to account, with the result that the unbeliever falls on his face, worships, and declares that **God is really among you.**

Several things need to be kept in mind. First, since Paul's argument here is restricted to the effect of glossolalia and prophecy on the outsider, he excludes their effects on the believer. Obviously, believers recognized speaking in tongues as from God, and it was for their sake Paul had demanded interpretation (v. 5). Second, the context of the scripture quotation (**thus,** i.e., for this purpose or to this end, "they will not listen to me," v. 21b) as well as the hypothetical reaction described in v. 23, make clear that the term **sign** in v. 22a denotes not merely the unintelligibility of the *content* of speaking in tongues—again, a quality it could take on also for the believer—but of the phenomenon as such: **If, therefore, the whole church assembles and all speak in tongues, and outsiders or unbelievers enter, will they not say that you are mad?** The outsider's argument ad hominem is still in vogue. The tongue speaker has frequently been described as suffering from a violent form of dementia or as a victim of a "recrudescence of psychic phenomena of a low stage of primitive culture."[92] Even the fundamentalist, shocked at the psychological interpretation of Christ's miracles or his resurrection, finds such an argument expedient in the face of uninterpreted tongues. One writes:

> Most of those susceptible to such contagious influence have been women of the more emotional, hysterical types, the stronger and more self-restrained have maintained their equilibrium. This makes the whole movement seem at least abnormal.[93]

The speaking to which Paul refers is not to be identified with unconscious or diseased conditions. The glossolalist had it in his power to leave off speaking when it profited no one. But from such an analysis as v. 23 reflects, from entering the game with such a towering handicap, Paul intended to spare the Corinthians. Further, if the phenomenon as such constituted a **sign,** then a sign to the outsider that he had been abandoned by God. What else could that Old Testament passage mean? But it is precisely this eventuality which the apostle intends to avoid! The purpose of the Isaiah quotation is not to celebrate the fulfillment of the prophet's prediction at Corinth, but to prevent it. For this reason Paul once more opposes prophecy to uninterpreted speaking in tongues, since prophecy, conviction, calling to account (note the exclusion of "foretelling" from Paul's definition) has faith for its purpose or consequence. This is the meaning of the second half of v. 22—**prophecy is not for unbelievers but for believers.** Hence it is not merely from the outsider's perspective that Paul takes up his argument here, but *for the sake of the outsider's coming to faith* that he pleads his case for prophecy against uninterpreted tongues. For Paul, some predictions did not beg for fulfillment, and the word of Isaiah in 28:11 was one of them. When these factors are not kept in mind, the section is at worst sadistic, and at best contradictory.

Practical Conclusions for Order in the Worship (14:26-33)

Now, having drawn the teeth from enthusiasm by setting the gifts of the Spirit within the conditions of historical existence, or better, by interpreting the Spirit as the one who warps his gifts to the life of the crucified, to the temporal, historical, to the ambiguous struggling for disclosure, Paul proceeds with specific instructions regarding the use of glossolalia and prophecy in the community's worship. Once more his theme reads: **Let all things be done for edification** (v. 26). For this purpose, glossolalia required restriction by numbers (**only two or at most three,** v. 27), by series (**in turn**), and by interpretation ("but if there is no interpreter, let him keep silent," v. 28). Paul obviously does not concede that the ecstatic can do nothing over against the power which dominates him. To prophecy, on the other hand, only the second restriction applies (**let two or three prophets speak . . . if a revelation is made to another sitting by**—the prophet obviously standing while speaking—**let the first be silent,** vv. 29a and 30, and **you can all prophesy one by one,** v. 31a). To the possible rejoinder that it would be wrong to dampen prophecy, Paul opposes a "teleological" view: If the prophet is silent today, the prophecy is not lost; the opportunity to speak will arise again. Further, some prophecy does not require "translation." Paul requires that it be "weighed" (v. 29b), adding that the prophet is master of his utterance (**the spirits of prophets are subject to prophets,** v. 32—the same accommodation to the popular notion as in v. 12), since God is not the author of disorder but of peace (v. 38). Instead of the animistic idea of the indwelling of an alien spirit in an alien house, the Spirit of God and the human will can be fused into a single, gathered power. But according to what criterion this weighing or evaluating? Certainly not that of mere agreement by "the others" (v. 29) with what is said. Truth is not arrived at by quantity. The answer must be: In accord with the definition of prophecy which Paul had already given in vv. 3-4 and 24-25: "Warning, convicting, calling to account, consoling, building up."

Let the Women Keep Silent (14:34-36)

If vv. 34-35 in this section are attributable to Paul, and not to the interpolation of a scribe, and suggested by the theme of "silence" in vv. 28 and 30, then they must be read in tandem with his concession in 11:5 and 13 to women's prophesying or praying in the public assembly. On the other hand, the verses are reminiscent of late ecclesiastical practice tailored to the Jewish model. There is one rabbinic tradition according to which the woman should not read from the Torah for the sake of the honor of the community.[94] The stricture suggests an interpolation by retrospection from 1 Tim. 2:11f., where the same verb "(not) to permit" appears (though in our passage in the passive voice), clearly referring to a prior decision (cf. 1 Tim. 2:12, "I do not permit the woman to teach") of which there is not the slightest trace here. Where or when had Paul given such a directive? (Paul's curious etiology in 9:7-10 applies to women's prophesying with head uncovered, not to their silence; further, his argument, for all its oddity, is theological and not chronological; but cf. 1 Tim. 2:13, "For Adam was formed first, then Eve . . ."; and, finally, his argument is relieved with the announcement of equality "in the Lord," 11:11-12, a feature displaced by the Pyrrhonism in 1 Tim. 2:15). But if the words are Paul's they cannot be construed as a rule to be universally applied. In other words, the section cannot begin with the majority of modern Greek texts and translations at v. 33b: **As in all the churches of the saints** (v. 34), **the women should keep silence**. . . .

An odd history attaches to the verse division. All older English texts of the New Testament, including the KJV and its revision in 1881, set a period at the end of v. 33, and began a new sentence or paragraph with v. 34. With the publication of the American Standard Version in 1900, the original division was altered, and the new sentence begun at v. 33b. Since then, all English versions of the New Testament have followed suit (the RSV, the NEB, the Jerusalem Bible; but cf. *The Living New Testament*). Curiously enough, Nestle's Greek text of the New Testament, first published in 1898, and in its subsequent editions used by the majority in Europe and America, contained the same verse division as appeared in English versions until 1900, while the Greek text of Westcott-Hort, first published in 1881, and in subsequent editions used by English scholars, evaluated the old division as on a par with the new. To what extent aversion to female occupancy of the pulpit contributed to the alteration can only be surmised. Incidentally, some Greek manuscripts of the New Testament place vv. 34-35 after v. 40, thus loosing them from any possible connection with Paul's statement in v. 37: **What I am writing to you is a command of the Lord.**

Again, if the words are Paul's, and require reading against the background of chap. 11, they apply specifically to the situation at Corinth, where feminist activity, if not spurred, then at least occasioned by the apostle's preaching, led to excesses and breech of order in the worship. (One Jewish writer states that v. 34 is understood properly when the frequent inappropriate disturbance in the women's section of orthodox synagogues is kept in mind, that Paul is thus referring to women who disturb the worship by talking, evidently to glean information regarding the liturgical events.)[95] But the chief reason for doubting the Paulinicity of vv. 34-35 lies elsewhere. In only one other instance in 1 Corinthians does Paul appeal to the Law in support of his argument, and to a quite specific portion of the Law—the Pentateuch (Deut. 25:4; in 9:9). From the context of vv. 34-35, it is impossible to determine whether or not Paul (or the scribe) has in mind the "Law of Moses" or a single passage from it, the Pentateuch, or the Old Testament as a whole. Further, Paul's appeal to the Law in chap. 9 takes its place on an ascending scale, climaxing in a "commandment of the Lord," and from all of which he chooses to derive no benefit! The point is not that Paul is antinomian. He will later write in Romans that the righteousness by faith, contrary to overthrowing, actually "makes the law to stand" (Rom. 3:31). Faith will have its consequence in the "keeping of commandments" (7:19), but, for such establishing or keeping, the Law had to wait, since only the revelation of righteousness apart from the Law could create that "new man" which the Law required. For this reason, the one in whom that "new man" was created, the new man who could now give the obedience for which the Law waited, displaced judicial decree as an orientation to life. In fact, such had never been the intention in the giving of the Law. However difficult it may be to systematize Paul's statements concerning the Law, one thing is crystal clear: Apart from faith in the crucified, there is no "keeping of commandments." And for this reason, it is to Christ (cf. 7:10), or to himself as "mercied by the Lord" (7:25, cf. v. 40) and not to the Law itself to which Paul makes final appeal.

One More Vigorous Word (14:37-40)

If v. 37 is not suggested by the interpolation of vv. 34-36 (**what I am writing to you is a command of the Lord**), then it is intended to set the signature to everything said of spiritual gifts from 12:1 onward. If elsewhere the apostle is careful to distinguish his counsel from a command of the Lord (cf. 7:10, 12, 25), here he insists that what he has written concerning prophecy and the gifts of the Spirit has behind it nothing less than the authority of Christ himself. Nor is this authority lodged in a tradition transmitted to Paul, and in this sense "from the Lord" (cf. 11:23ff.). This is evident from the verse following, identical with those "sentences of holy law" in 3:17; 5:3ff., and later in 16:22. In this section, then, Paul contends that the tests he requires of the spiritual gifts, the relation to each other in which he sets and ranks them, the "way" by which these gifts must travel, and even the order of their occurrence are neither to be judged by a system of ready-made values nor are directed toward his readers' goodwill, but are the decree of the Spirit, that is, of the crucified and exalted Lord as present who speaks through him and whom he serves as representative. The accent in v. 38 on understanding or not knowing makes clear, however, that the Lord's decree is not a merely external authority, which could exact only an external obedience, but that insight into its meaning is required, its absence attended by a curse. **So, my brethren,** Paul concludes this section, **earnestly desire to prophesy, and do not forbid speaking in tongues, but all things should be done decently and in order** (v. 40).

There was more involved at Corinth than a "chasm between charismatic virtuosity and moral value" (Fridrichsen). Spiritual virtuosity there was, and aplenty:

Only here [in chaps. 12–14], despite or alongside indications to the contrary, do we get an insight into the all but dizzying wealth of intellectual and spiritual life which must have filled the community, and to which Paul alludes, surely without exaggeration, in 1:4ff. By no means can we simply conceive the Corinthian community as a den of party strife, undisciplined sexuality, willful asceticism, and luxuriant gluttony. Certainly, that was all present in crude, unvarnished vitality, and most likely in delicately conceived and religious garb. But also, as we read in chaps. 12 and 14, what a profusion of high and highest possibilities, which Paul took with utter seriousness as *spiritual charismata!* It is an excess of spirits, powers, and gifts which occasions Paul's urgent admonition to *unity* in chap. 12, and to *order* and subordination in chap. 14. Extreme, most intense capabilities, even for the good and the divine (Paul at least regarded it so)—to the extent one may speak of powers of goodness and divinity in man—appear to be unleashed here, together with all sorts of demons from that pagan capitol, and which haunt the *ekklesia theou*, the church of God. And harder still than resisting evil there is Paul's other task, of mastering this explosion of Spirit and the spirits, of claiming and confessing a still higher point of view in face of all these highest possibilities.[96]

But at Corinth there was also a rage for the self as unengaged, and which led to a quest for perceptibility, for demonstrability, for proofs. How else could the "I" stand alone? And to that quest Paul opposed his "doctrine" of ambiguity (12:2; 14:7-19, 23; cf. 2 Cor. 6:8-9, "We are treated as impostors, and yet are true; as unknown, and yet well known; as dying, and behold we live!"). Tests were required of the charismata—the test of Christological confession (12:3); of love (chap. 13); of "building up" or of "mind" (chaps. 12 and 14). And it was these tests which hurled the charismatic back into the world, back to the historical and temporal, to corporeality, to the "other." But not even these tests could preserve the spiritual gifts from relativity. Prophecies would pass away, tongues would cease, and knowledge would pass away (13:8). The charismata were "in part" (13:9); they were not the presence of the eternal in time, but rather the manifestation of the Spirit in the temporal and provisional. They bound their possessor to ambiguity, thus to faith. But if so, then that meant that the "spiritual" and the empirical person were one and the same, that the concrete and to all appearances impious, ungodly and the justified person were one and the same, that Christian existence was characterized by an inevitable movement toward a goal which for all that was nevertheless hidden, begging for disclosure. "We ourselves, who have the first fruits of the Spirit, groan inwardly as we wait for adoption as sons, the redemption of our bodies" (Rom. 8:23). And the event which established such existence was the cross of Christ. And if that was true, then, despite all the tests, there could be no perceptible difference between the charismatic and the fakir. "Faith, hope, love *abide*, these three"!

The later church could no more live with the ambiguity than could the Corinthians. The church chose to remember what Corinth had forgotten—the Paul who renounced the apprehension of God in some other world than the world we know, the Paul of good order and care for the body. And it chose to forget what Corinth remembered—the Paul who wrote "strive to prophesy, and do not forbid speaking in tongues." Ecstatic experience, tongues, giving thanks, praying "with the spirit," warning, consoling, convicting, calling to account—it was all suppressed.

■ The Resurrection from the Dead (Chapter 15)

As more than one reader-interpreter has noted, everything Paul has written till now has its rationale here. Everything said thus far of God, Christ, or the Spirit, of Christian existence for "the other" in the world, has its premise in what is confessed here, and stands or falls with what is announced here. The chapter is thus not to be construed as a "climax" or conclusion to the epistle, as though it gathered up in a reprise everything said or written till now. It is the heart or hub of the letter from which everything has radiated. But if that is true, then the chapter does not furnish a qualification to what precedes, as though it were the "happy ending," the "in spite of all" attached to an otherwise gloomy tale. Then what Paul has said concerning the "word of the cross" must not merely be intimately connected with what he writes here of the resurrection of the dead, or relate to it only as effect to cause. Then the word of the cross and the word of the resurrection are not two poles or extremes, each attracting adherents separately from the other. Then they are not even two perspectives or two points at either end of a spectrum. All talk of the one, of a "theology of the cross" as somehow deriving its meaning from the other, from a "theology of the resurrection," or of its giving meaning to the other, or of its greater suitability to the "nihilism" of the age than the other—though without having lost sight of the other—and all reference to a "theology of the resurrection" as furnishing the support or proof for the other would have struck Paul as perverse. As though a "theology of the cross" were spared concreteness, visibility—"Why am I in peril every hour?" (v. 30), and a "theology of the resurrection" were spared ambiguity—"if in this life we are only those who have hoped in Christ, of all men we are most to be pitied" (v. 19; compare RSV)! What his Corinthian opponents or his interpreters have put asunder, for Paul was not only joined together but one and indivisible. The proclamation of the resurrection is at the same time and in the same breath the word of the cross; the word of the cross is at the same time and in the same breath the proclamation of the resurrection. And precisely how this can be so, Paul will show in this remarkable chapter.

Why did not Paul lay bare the beating heart of the matter earlier, as, for example, he did in Romans (cf. 3:21)? The answer cannot simply lie in the epistle's structure as determined by responses to reports and questions. Paul was not hidebound to protocol—he could write what lacked stimulus in hearsay or written query from Corinth, and for all its "occasional" character, the letter till now is not without a certain coherence. The theme of engagement, alignment, of "corporeality," life for the other, the battle with enthusiasm lies between every line. The question could just as well read, Why should Paul end every letter with a "finally, my brethren," or with drawing the "practical" or ethical consequence from doctrines stated earlier—a reading of Paul against the background of Romans, but for all that a misreading? The heart of our "first" letter to Corinth lies here—perhaps because his readers required 14 chapters of preparation. Paul's word in 3:2, "I fed you with milk, not solid food; for you were not ready for it, and even yet you are not ready for it," is not a promise to conceal. At any rate, Paul wanted his entree here, and it would not be the last time a New Testament author would transgress the law of the dinner table and reserve the most solid food for last (cf. Mark 15!). And, apparently, even the tradition yielded some precedent for it—"every man serves the good wine first; and when men have drunk freely, then the poor wine; but you have kept the good wine until now" (John 2:10).

The chapter is divided into six sections (1) vv. 1-11 contain the introduction and gospel of the resurrection; (2) vv. 12-19 contain Paul's argument for the resurrection; (3) vv. 20-28 comprise an excursus on the reality of the resurrection; (4) vv. 29-34 return to the argument interrupted at v. 20; (5) vv. 35-49 contain a description of the way in which the dead are raised, and (6) vv. 50-58 describe the destiny of those still alive.

Introduction and Gospel of the Resurrection (15:1-11)

Introduction (15:1-2)

In the Greek of v. 2, a dependent clause (**in what terms**—or wording—**I preached to you**) is set ahead of a main clause (**if you hold it fast**), which presents the translator with at least two options: *(a)* to set the dependent clause at the very beginning of the sentence in v. 1, as does the RSV, or *(b)* to treat it as an interruption of the main clause, though complementary to the relative clauses preceding. The second option is preferable, and would make the sentence read: "Now I make known to you, brethren, the gospel which I preached to you, which also you received, in which also you stand, by which also you are saved, as (in the terms) I preached to you—if you hold it fast, unless you believed in vain."

This is the seventh and last time Paul will characterize his preaching by use of a noun in the absolute—**the gospel** (cf. 4:15; 9:12, 14 [twice], 18, and 23; the verb "to preach the gospel" appears in 1:17; 9:16; and 18)—thus distinguishing it from any other. Earlier, Paul had given definition to the gospel as "Christ and, indeed, this one crucified" (2:2; cf. "the gospel of Christ" in 9:12); as the "secret and hidden wisdom of God" (2:16-17); as the "mysteries of God" entrusted to him as steward (4:1), and thus as his "ways in Christ" (4:17; cf. Paul's reference to "my gospel" in Rom. 2:16 and 16:25). The reference in 15:1 to **the gospel** is thus anaphoric, harking back to something already named or recognized, so that the phrase "I make known to you the gospel" cannot denote the disclosure of something totally new (cf. the RSV, **I**

Chapter 15   *1 Corinthians*

would remind you . . .). In what follows, then, Paul will excerpt that portion of his gospel from which this chapter draws its life.

The introduction has its dark side. The main clause in v. 2 is followed by a condition, **unless you believed in vain,** that is, "for no reason." The pronoun could just as well have appeared in the first as in the second person—"unless we believed in vain." Paul was not a fanatic. His service to the gospel was not such as to disallow alternatives. The "necessity" which had been "laid" on him (9:16) did not exclude amazement at its incomprehensibility. He knew that what he preached defied all sense and all reflection. That reference to Jews and Greeks in 1:22 ("for Jews demand signs and Greeks seek wisdom") was not racist—if that were all!—but referred to a world oriented to perception and conception, and which Paul opposed with "what no eye has seen, nor ear heard, nor the heart of man conceived," with what, presumably, only God could know (2:9-11). Paul had belonged to that world. To a Jew, abandoning the Torah spelled abandoning the universe which the Torah created and sustained, abandoning the history to which the Torah gave origin and goal. It meant the collapse of identity, of the "I" directed and oriented to Torah, meant chaos and an end to God. And Paul was a Jew. The alternative to Paul's gospel did not escape him. His life was harnessed in a dialectic of wisdom and foolishness, life and death, God in Christ and the nothing, future and annihilation. If on this side of Damascus, this side of his "call," he did not suppress what he had once hated—the crucified Jesus as Messiah—but embraced it in the acknowledgment of that hanged creature as Lord and God; if he "never burned what he had prayed to, and never prayed to what he had burned," neither did he suppress the nothing which formed the gospel's other half: "If in this life we are only those who have hoped in Christ. . . ." Again and again the "if," the dark, the nothing would find expression—in the announcement that God had chosen "things that are not, to bring to nothing things that are" (1:28); that he carried about in his body the death of Jesus (2 Cor. 4:10); that he was strong when he was weak (2 Cor. 12:10), or, finally, that justification was of the godless (Rom. 4:5, 17). And if Paul's preaching was "in demonstration of the Spirit and of power" (2:4); if the rule of God he announced did not consist in prattle but in power (4:21); if he made claim to miracles and to tongues "more than you all" (14:18), he knew well enough the panhuman character of that power, knew that it was capable of being construed as one more religious phenomenon (12:1). Finally, Paul knew that the test or criterion of its genuineness lay in what could not be proved: "No one can say 'Jesus is Lord' except by the Holy Spirit." The dialectic was never suppressed; the dark side, the alternative, the nothing, was never lost sight of—it was Paul's inheritance from his encounter with Christ, the event which had plunged him into chaos, but had also saved him from it.

What follows, then, with all its proximity to the event, is no less what "no eye has seen, nor ear heard," no less vulnerable to the judgment of sense or of "wisdom."

The Credo (15:3-8)

The section contains a credal statement appropriated by Paul, and over against others inserted at 8:6; 9:1; 11:23-25; and 12:3 (possibly also 6:14) is singled out for first place: **For I delivered to you as of first importance** (RSV; the adverbial phrase denotes rank, status) **what I also received. . . .**" According to majority opinion, the credo (composed at Jerusalem? originally in Aramaic? between A.D. 33 and 35? appropriated by Paul soon after the Damascus encounter?) begins at v. 3b and ends at v. 5. The structure of the credo is symmetrical. The three events—Christ's death, resurrection, and appearances—are marked off four times by the conjunction **that** or **and that:**

> . . . *that* **Christ died for our sins in accordance with the scriptures** (v. 3b), *and that* **he was buried,** *and that* **he was raised on the third day in accordance with the scriptures** (v. 4), *and that* **he appeared to Cephas, then to the twelve** (v. 5). . . .

Several expressions in the formula rule out Pauline manufacture. First, the phrase **for our sins** is a substitute for Paul's usual "for us," simply translated "on our behalf." In fact, the phrase suggests an interpretation of Christ's death subsequent to that reflected in the word "for us," and which construes Christ's death as an atonement "on account of our sins." From this, then, there was but a small step to interpreting that death as a substitutionary satisfaction, as occurring "in our place." Paul does not shrink at such language, though not without altering it (cf. Gal. 1:13), or concentrating on the *effects* of that atonement (cf. Gal. 3:13-14; 2 Cor. 5:21). His preference, however, is clearly for the simpler "for us" (cf. 1 Thess. 5:10; 1 Cor. 1:13; 2 Cor. 5:14f.; Rom. 5:6-8; 14:15; etc.). Whether or not the phrase **for our sins** derives from Palestinian, Jewish-Christian reflection against the background of such Old Testament texts as Isa. 53:5 can only be surmised. Next, the phrase **in accordance with the scriptures** (vv. 3-4) is never used elsewhere by Paul in such a context, and has induced more than one scholar to hunt about in the Old Testament for its referent (Hos. 6:2; Jonah 2:1; Dan. 12:7?). The vagueness of the expression suggests a liturgical context removed from anxiety over adducing proofs or evidence, and for which the entirety of Scripture is made to culminate in the death and resurrection of Christ in one grand expropriation or tour de force. Finally, the reference to Christ's being raised **on the third day,** and his appearance **to Cephas** is of a piece with oldest Palestinian (Judean or Galilean?) tradition respecting the "discovery" of the resurrection and the primacy of Peter as the first "authentic" witness to Christ's appearance, as well as gatherer of the community (Paul's reference to the "prince of apostles" by his Aramaic name always occurs in the context of his discussion of Jewish-Christian tradition or piety; his reference to the apostle by his Greek name, Peter, occurring in the context of his discussion of the Gentile-Christian mission; cf. the alternation of names and their corresponding contexts in Galatians 2). The Evangelists have variously drawn on this tradition (Mark's less precise "after three days" in Jesus' passion predictions is warped by his coevangelists to the reigning tradition, cf. Mark 8:31; 9:31; 10:34; and parallels; the ranking of Peter as the first witness to the risen Lord is reflected in Luke 24:34; cf. also 22:31-32, and Mark 16:7; Matt. 16:18-19 and John 21:15-17).

The credo omits mention of the empty tomb (cf. Mark 16:1-6; Matt. 28:1-6; Luke 24:1-11, 22-24), to say nothing of appearances to the women (Matt. 28:9-10; the spurious ending in Mark 16:9-11; cf. John 20:11-18). Further, the credo lacks all the apologetic reflected in the Evangelists' countering Jewish suspicion or alluding to Jesus' physical appearance (Matt. 28:11-15; Luke 24:36-42; cf. John 20:26-29). Reasons adduced for the omissions are legion, and none of them is more than a hypothesis.

Verses 6-8 add a series of resurrection appearances, concluding with the words, **last of all, as to one untimely born, he appeared also to me.** There is nothing in the Gospels or the remainder of the New Testament with which to compare the appearance to the 500 or to James. An appearance of Jesus to James appears in a totally incredible report from an apocryphal "Gospel of the Hebrews" cited by Jerome. The appearance to "all the apostles" may, however, have its echo in Matt. 28:16ff. and Luke 24:36ff. Speculation regarding these verses as reflecting a "Galilean" tradition (where else could Jesus appear to more than 500 **at one time?**) as opposed to or supplementing "Jerusalem" tradition in vv. 3-5, or as calculated to give the entire section Galilean coloring, takes us no further than the adducing of reasons for omission of all reference to the women and the empty tomb. Paul cites the credo as delivered, and the tradition as known to him, both linked by the repeated temporal adverb **then** (vv. 5b, 6, 7), but more significantly by the word translated in the RSV **he appeared** (vv. 5, 6, 7 and 8). The translation is eminently correct. The verb, occurring in the intransitive passive ("he was seen"), denotes a revelatory event or encounter, the accent falling on the subject hidden in the verb, not on the person encountered and referred to in the dative (**to Cephas . . . to the twelve . . . to more than five hundred . . . to James . . . to all the apostles . . . to me**). In other words, the emphasis lies on the appearing, not on the seeing. In fact, the term **he appeared** allows no inference whatever to be drawn regarding the mode or manner of

Cephas's perception of the Risen Lord, whether as "objective" or as "subjective," as mediated through sense or through inward, "spiritual" awakening. The same accent, the same initiative, the same "pleasure" of God to which Paul assigns the "revelation of his Son to me," and the same disinterest in the manner of its perception as is reflected in Gal. 1:16, is reflected in the credo and the tradition cited by Paul here. If the word *vision* were not long associated with what is self-induced, it could serve to describe what for Paul and earliest Christianity marked an encounter to which no category of human sight was equal or could even furnish preparation, but which for all its discontinuity with human experience still denoted a continuity in corporeality ("it is sown a physical body, it is raised a spiritual body," 15:44).

And **last of all, as to one untimely born, he appeared also to me.** The word translated **untimely born** appears most often among Greek physicians, and denotes a birth before full term, as in an abortion, or as arising from other, "natural" causes. The accent lies on the unripeness of the fruit of the womb, thus on its incapacity for life. It could easily have served as an epithet or expression of scorn. Whether or not aimed at Paul by his opponents, he takes up the term, applies it to himself. He had not been a disciple, but an enemy of "the Way." His encounter with Christ had been out of time, something unnaturally induced, a violent wrenching from one existence and exposure to another for which he lacked all preparation. Whatever presuppositions he had entertained over against that existence were all "negatively qualified." In Luke's terms, he had "breathed threats and murder against the disciples of the Lord" (Acts 9:1). But for all its unnaturalness and violence—and now Paul sets his pre-Damascus existence in dialectic with the event which ranked him with Cephas, the Twelve, the 500, James, and all the apostles—in that event Christ had brought himself to appearance: **He appeared also to me.** Despite the incongruence, Paul was an Easter witness. With v. 8, the chain of witnesses is complete, and Paul its last link.

There is nothing odd in the apostle's including himself in his gospel, his kerygma, in appending himself to the credo or the tradition. There is not a single author of the New Testament whose gospel has not in some fashion taken on his own flesh and blood, for whom the tradition of the sayings and doings of Jesus has not assumed his own lineaments. The words in Acts 3:15, "to this we are witnesses," in which are wedded the announcement that God has made his salvation, the recapturing of the world he created, contingent upon the person of his choice, and the existence surrendered to that choice, characterizes the totality of New Testament authorship. Precisely because of this peculiarity which attaches to the Gospel genre, attempts at disassociating the message from its author never enjoy consensus in the long run. The wedding of the historical event (**Christ died . . . was buried . . . was raised on the third day**) to its interpretation (**for our sins in accordance with the scriptures**) prevented the event from dissolving into brute, naked facts quarried for the sake of mere assent, and prevented the interpretation from degenerating into a myth calculated to serve mere religious aspirations. And that wedding had its impulse, its stimulus, and its occasion in the worship and confession of the community.

But does not the enumeration of witnesses in this section contradict that assertion? Why else the appeal to a series of six, if not to separate the objective and historical, to single out what is amenable to research from the web of its interpretation, and in order to give faith some cogent reason for believing? **He appeared to Cephas . . . to the twelve . . . to more than five hundred . . . to James . . . to all the apostles . . . to me.** Are these not proofs? If not for Paul, and evidently not for the Corinthians—who did not challenge Christ's resurrection, but rather their own (cf. v. 12!)—then for whom? Perhaps the enumeration could furnish yet others stimulus to a research which could result in establishing something which no historian would deny and still remain credible, reputable? Historical research has long been a way by which the Christian community has asserted the sovereignty of God who made his revelation contingent upon a particular person, place, and time. In essence, it is the confession that faith does not feed upon itself. For that reason alone, even if there were no other, historical study would deserve continual pursuit. But the pursuit will always leave the historian vulnerable. And it is precisely this vulnerability in which the wisdom of God is preached toward which v. 6 points: **Then he appeared to more than five hundred brethren at one time, most of whom are still alive,** *though some have fallen asleep.* Whatever the encouragement to Paul's contemporaries to ascertain the facts (**most of whom are still alive**) it was balanced by events which rendered the ascertainment problematic (**though some have fallen asleep**). And now, where are the **most**?

Paul "Last of All" (15:9-11)

In v. 9, Paul expands on the first member of the dialectic in v. 8 ("as to one untimely born"), and in v. 10 on the second ("he appeared also to me"): **For I am the least of the apostles . . . and his grace toward me was not in vain.** The discontinuity between what he had been and what he became was great enough to set Paul among "the things that are not" used to bring to nothing "the things that are" (1:28). Paul's admission, **I am . . . unfit to be called an apostle** is thus not to be set down to modesty or self-deprecation. The issue is not introspection or personal inventory but theological reflection. Together with its rationale—**because I persecuted the church of God**—the phrase focuses the gulf which the event ("he appeared also to me") created between itself and Paul as "last" or "least." Ironically, but not only ironically; naturally, understandably, in a world where one demands signs and another wisdom, that lostness or lastness had not been due to mere intolerance, to Paul's attempt to warp the world, or whatever part of it he could manage, to the shape of his own will. It had resulted from religious devotion, from a commitment to God. Earlier, in the first of two glimpses into his former life (the second in Phil. 3:4-5), Paul had written: "I persecuted the church of God violently and tried to destroy it; and I advanced in Judaism beyond many of my own age among my people, so extremely zealous was I for the traditions of my fathers" (Gal. 1:14). The relation between religion, the pursuit of the Torah, the worship of God, and the persecution of the "church of God" had been one to one.

To the event that had created the chasm, the discontinuity between what he had been and what he had become, Paul gives the name **grace.** Earlier, he had used the term in reference to himself—"according to the grace of God given to me" (3:10)—but without linking it to the event which it identified. Earlier still, in Galatians, that event had been on the tip of his tongue, then slipped off in an allusion: "When he who . . . had called me through his grace was pleased to reveal his Son in me" (Gal. 1:15). But here, **grace** and the event which had laid that "necessity" on him (9:16) are fused, forged together, with nothing left to the imagination. "He appeared also to me" . . . **by the grace of God I am what I am**. . . . Not Damascus and ineluctable fate, not "the revelation of his Son" and a necessity of compulsion, but "he appeared" and **by the grace of God,** as a result of which his boast or reward could consist only of thanks (9:17-18). And as for "thanks," "gift," charismatic gift, or even "collection" (16:13), they all derived from the same parent root, from "grace." Scores of times, the discontinuity which that word **grace** spelled for Paul would be reflected, refracted, mirrored, hinted at, and alluded to in his letters, and finally, not merely in reference to himself, in defense of his kerygma or apostleship, but as signaling the existence of those who had "received," "stood in," and "held fast" what he had preached—"Grace to you and peace from God our Father and the Lord Jesus Christ" (1:3); "the grace of the Lord Jesus be with you" (16:23). And in between their own Damascus: "But you were washed, you were sanctified, you were justified in the name of the Lord Jesus Christ and in the Spirit of our God" (6:11).

And **grace,** that favor of God toward Paul, not merely created but sustained the discontinuity: **By the grace of God I am what I am, and his grace toward me was not in vain. On the contrary, I worked harder than any of them, though it was not I, but the**

grace of God . . . with me. There is no mistaking it now—the subject of Paul's existence is not Paul but grace. Grace holds together that congeries of atoms called "Paul," gives to it the continuity from one moment to the next, so that the Paul of the last moment can be summoned up or recalled in the next, and the Paul of the next moment arched toward a summoning in a moment still to come; so that in whatever moment, with all the shifting and changing, and in a world whose shape is passing away, with the loss of perception of a trillion stimuli battering his senses in each millisecond of life, he can still say "I," can still say "I am what I am." Grace was the subject, grace the actor, grace the creator of the distance between "then" and "now," the grace of God. (The proposition **with** in that **grace of God . . . with me** belongs to **grace** and not to **me,** since grace is never for itself but always a "grace with"). And in grace lay the explanation for this man's racing through a continent, hungering and thirsting, ill-clad, buffeted and homeless, laboring with his own hands, blessing when reviled, enduring when persecuted, conciliating when slandered, tumbling through the Near East and Europe like the rain-washed filth down their cities' streets, "the refuse of the world" (4:11-13). **I worked harder than any of them.** "Naturally," writes one commentator, "not all of them together, but 'more than any one of them.'" Why not the lump sum—Apollos, the Twelve, even the 500—since grace was the actor? Grace had sniffed the competition and broken the tape.

Still, the race had been a relay, not a marathon. "He appeared to Cephas, then to the twelve. . . ." None of "them," none of those who had been "first" or "most" in bearing the tradition had been outrun or left behind. "By grace" they belonged to Paul ("whether Paul or Apollos or Cephas . . . all are yours," 3:22), as close to him as the not-I which embraced them, which had made them all a "self" together: **Whether then it was I or they, so we preach and so you believed** (v. 11).

The Argument for the Resurrection (15:12-19)

Now, following the reference to his solidarity with "any of them" in gospel proclamation (v. 10), Paul advances to a Corinthian challenge to it. Verse 12 does not state the challenge in a simple declarative sentence, but sets it in the interrogative following a conditional clause that assumes the reality of its premise. The result is a challenge to the challenge, hurling it against the common testimony: **Now, if Christ is preached as raised from the dead,** as in fact he is preached (the force of the conditional clause), **how can some of you say that there is no resurrection from the dead?** More, the indefinite pronoun in the interrogative clause pares down the opposition—"how say *some* of you?" Not all are in opposition, or at least not all are bold enough to draw the logical conclusion from their assumptions (only too apparent thus far) and give it expression in a clear denial. But if, as v. 11 makes clear, the credo and the tradition respecting Christ's resurrection are not at issue ("thus we preach and thus you *believed*," v. 11), then where does the challenge lie, and how can it constitute opposition to the announcement that Christ was raised? The argument in vv. 13-19 gives the answer.

The argument, consisting of two series of three conditional clauses (**if . . . then,** vv. 13-15 and 16-19; note the chiasma in vv. 14-15: **if . . . then; then . . . if**), begins with the startling announcement that **if there is no resurrection from the dead, then Christ has not been raised.** The challenge, the opposition at Corinth had been to the resurrection *from the dead*. Those eager to describe Paul's Corinthian opponents as "Gnostics," as the advocates of a discrete worldview or view of the self as expressed in a discrete mythology, suggest that at this point the apostle has incorrectly assessed the situation and assumed that denial of the resurrection was tantamount to assuming that death ends all. It is true—for the Gnostic, death did not end all. The soul or spirit, that which shared identity with deity, was immortal. It was rather the physical, the corporeal, that antithesis of spirit or "prison" of the soul which thrust it into unconsciousness of its true origin and home in deity, which required putting off. From such a perspective, the Gnostic could have assented to Paul's word that "flesh and blood cannot inherit the kingdom of God" (v. 50). It is possible that Paul erred, that he construed a present resur-

Chapter 15   *1 Corinthians*

rection "in the spirit" and thus a denial of a future bodily resurrection as a denial of resurrection as such, that the "second" letter to the Corinthians reflects a clearer, more mature appraisal—assuming, of course, as a majority today does, that the situation at Corinth between the two letters had remained more or less constant. In 2 Corinthians Paul appears to meet the Gnostic aversion to corporeality squarely with his analogy of the tent: "Here indeed we groan and long to put on our heavenly dwelling, so that by putting it on we may not be found unclothed. For while we are still in this tent, we sigh with anxiety; *not that we would be unclothed, but that we would be further clothed*" (2 Cor. 5:2-4). There is, of course, no evidence that the situation had in fact remained constant, so as to allow an interpretation of the "first" in light of the "second" epistle.

But it is also true that Gnosticism could not always maintain its antifleshly stance. For example, in the literature of the Valentinian sect, so called after its prophet and leader, who was expelled from the Roman church in the second century, the resurrection of the dead is affirmed—which indicates that the popular assessment of Gnosticism or of Gnostic teaching as somehow monolithic or uniform is wide of the mark. But more important, it indicates that the point at issue between Gnosticism and New Testament Christianity was not always the rejection of the doctrine of the resurrection in favor of the immortality of the soul, but of the *interpretation* of that doctrine. A pair of examples should suffice. In the *Gospel of Philip*, two definitions are apparently assigned to "flesh," the one true (sacramental) flesh of Jesus, and the other its copy, earthly and human. The one will inherit the kingdom, the other cannot, but it must nonetheless rise so that the ascending soul may be stripped of it and put on its heavenly garment. In an exposition of 1 Cor. 15:50 the author writes:

> Thou sayest that the flesh will not rise; but tell me what will rise, that we may honour thee. Thou sayest the spirit in the flesh, and it is also this light in the flesh. But this too is a logos which is in the flesh, for whatever thou shalt say thou sayest nothing outside

the flesh. It is necessary to rise in this flesh, in which everything exists.[97]

In the so-called *Epistle to Rheginus*, the term "resurrection" is applied to deliverance from the tomb of the body, but not to a release from corporeality:

> For if you were [once still] not in the flesh, but [first] received flesh when you came into the world, why should you not [also] receive flesh when you ascend into the aeon?[98]

As for the "docetic" wing of Gnosticism, according to which the eternal, preexistent "Christ" merely appeared to take on human flesh, the announcement that Christ had been raised would have been a contradiction in terms, since only Jesus of Nazareth, not "the Christ" who abandoned him at his crucifixion could die. The "historical" Jesus whom some interpreters allege the Corinthians to have cursed (cf. 12:3) was none other than the one they had exempted from their denial—the Christ of Paul.

In the literature of Gnosticism, "flesh" or "body," "death" and "resurrection" were variously interpreted (sometimes in contradictory fashion by the same author). For this reason, the reference in 2 Tim. 2:18 to those who hold that "the resurrection is past already," a passage regarded together with 2 Corinthians as shedding light on Paul's opponents here, could apply to sectarians who spoke of death as "ignorance" of God (cf. v. 34), of resurrection as the soul's "awakening" within the tomb of its flesh—but without denying its putting on a new body in its ascent toward its heavenly home. But it could equally apply to those who simply opposed the idea of a future resurrection with that of the immortality of the soul (to say nothing of those whose death ceremonies were calculated to furnish the soul a new body with which it would ultimately enter the realm of light). The decision that Paul incorrectly assessed the challenge to his gospel here could involve reading into his response the evidence for a full-blown system for which we are still searching. And even should such a system have existed, the probability that Paul had it in mind, apart from his having misinterpreted it, and this despite his use of terms suggestive of Gnostic influence, still needs proving.

There were others, of course, lacking Gnostic affiliation, who denied the resurrection—physical, psychic, or spiritual. In his account of Paul's Areopagus speech, Luke writes that the apostle's audience mocked "when they heard of the resurrection of the dead" (Acts 17:32), and in his account of Paul's defense before Agrippa, Paul is made to exclaim, "Why is it thought incredible by any of you that God raises the dead?" (Acts 26:8,23). Five hundred years before Christ, Aeschylus had put those words into the mouth of the divine Apollo: "But when the dust sucks up the blood of the man once dead, there is no resurrection."[99]

In any event, Paul had construed the challenge at Corinth to read: "He but not we," to which Paul then replies in the two triple conditional clauses: "If not we, then not he! (v. 13). And if not he, then we have preached for nothing. Then our setting you all to a thrumming and vibrating which that preaching was calculated to induce, was nothing but an echo to a silence (v. 14). And as for us who have preached, we have been found out, exposed as perjurers, since we took the stand and swore that God had done what he did not do—if not we! (v. 15). For if not we, then not he! (v. 16), and if not he, then your faith is a nothing, and the mastery, the conquest it promised, to which nothing in the world, no religious asseveration, no religious inspiration is the equal, has been a fraud—**you are still in your sins**—and the dead 'in Christ,' those whom we all believed shared with us his life and could never fall beyond his reach, their graves symbol merely of a 'little death' and promise of an end to churchyards, those dead have perished, are gone for good and all, for there is nothing about death, nothing at all that gives occasion for optimism, if not he! (vv. 17-18). If in this life we are only those who have hoped in Christ [not as in the RSV, **if for this life only we have hoped in Christ**—the copula 'we are' can be independent, so that the participle, 'have hoped,' can be an adjective, a supplementary or adverbial participle; the expression does not reflect an appetite for more than for this life, but reckons with the possibility that hope for either this life or another has been deceived], then we have thrown away what chance we had to wring what we could from this life for a nothing, and are most to be pitied (v. 19). If not we, then not he, and if not he, then nothing at all!"

If not we, then not he. How to wrench a positive, how to prove a case from two negatives? And who would be convinced? But the weakness of the argument does not lie simply in its begging the question. It lies much further back, further even than in what "we preached" and "you believed," that is, that "God raised Christ," and that with that event all of human history, every little life before and after it had been embraced. The vulnerability of the argument lies in its premise, the assumption that the statement concerning the activity of God, his raising of Christ from the dead, forces to an inference about God, his nature, about God as he is in himself, about God "as such," an inference which brooks no separation between God as he is and the activity of God, so that the subject "God" could be supplied with an infinite number of predicates which still left God alone and undefined: "God acts in history," "God judges," "God loves," "God raised Jesus from the dead," etc. Again, the premise, the assumption is that in that raising God has not merely revealed what he does, but who he is—not a God who is "also" or "at the same time" for us, or a God who is for us "in addition" to whatever else he may be, but a God whose name, that which expresses what he is in himself, is "for us." But if a wedge can be driven between what God is and what he does, if the raising of Christ can be disassociated from what God is, set down merely to an event in which he is "involved," however passionately, but in which he is still left undefined; if that event is not God's own "interpretation" of himself, then the raising of Christ can be exempted from that "for us," exempted, say, as a demonstration of omnipotence, of almightiness, of power. Then it can be separated from our raising. Then it would be possible to say, "he, but not we." Then the raising of Christ could simply be an "answer" to Christ's death, a corroboration of his Messiahship, and not the disclosure of God's nature as "for us" in the cross. There is the premise by which the argument stands or falls—that God has not simply appeared or acted or come down or condescended or "made himself known" in the event of Christ's death and resurrection (and if he is "for us," then that can be only one event) but has said "this is who I am." If God is "for us," if "for us" is his name, then "we because he." But if not, then "he, but not we."

The Reality of the Resurrection (15:20-28)

This section has often been described as an excursus, an interruption of the argument to be resumed at v. 29. In fact, there is nothing "off course" about it. It is first of all Paul's interpretation of the credo's "he was raised" in v. 11. Second, it is Paul's refutation of the enthusiast's interpretation of that credo, the notion that no distance, no disjunction lies between that "if we" and "then he," nothing to make of that "if we" (and therefore the "then he"!) a true condition, something to be assumed, believed, and hoped for. Then the "we" has already been anticipated in the "he." Then the resurrection has indeed already occurred. But if so, if tomorrow is already here, if there is no disjunction, no interval between "we" and "he," then God has not made himself captive to our temporality, has not made our time his time. Then every yesterday and tomorrow is always present to him, then he has nothing to wait for, not merely to be acknowledged to be the one he is, but to be the one he is—then God is not for us, but another. If the essence of God, the nature of God is "for us"; if he gives himself totally to us and is known by us as one who is and will be altogether for us; if nothing more lies beyond this revelation, though not even an eternity could suffice to exhaust what it means; if he has no other quality or attribute beyond what he has disclosed to us; if in his self-interpretation he has said everything to be said about himself, then to his Godhead being for our time, our history also belongs. Then he must wait, not because of (!), but *for* us. Then faith, then hope can be the only access to this God for us, this God who has taken on our time, this God who waits. But if by faith, then by suffering and endurance (Rom.

5:1-5), by suffering the disjunction between "we" and "he," now and then, then by waiting, by the cross.

The sentence structure seems clumsy, wooden, but the thought is clear enough. Verses 20-22 interpret the credo: **But in fact** (cf. 12:18 and 13:13—the little phrase marks a caesura, an "exhalation") **Christ has been raised from the dead, the first fruits of those who have fallen asleep** (again, that euphemism for the Christians' decease; cf. 7:39; 11:30; vv. 6 and 18 in this chapter). That predicate **first fruits** conjures up a welter of associations. The context is the old harvest festival, long neglected in the time of the kings, then revived and linked to the Sinai events. Seven weeks after the beginning of Mazzoth, "unleavened bread," in the third month of the Jewish year, the first sheaves of grain and the firstborn male of the herd were dedicated to Yahweh (cf. Exodus 23–24; Leviticus 23; Numbers 28; and Deuteronomy 26). If Rabbinic tradition reflects the ancient tradition, the harvesters, returning from field and farm, and flocking to Jerusalem's temple, were greeted with shouts and trumpets. At the forecourt of the temple, each one prayed, "I will exalt thee, O Lord, for thou hast set me up and not made mine enemies to triumph over me." In the temple proper, the priest then waved the firstling before the altar, and the harvester recited Israel's oldest credo from beginning to end (Deut. 26:5-10: "A wandering Aramean was my father . . ."), set the firstling by the altar, bowed himself down, and left.[100] But the ceremony not merely symbolized Yahweh's ownership of the land and its yield. That offering hid an ancient substitution of beasts for humans, congealed in the narrative of Abraham's offering his only son (Genesis 22), thus an occasion for projecting the metaphor into the future: Isaac received back and thus a race as numerous as the stars of the heaven and the sand by the sea, by which all the nations would bless themselves (Gen. 22:15-18). Christ, "Isaac bound"—it would not be the last time the "binding of Isaac" would serve as foil for the God "who gives life to the dead" (cf. Rom. 4:17; Heb. 11:17-19; John 3:16; etc.)— and thus the whole harvest, **those . . . who have fallen asleep.** "If he, then we . . . !"

Chapter 15   *1 Corinthians*

For as by a man (supply "is" or **came** with the RSV) **death, by a man . . . also the resurrection of the dead. For as in Adam all die, so also in Christ shall all be made alive** (or, "so also all who are in Christ shall be made alive"—the inference is not to be drawn that only believers will be raised; Paul merely has his readers, believers, in view). Verses 21 and 22 comprise a parallelism: **By a man came death,** and **by a man has come resurrection** (v. 21) are parallel to **as in Adam all die,** and **in Christ shall all be made alive** (v. 22). One commentator asks, "On what does the conclusion rest that the resurrection from the dead must also come by way of a man?" and answers, "the beginning and end of time must exactly correspond." But nowhere does Paul advocate the notion that with the coming of Christ humanity is returned to "square one." Note the Adam/Christ analogy and its collapse in Rom. 5:12-21: "If, because of one man's trespass, death reigned through that one man, *much more* will those who receive the abundance of grace and the free gift of righteousness reign in life." "By a man . . . in Adam," "by a man . . . in Christ." The references are to the human (all questions of a "historical Adam" aside!), to the temporal. If God is for us, then the divine is not at odds with the human. Then the eternal is not the antithesis of time, then the antithesis, the hostility must lie elsewhere—to "death," to "all" dying—then the saving, the reclamation of the human and temporal will occur by their being embraced in the human and the temporal, "by a man." Here is where the conclusion rests. And here is where the enthusiast, that anticipator of the "then" in the "now," that denier of the disjunction in time gets his comeuppance. And if that Adam/Christ analogy should somehow give occasion to metaphysical speculation, according to which the first in the series automatically contains what is to follow (**in Adam all die . . . in Christ shall all be made alive**), or to the mystical or Stoic notion of a "life relation" of the two series with their "heads," Paul had already established existence "in Christ" as occurring through an historical event, a body ("for by one Spirit we were all baptized into one body," 12:13), that body established by his death ("on the night when he was betrayed took bread, and said, 'This is my body,'" 11:24), and necessitating the obedience of faith ("which also you received, in which also you stand, by which also you are saved . . . if you hold it fast," 15:1-2). And as for existence **in Adam,** Paul would later make clear that "sin came into the world through one man and death through sin, and so death spread to all men because all men sinned" (Rom. 5:12). The possibility of construing that phrase "shall all be made alive" in v. 22 in any other way than in face of mortality, corruption, dissolution, nothingness, fractures on the phrase from **the dead** in v. 21.

The background of vv. 23-28 is that of Jewish apocalyptic, with its recitation of the events of the end-time seriatim. First the Messiah; then those who are his; then **the end** (another, third stage, or to be read as a further definition of "his appearing," thus "at last" or "finally"?), when the kingdom is delivered to the Father. Verses 24 and 28 are parallel, and give to the section its "frame." Not one item in the series could not have derived from speculation on the "Day of the Lord" between the Testaments—with one exception, signaled in the temporal adverbs and clauses in vv. 24 and 25, climaxing in v. 28: "When," "until," "when . . . then!" The hallmark of Jewish apocalyptic, the idea of the visible manifestation of God for judgment and salvation in the end-time, has been qualified. The series has been foreshortened in the announcement that the end has already penetrated to the present, that Messiah has already begun his rule; that the demons which the Messiah of apocalyptic would expel in the end-time (the **rule** and **authority** and **power** of v. 24), are already being crushed, put under his feet (v. 25, the subject of Ps. 11:1, cited here, has been altered to read, "until he," that is, Christ, "has put his enemies under his feet"); that **the last enemy, death,** is as good as dead (hence the present tense of the verb "to destroy" in v. 26); that, in fact, Messiah has made everything his fief (v. 27a; again, the subject of Ps. 8:7 cited here has been altered to read, "he," that is, Christ, **has put all things in subjection under his feet**). **All things** but God (the correction in v. 27b would be nonsense if God were the subject of v. 27a, as the RSV translates), who had determined this reign (Christ "*must* reign," v. 25), had subjected all things to Christ's subjecting (vv. 27b, 28).

But Messiah's reign has not merely penetrated the present. It is restricted to the here and now, its boundary described by the event forming the "frame" in vv. 24 and 28: **Then . . . the end, when he delivers the kingdom to God the Father . . . when all things are subjected to him, then the Son himself will also be subjected to him who put all things under him, that God may be** all in all (RSV, **everything to everyone**). So the kingdom of God the Father is in coming, not in having come. So the Son, to whom everything is subject, still struggles to thrust his enemies through that hole beneath his throne. So, though "as good as," nothing is complete, finished, and God is not yet but is still to be "all in all." Still to be, not because God needs the subjection in order to be what he will be, not because he requires time and history to achieve "self-realization," not because he could not do without the world or humanity in order to be God, but because "from eternity" he determined to be the God who would not yet be the God he would be, determined to be a God still to be "all in all," because "from everlasting" he willed for himself the disjunction between "now" and "then" which denotes human existence, willed to be for us, willed to be grace. But if by grace, then through faith, then nothing yet seen of eternity in time; nothing of the "then" in the "now"; nothing demonstrable which would not be capable of a thousand-and-one interpretations, and nothing "worldly wise"—all of it a "stumbling-block to Jews and folly to Gentiles," all a premise, an assumption, a confession "revealed to us through the Spirit" (2:10).

Return to the Argument: The Corinthians' Inconsistency (15:29-34)

Following his announcement of the reality of the resurrection of Christ, in whom "all shall be made alive," Paul first turns to a curious inconsistency in Corinthian practice which supports that announcement. **Otherwise**—if he, but not we; if he was raised, but we shall not be—"what will they do who are baptized for the dead; if the dead are not raised at all, why then are they baptized on their behalf?" This verse may be the most difficult in the entire epistle. Scarcely one word of it has escaped questioning and debate.

One thing is certain: Paul's question is calculated to exploit the gulf between what "some" say ("there is no resurrection from the dead," v. 12) and what they do (assuming the identity of subjects in vv. 12 and 29, cf. v. 34). "What will they do?" (not, **what do people mean?** RSV), that is, once they have tumbled to the inconsistency, or, what future do they have who deny the resurrection from the dead and yet are baptized for the dead? But what does **baptized** mean? To construe it as metaphorical in light of Paul's reference to his dying "daily" in v. 31, helps little. Whether a baptism by water or a martyrdom, a vicarious act is involved, and either "baptism" out of all harmony with Pauline teaching. Let the simplest reading stand: "Some [how many?] undergo water baptism [a second time] for the dead." And what does that "for" in "for the dead" mean? Does it mean simply "for the good of," or, as one author has suggested, can the magic be removed from this act by reading "in the place of," no conclusion then to be drawn regarding the beneficiary's taking profit from it?[101] The suggestion smacks of Mormonism, according to which any member of the sectarian's unaffiliated, deceased relatives may elect to choose or reject a baptism on their behalf. In early Christianity, if only among heretics, vicarious baptism "on behalf of," "to the advantage of," "for the good of the dead" cannot be denied.[102] But does Paul approve? On the assumption that he does, and that *for this reason* magic is out of the question, the conclusion to be drawn is that every reference in this letter and in every other to Baptism cannot be to an event which creates union with Christ, but rather to an event which merely expresses, "proclaims" or "confesses" a union already effected. But if so, and if that union should be with the death and resurrection of Christ, then the magical component is merely shifted from a "baptism for the dead" to Christ as a "collective," as "archetypal man," in whom we were all once somehow redeemed (the notion of this myth of

Chapter 15   *1 Corinthians*

the archetypal man as single, original, and discrete has long since been exploded), or, to an "objective justification," faith in the one instance relating to that event as echo to sound, and in the other as assent to the event's having occurred.[103] But there is another alternative to magic than to deny the present for the past; another alternative to denying the once-for-allness of Christ's death than to assert that "our 'old man' hung together with Jesus then (!) on the cross,"[104] another option to construing Baptism as an act *ex opere operato* than to construe it as simply "disclosing" the significance of the past. The alternative reads that in Christ's once-for-all death a "body" was created by God, of which Christ is head, and incorporation into which occurs through the Spirit in the Baptism, requiring, effecting the obedience of faith, a faith which not merely calls to mind or assents to that once-for-all event—curiously, here, "salvation-historical theology" and its parent orthodoxy join hands—but unites to the Christ who endured that event as in one flesh. The "wisdom of God" which has been revealed is neither nature nor history which can be known. The revelation is not a knowing but a "being known" (8:12-13; 13:12). Nor is faith a "making sense" of the revelation, for in the revelation God remains a mystery, unapproachable by reason because he is a person, a "Thou," the Other. By faith that Other has become known, become mine. And beneath it all the everlasting Pauline assumption that life, existence, is never that of a single self, but always "in" or "with." Only to the one for whom the self is self-contained could such talk smack of "mysticism."

So then, does Paul approve? But if so, why not make the approval explicit? (Or, does he disapprove, in v. 34: "Be sober as is right for you and do not sin, for *some* [!] have ignorance of God. I say this to your shame"?) Approve or disapprove; arguments for the one or the other, like all arguments from silence, prove nothing. The point is the inconsistency of "some" at Corinth. And if so, then perhaps Paul has assessed the situation correctly after all. The issue was not resurrection, psychic or spiritual, not even resurrection as physical—at least as some Valentinians were alleged to construe it—but resurrection "from the dead," from mortality, corruption, from ashes and silence to the body "which is to be" (v. 37), to corporeality, humanity.

From Corinthian inconsistency as yielding negative support for his gospel of the resurrection Paul moves to drawing conclusions from its denial, and in the interrogative form taken up at v. 29. **Why are we [not I, RSV] in peril every hour?** [v. 30]. **I swear [not protest, RSV], brethren, by my boast [not pride, RSV] in you which I have in Christ Jesus our Lord, I die every day** [v. 31; in the original, the pronoun **you** appears in the accusative case, but as the latter part of the verse makes clear, it is a substitute for the objective genitive]. **What do I gain** [literally, 'what is the profit to me'] **if, humanly speaking, I fought with beasts at Ephesus? If the dead are not raised, 'Let us eat and drink, for tomorrow we die'"** [v. 32].

The question in v. 30, **why are we in peril?** and the oath followed by the asseveration in v. 31, **I die every day** (in the original the order is reversed) comprise an autobiography. To the moment of writing, Paul could not carry on his work without endangering his life, and, often enough, that of his coworkers (included in that "we," cf. Rom. 16:7; 2 Cor. 8:22; Phil. 2:30; Philemon 23). That phrase attached to the outburst of pathos in the oath—**by my** boast **in you which I have in Christ Jesus our Lord**—is calculated to detach the boast from the confidence of the self-made man. The same attitude is reflected here as in 9:15. The apostle's activity, thus his pride, was anchored alone in what God did through him, that is, anchored in the "necessity" to which he had consented, by proclaiming the gospel free of charge (chap. 9), and by announcing it in face of danger and peril of death (chap. 15).

Is the reference to fighting with **beasts at Ephesus** to be taken as metaphor? Nowhere in his list of trials (2 Cor. 11:24-25) does Paul make mention of a legal indictment which carried such a penalty, aside from the fact that a Roman citizen could never be sentenced to such combat. The reference could thus be simply a figure drawn from the arena to describe Paul's response to his "necessity," and as for "Ephesus," city of Artemis-Diana, no other place-name would better suit the metaphor. "Ephesus" meant riot and uproar, plots and treachery, reaching as far as Jerusalem (cf. Acts 19:23-41; 21:27-36), but it also meant endurance and courage (cf. Acts 20:20, 27). The clause, however, could still be construed literally, that is, as a condition contrary to fact: "If I had fought with beasts at Ephesus, what would I gain?" Then, perhaps, that otherwise puzzling phrase, "humanly speaking," becomes clearer: "What would I gain, if, humanly speaking—that is, if men had had their way—I had fought . . .?" When Luke in good classical style writes that during the riot in the Ephesian theater "some yelled this and others that," "this" or "that" may easily have included the roar "To the beasts!" (*ad bestias*, cf. Acts 19:32). "What would I gain [in the original, 'what use, what profit is mine']?" The scholars are anxious to exculpate Paul of any opportunism. Let the "opportunism" stand. There is precedent for it. The question is from Paul's own Bible, the LXX of Isa. 22:13: "Eat, drink, for tomorrow we die."[105] There is a world of difference between the religion instructor's disinterested, balcony view of the next life, and that of a man with death all around.

At Corinth, denial of the resurrection and libertinism went hand in hand—but at Corinth! An apostle who never balked at proclaiming "whatever was true, honorable, just, pure, lovely, gracious" from the Graeco-Roman world, and in a minute would do so again (cf. v. 33), who acknowledged that "the nations" evidenced the work required by the Law as "written in their hearts" (Rom. 2:14-15) could never be called to testify that unbelief or absence of faith automatically spelled immorality, without denying that God had not abandoned the world. And he could never have embraced that "doctrine" of the ambiguity attendant upon human existence, rooted in the event by which "the wisdom of God" had appeared under the sign of "foolishness," if he had believed that the difference between the one *in* and the one *apart* from Christ was determined by anything or anyone other than the one "in whom" that one existed, that it was discernible to human science. And he would never have acknowledged the pan-human character of the "gifts of the Spirit," or struggled to assert that his waiver of rights was the mark of his apostleship, his "necessity," the sovereignty of the crucified in him, in face of attempts to set it all down to historical accident ("by the boast which I have in you in Christ Jesus, I die daily!"). But it was at Corinth that "some" had said "meats for the belly, and the belly for meats" (9:13); at Corinth that they had profaned the Supper and participated in pagan cultic meals. At Corinth denial of the resurrection from the dead and license went hand in hand.

The section closes with a series of imperatives and a bitter indictment (vv. 33-34). The first imperative (**do not be deceived**) is followed by a maxim from a comedy (*Thais*) of the poet and playwright Menander (342–290 B.C.), the Ben Franklin of the ancient world: **Bad company** (or, "evil speaking" which takes only death into account) **ruins good morals.** Of the two imperatives in v. 34, the first (in the aorist tense) is "ingressive," summoning to an action or attitude in contrast to what prevailed till now— "be rightly sober," or "be sober as is right for you." The second imperative (in the present tense) is "durative," summoning to a continued action—"do not sin." The antithesis struck by the two imperatives is between sin and a sobriety (a **right mind,** RSV) which allows no inconsistency between praxis and theory, faith and life. **For,** or perhaps better, "indeed," **some have no knowledge of God** (the original reads, "have an ignorance of God"). **I say this to your shame.** The ignorance was something actively pursued; it was the attempt to alter "if he, then we" to read "he, but not we," to make a nest for that alteration in a life for the self, thus to deny the nature of God as "for us," for our time, our history, and thus his claim to our corporeality.

How the Dead Are Raised (15:35-49)

The section is dominated by the question put in v. 35. Aside from the richness of rhetorical devices (cf., e.g., the chiasma in vv. 40 and 41; the series of antitheses, the repetition of words at the beginning of successive clauses, and the assonance, i.e., the identity of vowel sounds, in vv. 42-44, etc.), there is a heap of anthropological and other terms, such as **body** (vv. 35, 37, 38,

Chapter 15 *1 Corinthians*

40, 44); **flesh** (v. 39); **glory** (vv. 40-41, 43); "soul" (v. 45, translated **being** in the RSV); **spirit** (v. 45); **image** (v. 49), and adjectives such as "souled" (v. 44, translated **physical** in the RSV); **spiritual** (v. 44); **of dust** (vv. 47-49), and **heavenly** (vv. 48-49)!

But some one will ask, "How are the dead raised? With what kind of body do they come (rise)?" (v. 35). Paul's adversary, that anonymous "someone" who has haunted the discussion since v. 12, obliquely attacked for inconsistency and the resultant damage to "good morals" (vv. 29, 33), directly charged with an invincible ignorance of God which should leave the Corinthians red-faced (v. 34), gets full return for whatever scorn he may have heaped on Paul's gospel (refracted in that word "folly" in 1:18, 21, 23-24; 2:6-16): "You fool!" Then, taking up the analogy of the seed and the sower, the latter part of which he never lets go (cf. vv. 42-44), Paul strikes at the notion of the automatic persistence of life.

The seed does not come to life without death (v. 36), and what is sown **is not the body which is to be,** but a "naked kernel" (v. 37). The word "naked" is a double entendre. It denotes the "mere" seed (RSV, **a bare kernel**), the buried body, but in the mind of Paul's contemporaries it represented whatever was fated to persist—whether or not the deity willed otherwise—once the body fell prey to worms: the "soul." Paul asserts: "There is no continuity between what is sown, between the 'soul' and the body to be!" The point will take rawest shape in midst of the Adam/Christ contrast in vv. 45-49, in that antithesis between the "psychic" (RSV, **physical**) and the "spiritual" in vv. 45-46. On the face of it, the notion of discontinuity between the seed and the plant is nonsense, and takes its place with that other offense to horticulture in Rom. 11:17-24. But in neither instance is the move from agronomy to Christian existence, but exactly the reverse. The analogy is warped to what it serves, and here it is made to fit the assertion of discontinuity, the contention that there is no resurrection unless "from the dead." What that warping and twisting of the figure to serve its topic means is that there is, after all, no analogy in nature to the activity of God envisioned here, but only a refraction; no possibility of inferring the "wisdom of

God" from what can be observed in the world. Quite the contrary, what can be seen in the world, the speech that identifies that observation, "every thought," needs "taking captive to obey Christ" (2 Cor. 10:5). And the fact that it is even capable of being taken captive, of being "conquered," pressed into the service of the "wisdom of God," does not lie in the power of that thought, but in the power of the God who made it. For this reason, what follows in that catalog of "flesh," "bodies," and "glories" in vv. 39-41 is not a proof from nature or the cosmos. The resurrection from the dead does not "rest" on this variety of forms (cf. Lietzmann on the passage). Paul is not attempting to show that the resurrection is "ontologically possible" (cf. Conzelmann on the passage). The catalog is not even a proof for the existence of God. Paul, like his Jewish and Greek (!) contemporaries, made no use of the "ontological argument" for the existence of God, which moves from the cosmos to the Creator, from the "watch" to the "watchmaker." The arguments and remonstrances of a Cleanthes in David Hume's *Dialogues Concerning Natural Religion* reflect a mentality totally unlike that of Paul or his contemporaries. Only skeptics denied that God could be known, and simply because they denied the possibility of any objective knowledge. The "fool" of v. 35, and "some" who have "no knowledge of God" in v. 34, are what they are in light of the "wisdom of God," not his unknowability. So the "catalog" in vv. 38-41 proves nothing. It is rather a witness to the creative will of God manifest in the unlimited and inexhaustible variety of the cosmos. To this, v. 38 gives the clue: **God gives it a body as he has chosen.** For this reason, the adverb "thus" (**so**) in v. 42 does not signal the conclusion to a logical argument or syllogism begun at v. 39. It introduces a correlative: Just as God has willed one "flesh" for humans, another for beasts, and still others for birds and fish, so he has willed the resurrection from the dead. (The term **flesh** in v. 39 is not used pejoratively, as marking hostility to God, but refers to what is altogether earthly, thus synonymous with **of dust** in vv. 47-49; for this reason only, it is substituted for "body"). Just as God has willed a distinction between celestial and terrestrial "bodies" and their "glories" or "brilliance," so he has willed the resurrection from the dead. (The term **flesh** in v. 40 would not have suited the description of the celestial or heavenly; or did Paul choose "flesh" in v. 39 because he conceived the **glory of the terrestrial** as dimmed by its transitoriness? At any rate, the object throughout these verses is the **body**—**flesh** and **glory** denote a distinction in kind and quality.) Just as God has willed a distinction in brilliance even among celestial bodies (a **glory of the sun . . . the moon . . . the stars; for**—or better, "and even"— **star differs from star in glory,** v. 41), so he has willed the resurrection from the dead. **God gives it a body as he has chosen!**

Following his "analogy" and his witness to God's power, Paul now proceeds to answer the question of the "how," and in a series of four antitheses, punctuated with repetitions of words at the beginning and an identity of sounds at the conclusion of each phrase (an assonance which cannot be observed in translation):

It is sown in corruption, it is raised in incorruption.
It is sown in dishonor, it is raised in glory.
It is sown in weakness, it is raised in power.
It is sown a soulful body, it is raised a spiritual body (vv. 42-44).

Where is the subject in the antithesis, or where does the continuity lie between what is sown and what is raised? It does not lie in the body. "Body" appears on either side of **sown** and **raised,** but between the two lies "corruption," **dishonor,** and **weakness;** between the two lies death, not only of the physical but of what was thought to possess immortality, the "soul." The first member in that fourth antithesis is not a **physical body** (RSV) but a body with its own kind of soul, a "soulful body." Between **is sown** and **is raised** lies an infinite gulf which the body cannot span. But that can only mean that between the two lies a miracle, an "incorruption," a **glory** and a **power** to which not body but something else must furnish the clue. Someone else must give the promise or guarantee. The subject of the antitheses, tucked away in the passive voice of those verbs **is sown** and **is raised** is God. The continuity lies with God, with the power of God who wills **body,** wills corporeality either side of the gulf.

Note the tense of the antithesis: **is sown . . . is raised.** Does Paul conceive "what is to be" as so certain that it might as well be "is"? Or, again, "if there is a soulful body, there is also a spiritual body" (v. 44b). Does Paul conceive the **spiritual body** as already in existence, like a garment waiting to be put on (cf. vv. 53-54)? Perhaps. But the tense is also required by an event already occurred, and registered in the Adam/Christ contrast: **Thus it is written, "the first man Adam became a living** soul" (RSV, **being**); **the last Adam became a life-giving spirit** (v. 45). The quotation from Gen. 2:7 appears misplaced. On the face of it, v. 46 should have followed v. 44b: "If there is a soulful body, there is also a spiritual body. But it is not the spiritual which is first. . . ." But as important as the question of first and last was for Paul, what made the first first and the last last, and thus demanded the present tense in those antitheses (**is sown . . . is raised**), had the priority. If there is no promise of the "incorruption," **glory,** and **power** of what is raised in the "corruption," **dishonor,** and **weakness** of what is sown, it is because there is no promise of the "last Adam" in the first, no omen or guarantee of the **life-giving spirit** in the "soulful body." If there is continuity between what is sown and what is raised, then because the last Adam "was made"—this is the force of that verb **became** at the head of the scriptural quotation—**a life-giving spirit.** Between the two the same subject, the same power. In an old hymn, and in the opening lines of what proved to be his last will and testament, Paul would ring the changes on that word **was made:**

> Therefore God has highly exalted him and bestowed on him the name which is above every name, that at the name of Jesus every knee should bow, in heaven and on earth and under the earth, and every tongue confess that Jesus Christ is Lord, to the glory of God the Father (Phil. 2:9-10).

> Paul, a servant of Jesus Christ, called to be an apostle, set apart for the gospel of God which he promised beforehand through his prophets in the holy scriptures, the gospel concerning his Son, who was

Chapter 15   *1 Corinthians*

descended from David according to the flesh and designated Son of God in power according to the Spirit of holiness by his resurrection from the dead, Jesus Christ our Lord (Rom. 1:1-4).

Now to the order: **But it is not the spiritual which is first but the** "soulful" (RSV **physical**). Paul's contemporary, Philo, befuddled by the two creation accounts in Genesis 1 and 2, had decided upon two creations, first of the "heavenly man" (Gen. 1:27), made in God's image, and last of the "earthly man" (Gen. 2:7), a composite of clay and divine breath:

> There are two types of man: the one a heavenly man, the other an earthly. The heavenly man, being made after the image of God, is altogether without part or lot in corruptible and terrestrial substance; but the earthly one was compacted out of the matter scattered here and there, which Moses calls "clay." For this reason he says that the heavenly man was not moulded, but was stamped with the image of God; while the earthly is a moulded work of the artificer, but not his offspring.[106]

Paul drew no such distinction. Did he know of it? His omission of the term "molded" (RSV, **formed**) in his quotation of Genesis 2, but which for Philo marked the inferiority of the earthly to the heavenly man, raises the suspicion. But if he did know of it, he allowed for no distinction, or, better, he stood Philo's sequence on its head, made Philo's "last man" first and his "first man" last, and in doing so tore Philo's "heavenly man" from his preexistence to become an object of "sowing" and "raising." The phrase **became a life-giving spirit** in v. 45, as well as the phrase **the second man . . . from heaven** in v. 47, screen a reference to Christ's resurrection "from the dead," nothing less, nothing more. Or, had **some** of the Corinthians reversed the order? Had they taken to that myth, later to undergo a hundred variations, each with its own adherents, the myth that the irrational and unknowable God had created a **first man Adam** like himself (or was himself that "first man") who should be a model for the **last Adam**, taking residence in that earthly man and his offspring as their kernel or "soul"? If so, he drew the myth's teeth at the same point at which he would have drawn Philo's—at the point of time or history. The **life-giving**

spirit (v. 45), the **spiritual** (v. 46), the **man from heaven** (v. 47) was plunged from an existence which Philo described as "without part or lot in corruptible and terrestrial substance,"[107] "incorporeal [literally, 'bodiless'], neither male nor female, by nature incorruptible,"[108] an existence which the myth regarded as the direct antithesis of corporeality, to become **last** (v. 45) or **second** (vv. 46-47). And if the **first man, Adam,** "the living soul," the psychic or "soulful" man, the man **of dust,** then we: "As the man of dust, so those of dust"—no incorruptible seed hidden in the hull of the psychic, but **of dust,** from dust, remaining dust, and returning to the dust to become dust again (Ps. 103:4 and 78:39)! And if Christ, the **last Adam,** the **life-giving spirit,** the **spiritual,** the **second man from heaven,** then we: **And as is the man of heaven, so . . . those . . . of heaven** (v. 48). But those conditional clauses in v. 47 take their tenses and their sense only from what follows in v. 48. Between those two Adams, and those shaped or conformed to them (bearing their "image"—in Philo, a term reserved only for the "heavenly man"!), there is no entelechy, no progression or development from one to the other, no continuity in essence or substance, but only history and death. And yet, between those two also lies promise: **Just as we have borne the image of the man of dust, we shall also bear the image of the man of heaven.** (*Genesis Rabbah* 14.8 on Gen. 2:7b contrasts the man of dust in Gen. 2:7 with the resurrection Spirit of God in Ezek. 37:14—an argument to Paul's taste!)[109] And it can only be promise; the argument can only read "if he, then we," because for all their oneness, for all their unity in that one "body" (12:13, 27), only one part of that body (the **life-giving spirit,** v. 45) can give existence to the whole, to **those of heaven** (v. 48), and that he does so or will do so can never be seen, to say nothing of being achieved (the oldest manuscript witness to 1 Cor. 15:49 reads, "just as we have borne the image of the man of dust, *let us also bear the image of the man of heaven*"). "If he, then we" is neither a sign nor a wisdom to be sought or demanded. It is a promise to be believed. The sequence of the argument in vv.

12ff. has been reversed. There was never any question as to the "he" in that "if he, then we."

The Destiny of Those Still Alive (15:50-58)

Verse 50 is a Janus, facing both ways. It sums up the argument begun at v. 35 in respect of the dead, and furnishes the thesis of the argument commencing at v. 51 in regard to those still alive: **Flesh and blood cannot inherit the kingdom of God.** For **flesh and blood** read "psychic" or "soulful"; for "of dust," bearing the "image of the man of dust" (vv. 44b-49), read **mortal** (v. 50b). To that single goal of the resurrection from the dead— the kingdom of God, God's rule, God "all in all" (v. 28)—the "mortal," dead or alive, whatever can be "sown," planted "six feet under" and over it intoned "dust thou art, to dust thou shalt return," has no claimant's right. Verses 51-53 describe the destiny of those still living at Christ's return. How the apostle came to this knowledge he does not say, nor is it clear that he includes himself among those who will still be alive (all the manuscript witnesses not in support of our text rule out the possibility). He calls what he has to tell a **mystery,** the revelation of an event rooted in divine decree and occurring with divine necessity, but in a fashion inaccessible to human comprehension: **We shall not all sleep, but we shall all be changed.** The accent in that parallelism of v. 51 lies in the collective—**all** will be changed, and the change will be for the living what it will be for the dead. Neither will be at disadvantage, neither at advantage over against the other. In v. 52, Paul then draws on the language of apocalyptic to describe the "when" of the change—**in a moment, in the twinkling of an eye, at the last trumpet.** In the daily Shemone-Esre or Eighteen-Petition Prayer, the Jewish synagogue prays for the coming of the trumpet call: "Blow in the great Shofar for our liberation," a petition gathered with another which praises the God who raises the dead.[110]

On a Sunday in May 1545, Luther spent a third of his sermon on that trumpet:

> Trumpets are made from brass, used in the army, in battle. . . . The great angel will beat the drum. Then God will let trumpets blow, . . . a black cloud will come up, thunder and lightning, the whole earth will shake and everybody with it, till the last thunderclap—the drum roll to throw everything into a heap. Then, in a moment, you will be dead and alive. . . . Christ's voice is gentle, but God's is a trumpet that brings a house down in a second, so that it turns to mere dust. It smashes, then, and it happens in a moment. Then all creatures will shout to him: Hurrah, Hurrah! . . . Then we will be changed from the mortal to an immortal nature.[111]

And as if it were not yet clear why there needed to be a "sowing" and a "raising," why "flesh and blood" could not inherit the kingdom, Paul adds in v. 53: **For this perishable** (not, **this perishable nature** which reduces the force of the demonstration, RSV) **must put on the imperishable, and this mortal** (again, not **mortal nature**) **put on immortality.** The language is still that of apocalyptic thought, reminiscent, for example, of those references to the "garments of glory" or of "life" in 1 Enoch (62:15-16). In the original, the sentence begins with the verb "it must be," cipher or shorthand for an eschatological necessity decreed by God (cf. this theme in Luke and Acts). And the demonstrative pronouns in the parallelism of vv. 53 and 54—**this perishable, this mortal**—once more drive a wedge between the subjects on either side of the "change." There is no identity, no continuity between **perishable, mortal** and **imperishable, immortality**—only that "it must be."

The argument respecting the equality of the dead and living at the parousia flows into what is virtually a hymn, ending at v. 57. When what "must be" finally "is," then the "word which was written" will come to be. That "word" is a little "chain" quotation from Isa. 25:8 and Hos. 13:14, and to greater or lesser degree at variance with both the LXX and the Hebrew text (in his quotation of Hosea, Paul may have followed a text similar to that of a later competitor of the LXX, Theodotion). More important, that "word" appears to violate its Old Testament contexts. The setting of the Isaiah passage is Yahweh's feast for the nations come on pilgrimage to Zion. The time of suffering is over, and Yahweh will remove the veil from the faces of those mourning their dead in the last great historical struggles. If those faces should still show sorrow, he will wipe away their tears. Then Isaiah (or a later hand?) adds: "He will swallow up death forever" (Theodotion, "in victory"). The setting of the Hosea passage is a dialog between Yahweh and the prophet over Ephraim's (the northern kingdom's) guilt, a guilt "tied up" as in a scroll and "remembered." Most regard the dialog as ending in Yahweh's refusal to redeem: "Shall I ransom them from the power of Sheol? Shall I redeem them from Death? Here with your plagues, O Death! Here with your tortures, O Sheol!" (there is no direct correspondence between the Hebrew word for "plague" or "torture" and the term "sting" in the LXX and in Paul). But if the Hebrew of Hos. 13:14 should consist of a promise and not a threat—"from Sheol I will ransom! From Death I will redeem!"—the passage would express a faith in the power of God to penetrate where most believed he could not go (cf. Amos 9:2). In that case, the Hosea passage recontextualizes the passage in Isaiah, interprets the "swallowing" not of a cessation of struggle and war, but of God's power over death and the place of the dead, and Paul in turn recontextualizes Hosea's word in a confession of God's power to reach beyond Ephraim to all the dead.

Now **the sting of death is sin, and the power of sin is the law** (v. 56). The verse is not a gloss (cf. Weiss and Conzelmann on the passage), or a "little excursus" (cf. Lietzmann on the passage), the intrusion of antinomist sentiment into an otherwise coherent argument. It is Paul's "pesher," his commentary on the little word "sting" he found in his edition of Hosea 13, and gives the basis for the thanks in v. 57, itself a reminiscence of that little "chain." What gives to death its reality (to read a cattle-prod or scorpion into the word **sting** would stretch the figure beyond what it can bear) is sin, and what not merely discloses but even gives occasion to that reality, thus its power, though not freely but against its will, is the Law (cf. Rom. 3:20 and 7:7-12). And from this reality and this power "we" ("thanks be to God who gives *us* the victory") have been set free.

Now, the end of the believers' life can be viewed from a totally different point of view. From that rage for the self which strikes at every link, tears at every connection but that with itself, a range inflamed by the Law, by the command to be and do otherwise, a rage the consequences of which in action cannot be foreseen or controlled, so that it becomes a power which none can master, until at last it succumbs to the event which reveals the nothingness of such an existence by destroying it, from this power Christ's death and raising drew the **sting**. As Paul wrote earlier and would write again, to this power those who had become one body with Christ had died (Gal. 3:19-20, "I through the law died to the law, that I might live to God. I have been crucified with Christ"; Rom. 6:10, "Consider yourselves dead to sin and alive to God"), so that what remains is an end to life and not a horror. It is this death, this end to life which Paul calls a "sowing" and from this death the body will be "raised." Following this death, humanity, corporeality, will be "changed":

> Man as such . . . belongs to this world. He is thus finite and mortal. One day he will only have been, as once he was not. His divinely given promise and hope and confidence . . . is that even as this one who has been he will share the eternal life of God Himself. . . . He does not look and move towards the fact that this being of his in his time will one day be forgotten and extinguished and left behind. . . . He does not hope for redemption from the this-sidedness, finitude and mortality of his existence. He hopes positively for the revelation of its redemption as completed in Jesus Christ, namely, the redemption of his this-sided, finite and mortal existence.[112]

Thanks be to God, who gives us the victory through our Lord Jesus Christ!

The section concludes with the address used at the very beginning of the chapter, this time annexed to an adjective and personal pronoun: **My beloved brethren**. . . . From first to last, from gospel, from credo and tradition to the arguments for the resurrection from the dead, for its reality, to the exploiting of inconsistencies, to the answer to the "how," and finally to the "hymn," one circle of readers has always been in mind. "Some," the demurrers, the deniers, baptized for the dead, ignorant of God, corrupters of morals, the "fool"—they are all embraced in that address in v. 58: **My beloved brethren.**

Be steadfast, immovable, always abounding in the work of the Lord. The word is not a warning, nor is it a summons to comply with a rule or standard externally applied, a call to be what one would otherwise not be without that command, as though the indicative needed the attachment of the imperative, as though the "wisdom of God" could be heard and believed in the abstract, without a link to the moments of factual, historical life. If the hearing of that "wisdom" is faith, and if its connection with those moments is love, then faith and love are one and the same. Then the actions, the deeds of love—**the work of the Lord**—are anticipated in the hearing and believing (but not the reverse; faith, "receiving," "standing in," "holding fast the gospel," is always the presupposition for love, 15:12, and, without this, love is no longer a deed, but a "work," a performance, and thus worthless; if the knowledge of God rests on a "being known by God," 8:2f., then love rests on the love of God, cf. 2 Cor. 5:13). Then believing is never something over and done with, but always a becoming—not in terms of an approximation to an ideal ("be what you are," that is, "become in reality what you are ideally"), but because the subject of existence is everlastingly at work for the other in those who are his. Then existence by faith spells time for the other, space for the other, life for the other bound to the conditions of this world. Then that existence spells history, deed, corporeality, cross. And because the one who was buried, raised, and appeared, because the "first fruits" reigning, destroying all rule, authority and power, subjecting all things to himself, because the "last Adam," the "second man from heaven," because the "life-giving spirit" whose image we shall bear is the subject of existence, that work can never be "in vain."

■ Conclusion (Chapter 16)

The concluding chapter is composed of seven sections. The first section pertains to the "collection" (vv. 1-4); the second to

Paul's travel plans (vv. 5-9), and the third to Timothy's arrival and Apollos's delay (vv. 10-12). The fourth section contains the apostle's concluding admonitions (vv. 13-14); the fifth pertains to the reception of Stephanus and his company (vv. 15-18); the sixth contains greetings (vv. 19-20), and the last a conclusion in Paul's own hand (vv. 21-24).

The Collection for the Saints (16:1-4)

The verses have been slandered, dubbed as "external matters." But love, the "work of the Lord" is never something alongside of or, in addition to faith. Faith takes its shape in the act; the believer is always believer in the act, whether or not that shape is perceptible or demonstrable as the shape of faith. At issue is not proof but existence! And since the deed or act can never be a doing or acting in general, but is always occasional, stimulated, evoked, called up, necessitated by a specific "now" of a specific "other," and all for the reason that the one to whom faith has wed the believer is incessantly at work, reigning till all things are under his feet, then the answer to a quite specific, temporal, historical, earthly, mundane need in the other is no mere "external matter," but the love in which faith takes its shape. Then, when faith, on a hunt to take its shape in love, misses, overlooks, or ignores what can give it shape, it seeks for a disclosure of its possibilities. Corinth had asked, and Paul had disclosed: **Now concerning the contribution for the saints.**

This is the first time that Paul indicates how that promise he had made earlier to the Jerusalem conclave was to be carried out (cf. Gal. 2:10). It would not be the last (cf. 2 Corinthians 8–9, and Rom. 16:25-27, 30-31). Clearly, he had spoken of the collection for the Jerusalem poor while at Corinth, since the Corinthians had referred to it in their inquiries to Paul (**now concerning,** cf. 7:1, 25; 8:1(4); 12:1). Paul's instructions regarding the collection here lack the urgency and intensity of feeling expressed in 2 Corinthians (and Romans), occasioned by Corinth's neglect to finish the task. The comparison with the liberality of the churches in Macedonia; the appeal to Corinth to prove the gen-

Chapter 16   *1 Corinthians*

uineness of its love; the holding up of Christ as prototype ("though he was rich, yet for your sake he became poor"); the appeals to Scripture; the action undertaken to allay the suspicion he was feathering his own nest; the reference to his humiliation in the event the collection at Corinth was not completed; the sending of Titus and that anonymous "brother" to expedite matters, and the promise of enrichment through generosity—all this is lacking here. The verses merely outline a procedure laid down earlier for the churches in Galatia. Each Sunday (literally, "each first of Sabbath"—the Jewish week forming the basis), a freewill offering is to be received, a practice not yet current in early Christianity, and each contributing according to means. The procedure as outlined is eminently practical. The apostle would not only be relieved of appealing for funds on his arrival (other matters required his attention, cf. 4:21; 11:34), but the amount would exceed what could be gathered at a single offering. On his arrival, Paul would send representatives chosen at Corinth to Jerusalem, together with his letters of recommendation (the phrase which the RSV translates **I will send those whom you accredit by letter** would better read "I will send by letter whom you accredit"). Nothing reflects charges of fiscal irresponsibility (cf. 2 Cor. 9:20-21). Paul's decision to accompany the Corinthian delegation is still in the air, contingent upon "whether it is worth the effort" (RSV, **if it seems advisable**). What would be worth the effort? Certainly not the size of the collection, but the possibility that the collection could reflect more than a promise kept? The space and heat devoted to the affair in 2 Corinthians reveals more than impatience with Corinth's delay. The absence of any mention of the collection in his earliest letters (1 Thessalonians and Galatians), measured against Paul's later appeal to Corinth, and his final appeal to Rome to struggle with him in prayer that his (!) "service" to Jerusalem "might be acceptable to the saints" (cf. Rom. 16:31), suggests an alteration of the initial reason for the collection to an occasion for something greater than the alleviation of economic distress, that is, for a move toward reconciliation with those parties in the church which had opposed Paul.[113] Here, in 1 Corinthians, a promise to be kept still holds center stage, but not without the proviso: "If it is worth the effort for me to go also," **they will accompany me.**

Paul's Travel Plans (16:5-9)

Since the offerings were to be ready upon his arrival, the Corinthians needed to know when Paul would arrive. His itinerary corresponded roughly to a triangle. From Ephesus across the Aegean he would move north by land, put out for Macedonia at the Aegean's northernmost port, and from there move down to Corinth where he would presumably arrive in late fall, spending the winter at Corinth till the shipping lanes were open again. Corinth would then fit him out (the RSV reads, **so that you may speed me on my journey**). But for where? As yet, the trip to Jerusalem was still tentative (cf. v. 4). In fact, the entire itinerary has the scent of the tentative about it. The resolve in v. 5—**I will visit you after passing through Macedonia, for I intend to pass through Macedonia**—pales into a probability, reflected in the participle (translated **perhaps**), the disjunctive conjunction (**or**), and the conditional clause (**wherever I go**) in v. 6, and in the expression of desire ("I wish" or **I want**) or hope, climaxing in the so-called Jacobean condition in v. 7: **If the Lord permits** (cf. James 4:15). Paul is not master of his future. He is certain of only one thing, that he will remain in Ephesus till Pentecost (again a reference to his Jewish calendar), since a "great door" has been thrown open to him there. The metaphor in v. 9 has been twisted out of shape (the figure warped to its referent again! cf. 15:36-38) by the second adjective (translated, **for effective work** in the RSV), but the meaning is clear enough. God—the subject hidden behind the phrase **a door ... has opened to me**—has made possible an activity in proconsular Asia certain of results, and despite the opposition (**many adversaries**), Paul must exploit the "opening."

Paul's plans were altered. Timothy, sent on ahead to Corinth before the completion of the letter (cf. 4:17, and the verses in the following section), had evidently succeeded in his mission of reminding the congregation of Paul's "ways in Christ," for which reason the apostle drew up another, second itinerary. He would sail directly for Corinth, from there traveling north to Macedonia, would drop down to Corinth again, from there embarking for Jerusalem (cf. 2 Cor. 1:15-16). This second plan, much more to the Corinthians' taste, was not carried out, as is clear from their reproaching Paul for vascillation (cf. 2 Cor. 1:12ff.). The reason lay in the altered situation at Corinth, mirrored in "Second" Corinthians. To that situation, Paul first responded by letter (2 Cor. 2:14—6:13 and 7:2-4?), then by a visit which ended disastrously (cf. 2 Cor. 7:12). Paul then returned to Ephesus, penned yet another letter to Corinth (the letter of tears referred to in 2 Cor. 2:4; 2 Corinthians 10–13?) which eventuated in a reconciliation reported to him by Titus (cf. 2 Cor. 7:6f.), a report for which Paul was too impatient to wait at Ephesus, and so met Titus half-way at Macedonia (2 Cor. 2:12-13).

Timothy's Arrival and Apollos's Delay (16:10-12)

The injunction to see to it that when Timothy arrives he would have nothing to fear from the opposition to which Paul was exposed (the RSV carelessly translates, **see that you put him at ease**) makes clear Paul's letter will arrive at Corinth ahead of Timothy. It will require less time for the letter to reach Corinth by sea than for Timothy, already underway, to arrive by land (through Macedonia?). Timothy will then find himself in the position of acting as "translator" of the letter as well as interpreter ("to remind you of my ways," 4:7), his credentials consisting of his sharing the Gentile mission with Paul—**he is doing the work of the Lord, as I am** (v. 10b). But if Paul is his sole reference, the hazard of being daubed with the same brush as the apostle is real—hence the chain of imperatives in vv. 10 and 11: **See that . . . let no one despise him . . . speed him on his way in peace.** . . . The hazard was avoided; Paul's demands were met—an inference drawn from the drafting of the second itinerary (2 Cor. 1:15-16). Had other, unnamed persons accompanied Timothy, or were those "brethren" together with Paul (the prepositional phrase in v. 11b could be linked to the verb or to the pronoun)? No doubt the latter was the case, the **brethren** in v. 11 then identical to those in v. 12, that is, those with Paul and ready to return to Corinth.

If, following 4:6 ("these things . . . I have given shape as applying to myself and Apollos for your sake"), there should be a lingering suspicion that Apollos would have fallen in with his faction and Paul's detractors (1:12; 3:4), v. 12 should dispel it. The "Alexandrian" had been yoked with Paul; Paul had **urged** him (literally, "urged him muchly") to leave for Corinth with those anonymous "brethren," and Apollos had delayed. And the longer the delay, the less the opportunity for a triumphal entry, at least among his campaigners; the less the chance for self-aggrandizement at the expense of Paul. Timothy was already on his way, the letter about to be posted, and the reconciliation with Corinth would not be far behind. The reason for the delay is given in v. 12c: **It was not at all** the **will** that he **come now; but he will come when he has opportunity.** Neither the will nor the time were at Apollos's disposal. They were God's. Apollos was no more master of his future than was Paul. "What then is Apollos? What is Paul? Servants through whom you believed, as the Lord assigned to each" (3:5).

Concluding Admonitions (16:13-14)

The section contains five imperatives—"watch, stand fast in the faith, play the man, be strong. Let everything of yours [RSV, **you do**] be in love." The words are reminiscent of Ps. 30:25 in the LXX. But for a greeting and benediction, the epistle might well have ended here. In 1 Thessalonians, 2 Corinthians, and Philemon, a similar cluster of imperatives draws the letter to a close, a feature imitated in the Pastorals (cf. 1 Timothy 6 and Titus 3). But what follows Paul's admonitions here may also be set down to matters of style, and not merely to second thoughts, as is indicated in Gal. 6:11-17, and its imitation in the Deutero-Pauline letters (cf. Eph. 6:21-22; Col. 4:7-9; 2 Thess. 3:14-15 and; 2 Tim. 4:9-18).

If the distance between believing and doing, between what we are and what we will be, is not bridged by a summons to which we respond as to an external command, but lies in the very nature of what God has given—himself, pressing us toward a consummation yet to come—why the imperative? The hallmark of Christian existence is hiddenness, a hiddenness established in that event of the cross. For this reason, the admonition, the exhortation, the imperative can appear as command, for the world, what can be seen, touched or handled, what can be thought or perceived, promises life in isolation, even in—particularly in—the name of God or religion. Lured by the promise, the community of Christ needs "reminding," needs a word—"watch, stand fast!"—the word that the subject of our life, our existence, is the crucified Lord who has established the mode of the cruciform, death to the rage for selfhood, as the only mode of our conformity to him. But the beating heart of the admonition is the promise. We are, we already are, the sign of the humanity of the crucified Lord in this world. And one day we shall bear the image of that "man of heaven." In terms which the advocates of at least one popular Christian movement would understand,

> one does not own faith as a possession, in the sense of a conviction already reached, but only in enacting the decision of the moment, and one does not have it *alongside of* other decisions, but *in* them. The believer is therefore never a finished product, but is always becoming.[114]

For Paul, we press on, not by ordering life to an extrinsic standard or mandate, but because Christ has made us his own, because "God will supply every need . . . according to his riches in glory in Christ Jesus" (Phil. 3:12; 4:19).

Stephanas and His Company (16:15-18)

The same appeal to respect those who labored among them as Paul makes here on behalf of **the household of Stephanas** he had made to the Christians at Thessalonica (cf. 1 Thess. 5:12-13). Paul describes Stephanas and his "family" as the "first-fruits" (RSV,

first converts) of Achaia, a term he had used earlier of Christ (15:23), and against the same background—the festival in acknowledgment of Yahweh's ownership and its hidden promise. Stephanas was "firstling" and there was more to follow from that proud country now a vassal of Rome. Was it for the sake of what he believed it tokened, the future which he believed it promised, that Paul had broken his rule and baptized the household of Stephanas (or Crispus and Gaius, cf. 1:14-16)? **To such,** Paul adds in v. 16, **be subject . . . and to every fellow worker and laborer**—the merest hint at ecclesiastical rank, and severely qualified by reference to those in authority as having "put themselves at the disposal of the saints" (v. 15). Nowhere does the apostle establish order in his communities in statistical fashion; he assigns authority only to service become concrete, for only in such service does Christ announce his promise and lordship. "Therefore, for this reason"—for the reason of service become concrete; service to Paul and to Corinth—"pay heed to such" (v. 18b). Did Paul's struggle against singling out individual elect persons, his attempt to establish all responsibility and service in the community on the principle that every believer was a charismatic—that love was the bar before which every gift had to appear and be judged—did it finally destroy the tradition rather than encourage it, and lead it once again to enthusiasm, to singling out individual, elect persons?[115] **I rejoice at the coming of Stephanas and Fortunatus and Achaicus,** Paul writes, **because. . . .** How should the reason read: as a reproach for something held back, or as the recognition of an involutary separation? The original allows for either reading: "Because these compensated for what you lack" (cf. 2 Cor. 8:14 and 11:9), or **because they have made up for your absence** (cf. Phil. 2:30). The verse following (v. 18) appears to require the second reading: **They refreshed my spirit as well as yours.** Curiously, the three emissaries referred to in v. 17 are not named together in chap. 1, and in this chapter there is no mention of Chloe's people (cf. 1:11). The epistle was not penned at a single setting, so it is conceivable that the deputation from Chloe had recently departed from Ephesus, and that Stephanas, Fortunatus, and Achaicus had only recently arrived there.

Paul's Greetings (16:19-20)

Now the apostle sends greetings from the congregation in proconsular Asia, from **Aquila and Prisca** (Priscilla), forced to flee Rome following Emperor Claudius's expulsion of the Jews in A.D. 49, and who attached themselves to Paul at Ephesus (cf. Rom. 16:3-4; had the couple by this time returned to Rome?), and from "all the brethren." With one exception (Rom. 16:22, "I Tertius, the writer of this letter, greet you in the Lord"), all salutations or greetings from Paul's coworkers to his addressees are relayed by him alone (cf. 1 Thess. 1:1; Gal. 1:2; 2 Cor. 1:1; 13:13; Phil. 1:1; 4:21; Philemon 1, 23; and Rom. 16:21). The implication is that the apostle to the Gentiles speaks for all because he outranks them all. The invitation to **greet one another with a holy kiss** (cf. 1 Thess. 5:26; 2 Cor. 13:12 and Rom. 16:16; cf. also 1 Peter 5:14) suggests the gathered assembly as context for the reading of Paul's letter. In addition, the invitation together with the anathema and *maranatha* in v. 21 suggest fixed forms derived from the primitive community's Lord Supper liturgy (cf. Rev. 22:14-15, 17, 20). The **holy kiss** (scarcely an erotic act, but appropriated from ancient family custom and performed at worship) had theological significance. It signified forgiveness given and received as presupposition for participation in the Supper, and together with the Supper announced the unity of the community as the family of God of the end-time. So, at least, it was construed by the later church which set it at various points in its eucharistic liturgy, only to restrict it later to the same sex or to the clergy, and finally to abandon it.

The Conclusion (16:21-24)

Following the greeting in his own hand (cf. Gal. 6:11 and Philemon 19), Paul once more has recourse to that prophetic "sentence" of sacral right or holy law, by which he not merely warns but proclaims the Judge as already present. This time, however, the sentence takes the form of an anathema: **If anyone has no love for the Lord, let him be accursed** (v. 22). As noted above, the context of the sentence, as well as of what immediately precedes and follows, may well have been cultic. The suggestion that it was a formula used to exclude catechumens or the unbaptized from the Supper is macabre. The sentence is addressed to the entire community, none excluded. More important, just as in 3:17 and 5:3ff., so here the conditional clause (**if anyone has no love**) makes evident that the anticipation of judgment is in the service of grace, that is, calculated to allow time for repentance. That the "sentence" was construed in this fashion can be seen from the Lord's Supper liturgy of the *Didache*, a manual of church instruction from the second century (ca. A.D. 150), in which the sentence is absorbed by its motive: "If any man be holy, let him come! If any man be not, let him repent."[116] (Note the misapplication of the sentence in the author's caveat to editorial tampering in Rev. 22:18-19.) In the original, the exclamation at the conclusion of v. 22 and translated **our Lord, come!** in the RSV, is Paul's transliteration of the Aramaic *Marana tha* (or *Maran atha*), again suggestive of a liturgical context (just as, e.g., the "Abba! Father!" in Rom. 8:15; cf. Rev. 22:17,20). The meaning of the interjection is moot, depending upon whether or not the verb (transliterated *tha* or *atha*) is construed as imperfect ("our Lord, come!") or as perfect ("our Lord has come!"); whether or not the phrase is to be interpreted as an appeal or warning (our Lord has come, and thus exercises his judgment in the present, cf. 11:27-32), and if not a warning, either an appeal to the Lord to appear at his Supper, or to hasten his parousia. Is it possible that an originally eschatological utterance, an appeal to Christ to make speedy return for deliverance, later came to be set in a liturgical context, and was thus transformed into an appeal to the Lord to be present at the community's worship, at his Supper? Then it is probable that Paul tore it from its cultic context and restored it to its original setting. For an apostle who saw the "footsteps of Messiah" in the "present distress," was convinced that the time had "been shrunk," that the "shape of this world" was "passing away" (7:26-31); who saw victory already wrenched from death (15:55-57), and whose own speech was an anticipation of judgment, there can be little doubt that the prayer was for the cosmic drama to begin, its final act the subjection of the Son, and God "all in all" (15:28).

Paul concludes: **The grace of the Lord Jesus be with you. My love be with you all in Christ Jesus. Amen** (vv. 23-24). Paul ends his letter where he had begun (1:3)—with **grace**—just as in the remainder of his undisputed epistles (cf. 1 Thess. 1:1; 5:28; Gal. 1:3; 6:18; 2 Cor. 1:2; 13:14; Phil. 1:2; 4:23; Philemon 3, 25). The term or its congeners is used more than 100 times in Paul's correspondence. Despite its echoing the ancient Greek greeting, despite its use in the community which preceded him (a liturgical use, signaled in the frequent absence of the definite article?), Paul has made it his own, harnessed it to his gospel and its interpretation. **Grace** denotes the "wisdom of God" become temporal, historical, palpable, and concrete in the "Christ crucified." **Grace,** bound to no human presupposition, but the negation of every human preparation—a "stumbling block to Jews and folly to Gentiles." **Grace,** with no room for human struggle for the good. **Grace,** guaranteeing no status or rank, but a gift, a charisma, and given to all. **Grace,** the shape of the proclamation, the shape of the proclaimer—Paul's "fate"!—and the shape of the one to whom proclaimed. **Grace,** God's favor in the event of the cross. And to it, Paul joins his **love . . . in Christ Jesus,** that impossibility become possible, become actual, corporeal and "abiding"—because of **grace.**

NOTES

1. Schalom Ben-Chorin, *Paulus: Der Völkerapostel in jüdischer Sicht* (Munich: Deutscher Taschenbuch Verlag, 1984), p. 195.
2. Cf. pp. 15-20.
3. Lucian, *The Passing of Peregrinus* 13, in *Lucian*, trans. A. M. Harmon, LCL, p. 15.
4. *ANF*, 1:244.
5. *APOT*, 1:397-398.
6. *The Nag Hammadi Library in English*, ed. James M. Robinson (San Francisco: Harper and Row, 1977), p. 116.
7. Adolf Schlatter, *Die Korintherbriefe*, Erläuterungen zum Neuen Testament (Stuttgart: Calwer Verlag, 1962), p. 27.
8. Sermon on Genesis 3 (1525), WA 20:334-335.
9. Homer, *Od.* 17.218, in *Homer*, trans. A. T. Murray, LCL, 2:167.
10. Philo, *On Husbandry* 9, in *Philo*, trans. Colson and Whitaker, LCL, 3:113.
11. Ibid., 18, 80, 121, 131, on pp. 117, 149, 171, and 175.
12. *The Scriptures of the Dead Sea Sect*, ed. and trans. Theodore H. Gaster (London: Sacher and Warburg, 1957), p. 283 (1QM 18:6-11).
13. Rudolf Bultmann, *Der Stil der paulinischen Predigt und die kynisch-stoische Diatribe* (Göttingen: Vandenhoeck and Ruprecht, 1910), p. 65.
14. *Sib. Or.* 3.772-776, in *OTP* 1:379; cf. also Rev. 3:12.
15. Ernst Käsemann, "Sentences of Holy Law in the New Testament," *New Testament Questions of Today*, trans. W. J. Montague (Philadelphia: Fortress, 1969), pp. 66-81.
16. Cf. Schalom Ben-Chorin, *Paulus*, p. 104.
17. Seneca, *On Benefits*, in *Seneca: Moral Essays*, trans. John W. Basore, LCL, 3:461, 463.

1 Corinthians

18. Ethelbert Stauffer, *Jesus, Paulus und Wir* (Hamburg: Friedrich Witig Verlag, 1961), pp. 46, 48, 50.
19. Seneca, *On Providence* 2.9-10, in *Seneca: Moral Essays*, 1:11.
20. Adolf Schlatter, *Paulus der Bote Jesu: Eine Deutung seiner Briefe an die Korinther* (Stuttgart: Calwer Verlag, 1956), p. 164.
21. *Sanhedrin* 7:4a, in *The Mishnah*, trans. Herbert Danby (London: Oxford University Press, 1964), p. 391; but cf. *Kerithoth* 1:1-2, in which the sentence is commuted to a sin offering, if the offense was committed in error (pp. 562-563).
22. Cf. the reason for the prohibition against marrying one's mother-in-law, daughter-in-law, stepdaughter, or stepmother in the *Institutes* of the second-century Roman jurist Gaius, in *Elements of Roman Law by Gaius* 1.63, trans. Edward Poste (Oxford: Clarendon, 1890), p. 67.
23. Cicero, *In Defence of Cluentius* 14-15, in *Cicero*, trans. H. Grose Hodge (Cambridge, Mass.: Harvard University Press, 1979), 9.237.
24. For a discussion of the origins, form and situation-in-life of the catalogs of vices and virtues in the New Testament, cf., e.g., Philip Carrington, *The Primitive Christian Catechism: A Study in the Epistles* (Cambridge: Cambridge University Press, 1940); "Essay II: On the Inter-relation of I Peter and other N.T. Epistles," in E. G. Selwyn, *The First Epistle of St. Peter* (London: Macmillan, 1949), pp. 365-466; and Eduard Kamlah, *Die Form der katalogischen Paränese im Neuen Testament* (Tübingen: J.C.B. Mohr, 1964).
25. 1 Enoch 91:15, in *APOT*, 2:264.
26. *The Dead Sea Scriptures in English Translation*, p. 251 (1QpHab V, 4).
27. Cf. 1 Enoch 91:21-25, in *APOT*, 2:259.
28. Cf. Plato, *Georgias* 509c, in *Plato*, trans. W. R. M. Lamb, LCL, 5:475.
29. *OTP*, 2:117f.; cf. Jub. 22:14; 25:17; the Damascus Document 1:7f., in *The Dead Sea Scriptures in English Translation* (CD I), and also Enoch 5:7.
30. 2 Bar. 44:11-15, in *OTP*, 1:634.
31. Cf. Mark 7:21f.; Rom. 1:29-31; 13:13; 2 Cor. 6:6f., 9f.; 12:20f.; Gal. 5:19-22; Eph. 4:2f., 31-32; 5:3-5, 9; Col. 3:5, 8, 12; 1 Tim. 1:9f.; 4:12; 6:11; 2 Tim. 2:22; 3:2-5, 10; Titus 3:3; 1 Peter 2:1; 3:8; 4:3, 15; 2 Peter 1:5-7; Rev. 21:8; 22:15; Did. 2:6; Barn. 19; Pol. *Phil.* 2:2; 4:3; *Herm., Man.* 5.2-4; 6.2; 8.3-5; *Sim.* 6.9.15; Apoc. Peter 21-31.
32. Cf. Wis. 14:22ff.; *Sanhedrin* 10:2 in the Mishna, where the threat-formula, "have no share in the world to come," corresponds almost exactly to v. 9; cf. also the Manual of Discipline or Community Rule 4:9-11, in *The Dead Sea Scriptures in English Translation*.

Notes

33. Cicero, Plautus; cf., e.g., Plato, *Georgias* 525a, in *Plato*, p. 525.
34. Cf. *Pistis Sophia*, trans. G. R. S. Mead (London: John M. Watkins, 1947), pp. 213-218.
35. A. Schlatter, "Paulus und das Griechentum," *Das Paulusbild in der neueren Deutschen Forschung*, ed. K. H. Rengstorf (Darmstadt: Wissenschaftliche Buchgesellschaft, 1964), pp. 102-103.
36. *Epictetus*, trans. W. A. Oldfather, LCL, 2:244.
37. *The Meditations of the Emperor Marcus Antoninus*, ed. A. S. L. Farquharson (Oxford: Clarendon, 1968), 4.3, vol. 1, 52.
38. Cf. Rudolf Bultmann, *Theologische Enzyklopädie*, ed. Eberhard Jüngel und Klaus W. Müller (Tübingen: J.C.B. Mohr, 1984), p. 125.
39. Martin Luther, *Vom ehelichen Leben und andere Schriften über die Ehe*, ed. Dagmar C. G. Lorenz (Stuttgart: Philipp Reclam, 1978), p. 5.
40. Ibid., pp. 38-39.
41. *Ehe-Gabe, Eine Hochzeitspredigt gepredigt von Martin Luther* (Fürth: Flacius Verlag, 1984), p. 22.
42. *Vom ehelichen Leben*, p. 50.
43. *Ehe-Gabe*, p. 15; cf. pp. 7, 10, 21, 23, and also Luther's description of marriage and celibacy as God's gift in *Vom ehelichen Leben*, pp. 6, 13-14, 17-18, 34, 42, 45, 50-51, 53, 59; in his Vorreden, the Reformer described the antichrist as forbidding marriage; cf. *Luthers Vorreden zur Bibel*, ed. Heinrich Bornkamm (Insel Verlag, 1983), p. 121.
44. *Vom ehelichen Leben*, p. 41.
45. Ibid., pp. 15, 49.
46. *Ehe-Gabe*, p. 9.
47. 1 Clement 46:2, (The Apostolic Fathers, LCL, 1:87). trans. Kirsopp Lake.
48. *Vom ehelichen Leben*, pp. 25, 27, 28.
49. *Josephus*, trans. Ralph Marcus, LCL, 7:123.
50. *Epictetus*, 2.515.
51. Act V, Scene 1.
52. What moves Hector the Trojan to go out to battle against the Greeks is the possibility of the capture of his wife, Andromache, her plying the loom or bearing water against her will, thus of a "strong necessity" laid on her. Cf. Homer, *The Iliad*, trans. A. T. Murray, LCL, p. 295.
53. Cf. *As. Mos.* 8:1; 2 Bar. 25:1ff.; 48:31; 68:2; the Baraita or "addition" to the Mishna tractate *Sanhedrin*, cited in Strack-Billerbeck, *Kommentar zum Neuen Testament aus Talmud und Midrasch* (Munich: C. H. Beck, 1928) 4/2:981.

1 Corinthians

54. "Vorrede über den Propheten Daniel," *Biblia Germanica*, Wittenberg: Hans Lufft, 1545, pp. CX-CXI.
55. *Epictetus*, 2.489-491.
56. *Vom ehelichen Leben*, p. 25.
57. Cf. Roy A. Harrisville, *Romans*, ACNT (Minneapolis: Augsburg, 1980), p. 215.
58. *ANF*, 1:324.
59. *LW*, 35:382.
60. Gershom Scholem, "Volk des Buches," in *Sie werden lachen— die Bibel*, ed Hans Jürgen Schultz (Munich: Deutscher Taschenbuch Verlag, 1985), p. 100.
61. But cf. Blass-Debrunner, *Grammatik des neutestamentlichen Griechisch*, 16th ed. (Göttingen: Vandenhoeck and Ruprecht, 1984), §369,2, pp. 298-299.
62. Adolf Schlatter, "Das Gott wohlgefällige Opfer," quoted by Käsemann, "A Pauline Version of the 'Amor Fati,'" *New Testament Questions of Today*, p. 235.
63. Cf. Manes Sperber, "Verwoben ins tägliche Leben," in *Sie werden lachen—die Bibel*, p. 150.
64. Luther's Preface to Romans (1522), *LW* 35:367, 368, 370.
65. *Die Marburger Theologen und der Arierparagraph in der Kirche, Eine Sammlung von Texten aus den Jahren 1933 and 1934*, ed. Heinz Liebing (Marburg: Elwert Verlag, 1977), p. 41.
66. Cf. Dial. Trypho 70:4, in *ANF*, 1:234.
67. Cf. Str-B, 3:406-407.
68. Cf. *Agamemnon*, trans. Herbert Weir Smyth, LCL, p. 93.
69. Schlatter, "Paulus und das Griechentum," p. 108.
70. "On the Veiling of Virgins" 7, in *ANF*, 4:31-32.
71. Eberhard Jüngel, *Tod* (Gütersloher Verlagshaus Gerd Mohn, 1985), p. 143.
72. *Goethes Sämmtliche Werke* (Stuttgart: J. G. Cotta'schen Buchhandlung, 1968), 7:188.
73. Roy A. Harrisville, "Speaking in Tongues: A Lexicographical Study," *CBQ* 38 (1976): 35-58.
74. *Livy*, 2.32, trans. B. O. Foster, LCL, p. 325.
75. Anton Fridrichsen, *The Problem of Miracle in Primitive Christianity*, trans. Roy A. Harrisville and John S. Hanson (Minneapolis: Augsburg, 1972), p. 144.
76. Friedrich Schiller, *Gedichte, Eine Auswahl*, ed. Gerhard Fricke (Stuttgart: Philipp Reclam, 1980), p. 124.
77. Frank Chamberlain Porter, "Shorthand Notes on the Works of Benjamin W. Bacon," cited by Roy A. Harrisville, *Frank Chamberlain*

Notes

  Porter, Pioneer in American Biblical Interpretation (Missoula: Scholars Press, 1976), p. 23.
78. Schalom Ben-Chorin, *Paulus*, p. 41.
79. Günther Bornkamm, "Der Köstlichere Weg," in *Studien zum Neuen Testament* (Munich: Chr. Kaiser Verlag, 1985), p. 223. For what follows, I am indebted in large part to that excellent essay.
80. *Poetae Lyrici Graeci*, 2:17f., quoted by Bornkamm, "Der Köstlichere Weg," note 3, on pp. 217-218.
81. Bornkamm, "Der Köstlichere Weg," p. 225.
82. Herman Melville, *The Confidence-Man: His Masquerade* (New York: Bobbs-Merrill, 1967), pp. 3-8.
83. T. Issachar 4 (ca. 109–106 B.C.), *OTP*, 2:803.
84. 1 Esdras 4:35-40 (RSV).
85. Bornkamm, "Der Köstlichere Weg," pp. 227-228.
86. Ibid., p. 233.
87. For examples of ecstatic speaking in tongues, cf. Eddison Mosiman, *Das Zungenreden geschichtlich und psychologisch untersucht* (Tübingen: J.C.B. Mohr, 1911), pp. 59, 79.
88. Cf. David Hill, *New Testament Prophecy* (Atlanta: John Knox, 1979), passim.
89. Ludwig Feuerbach, *The Essence of Christianity*, trans. George Eliot (New York: Harper and Row, 1957), p. 127.
90. Philo, *The Special Laws* 4:49, in *Philo*, LCL 8:38-39; cf. *Who Is the Heir of Divine Things?* 249, 259, 263-266, in *Philo*, LCL 4:409, 411, 417, 419.
91. The quotation from Celsus in Origen, *Against Celsus*, 7.9, in *ANF*, 4:614.
92. Frederick G. Henke, "The Gift of Tongues and Related Phenomena at the Present Day." *The American Journal of Theology* 13 (1909): 206.
93. Arthur T. Pierson, "Speaking with Tongues—II," Editorial, *The Missionary Review of the World*, 30/9 (September 1907):683.
94. Tosepta *Megilla*, cited by Str-B, 3:467.
95. Cf. Schalom Ben-Chorin, *Paulus*, p. 109.
96. Karl Barth, *Die Auferstehung der Toten* 4th ed. (Zollikon-Zurich: Evangelischer Verlag, 1953), pp. 37-38.
97. *Gospel of Philip* 23, quoted in R. McL. Wilson, *Gnosis and the New Testament* (Oxford: Blackwell, 1968), pp. 74-75.
98. Quoted in Kurt Rudolph, *Gnosis*, trans. Robert McL. Wilson (Edinburgh: T. and T. Clark, 1983), pp. 192-193.
99. Eumenides 648 in *Aischylos*, ed. Oskar Werner (Munich: Ernst Heimeran Verlag, 1959) p. 228.
100. *Bikkurim* ("First fruits") 3:1-8, in *The Mishnah*, pp. 96-97.

1 Corinthians

101. Cf. Mathis Rissi, *Die Taufe für die Toten* (Zurich: Zwingli Verlag, 1962), pp. 54, 85, 89, 91.
102. Cf. Karl Staab, *Paulus Kommentare aus der griechischen Kirche* (Munster: Aschendorff, 1984), p. 8; cf. also Rissi, pp. 7, 11-14.
103. Cf. Rissi, *Die Taufe*, pp. 59, 70, 74-77, 79-82, 84-85, 89.
104. Cf. ibid., p. 82.
105. There are countless parallels to this saying in Greek and Roman literature, one of which is *not* from Seneca's *Controversiae*, Book 14, but *from Controversiae* 2, and which does not read "Let us drink, for we must die," but "Let us live—we must die"—an error perpetuated by commentators since the 18th century. Cf. *The Elder Seneca*, trans. M. Winterbottom, LCL, 1:349.
106. Philo, "Allegorical Interpretation of Genesis II," *Philo*, LCL, 1:167; cf. also "On the Account of the World's Creation Given by Moses," 134-136, LCL, 1:107.
107. Philo, "Allegorical Interpretation of Genesis II," *Philo*, LCL, 1:167
108. "On the Account of the World's Creation Given by Moses," 134, LCL, 1:107.
109. Jacob Neusner, *Genesis Rabbah, The Judaic Commentary to the Book of Genesis, A New American Translation* (Atlanta: Scholars Press, 1985), 1:156.
110. Cf. Str-B, 4/1: 211-212.
111. *D. Martin Luthers Epistel-Auslegung*, ed. Eduard Ellwein, vol. 2, *Die Korintherbriefe* (Göttingen: Vandenhoeck and Ruprecht, 1968), p. 303.
112. Karl Barth, *Church Dogmatics* III/2 (Edinburgh: T. & T. Clark, 1960), pp. 632-633.
113. Cf. Roy A. Harrisville, *Romans*, pp. 246-247.
114. Bultmann, *Theologische Enzyklopädie*, p. 145.
115. Cf. Ernst Käsemann, "Amt und Gemeinde," *Exegetische Versuche und Besinnungen*, pp. 118, 125-126, 134.
116. *Didache* 10:6, The Apostolic Fathers, LCL, 1:326.

ABOUT THE AUTHOR

Roy A. Harrisville is a graduate of Concordia College, Moorhead, Minnesota, and of Luther Northwestern Seminary; his Th.D. is from Princeton Seminary. He has served parishes in Minneapolis and Mason City, Iowa, and since 1958 has been professor of New Testament at Luther Northwestern. He has done research at leading theological centers in Europe and America.

Professor Harrisville is a popular and widely known lecturer, translator, teacher, and author (he has written, edited, or translated 20 scholarly books). In 1987 he gave the Hein lectures, *Ministry in Crisis: Changing Perspectives on Ordination and the Priesthood of All Believers* (Minneapolis: Augsburg, 1987). His commentary on Romans was the first volume in the Augsburg Commentary on the New Testament series.